The National Archives *A practical guide for family historians*

Gone but not forgotten:
in fond memory of David Williamson, Douglas Brown and
Durban MacGregor, three of my friends who died when this
book was in gestation

For John Powell, the man who made a difference

The National Archives

A practical guide for family historians

STELLA COLWELL

the national archives

First published in 2006 by
The National Archives
Kew, Richmond
Surrey, TW9 4DU
UK
www.nationalarchives.gov.uk

The National Archives (TNA) was formed when the Public
Record Office (PRO) and Historical Manuscripts Commission
(HMC) combined in April 2003.

A catalogue card for this book is available from the British
Library.

ISBN 1 903365 85 6
    978 1 903365 85 4

Book design by Ken Wilson
Typeset by Gem Graphics, Trenance, Cornwall
Printed in the UK by the Bath Press, Bath

Cover images: The National Archives © Hugh Alexander;
family image courtesy of Jane Parker

Contents

List of illustrations 6

Acknowledgements 7

About this book 8

1 INTRODUCTION TO THE NATIONAL ARCHIVES

Should you be at Kew or the Family Records Centre? 10

Things you need to know 11

Things to do before your trip to Kew 12

Be prepared 17

What do I do? A step-by-step reminder 19

Some practical advice 21

2 VITAL RECORDS HELD ELSEWHERE

Sources about Scots and Irish ancestors 22

Parish registers of baptism, marriage and burial 23

Wills proved locally in England and Wales before 1858 26

Wills proved in England and Wales from 1858 onwards 26

Electoral registers 27

Directories of names 27

Newspapers 29

Manorial records 30

County records 31

3 THE RECORDS A TO Z

Apprenticeship records 32

Army service records 35

Births, marriages and deaths of Britons at sea and abroad 55

Cemetery records 63

Census returns 66

Change of name 69

Civil War and Interregnum 70

Coastguard 73

Crime, convicts and transportation 77

Customs and Excise officers 83

Death Duty registers 84

Divorce petitions 87

Dockyard employees 90

Emigrants 92

Immigrants 101

Legal proceedings: civil actions 111

Maps, Tithe and Valuation Office records 117

Marriages – 'Fleet' and other clandestine weddings in London 120

Medieval ancestors – before parish registers 122

Merchant Navy 129

Nonconformists 138

Police: London Metropolitan Police and Royal Irish Constabulary 143

Railway workers before nationalization 146

Royal Air Force 148

Royal Marines 154

Royal Navy 158

State tontines and life annuities 166

Tax lists 170

Wills and other probate records 175

Some general comments and advice 186

Further reading 188

Useful addresses 194

Index 197

List of illustrations

Our home page at *www.nationalarchives.gov.uk* 14

The three search boxes 15

WO 97/1453 Army attestation and discharge 37

WO 363/v 60, f1049 Army service papers 45

BT 334/52, p61 Return of deaths at sea 58

RG 33/76, p96 Marriage registration, British Embassy, Paris 61

RG 6/1332, p224 A Friend's burial registration 64

HO 107/279/4, f6, p6 1841 Census of Coastguard 76

ASSI 44/168, pt 1 Report on Coroner's Inquisition 78

BT 27/1851 Ship passenger list 94

C 110/136 Chancery Masters exhibit 116

REQ 2/26/48, no 5 Pedigree produced to the Court of Requests 125

ADM 107/6 Royal Navy Lieutenant's passing certificate 162

E 179/164/513 m51r Hearth Tax return 172

PROB 1/20 Part of an original will 179

Acknowledgements

This new edition of the original book, called *New to Kew?*, was not written under the most ideal of circumstances. It is an example of armchair genealogy, as the updating and additional text were completed slowly and painfully whilst waiting for and recovering from major spinal surgery. As a result, I have a lot of people to thank for their support during a very frustrating time: chief among these are Guy Grannum, Roger Kershaw and Mark Pearsall, who checked the text, and they, Amanda Bevan, Helen Campbell, John Cassidy, Cecelia Doidge-Ripper, Gillian Kirby and Amy Warner all helped to fill in gaps. Emma Bayne, Alistair Hanson and Andrew Spence came to my rescue and sorted out the mystery of the crashed computer for me. Shirley Hughes very kindly looked up some specific document references, Sheila Knight sent me copies of printed material, Nora Talty-Nangle and Catherine Bradley did printouts when necessary. Thanks to our excellent online services, including our large army of detailed Research Guides, indexed digital images of some of our major genealogical sources and catalogues to our collections, I was able to experience what it is like to be a researcher off site as well as an on-site user on both sides of the help desks. The 'How to' leaflets from the Microfilm Reading Room at Kew, and the comprehensive series of family history handbooks compiled by my colleagues were of great help too. Amanda Bevan's *Tracing your Ancestors in the Public Record Office* has been a source of reference, and I also resorted to my own *Family Roots, Discovering the Past in the Public Record Office* and *Dictionary of Genealogical Sources in the Public Record Office*.

I'd particularly like to thank John Powell for fixing my spine, and Elaine Rush for ensuring I didn't feel a thing. Rebecca Dixon, Matt Manning, Jonathan Martin, Claire Race, Carl Roper and Marian Stephens then worked miracles on muscles I'd never heard of before to get me walking again. Caroline and Hans Bonkenburg, Shirley and Alan Lowe, Vicky Henry and my cousin Richard Colwell made my long stay by Lake Thirlmere unforgettable in so many ways whilst correcting the first draft. Tim Allen, Janice Bloomfield, Pat Brown, Bernard Casburn, Elaine Clarke, Steve Coker, Kathryn Coward, Barrie Lawrence, Dick MacGregor, Bill Merrick, Stuart Miller, Frances Mount, Alan and Ruth Riddleston, Kevin Seager, Kate Tatham and Mark Woolmore lent much valued practical support to keep me going. I'd also like to thank all my friends and colleagues for keeping up my spirits and making me laugh.

Finally, I would like to thank the production editor, Alfred Symons and the copy-editor, Liz Jones, for cutting the text down to size.

Any errors and omissions are mine.

About this book

In the following pages, I want to share with you some of the prime sources for family historians in the National Archives, at Kew, but there are many more, as you will find out for yourself as you get to know your way around the place.

The National Archives (known until 1 April 2003 as the Public Record Office) contains the historical administrative and departmental records of the central government of the United Kingdom as well as those of the central law courts of England and some for Wales. The records of our government's activities and decisions make it accountable to its subjects and they are admissible as evidence in a court of law, so they are the nation's memory, and a very long one too, for they span almost 1,000 years of continuous record-keeping.

You may not think that there is anything here to interest you amongst government archives, but you will be amazed at how much central authority has impinged on our lives since early times. Have a look at the alphabetical list of records on the Contents page at the front of this book to get some idea of the vast range of subject areas covered by government and our central law courts. We hold some private records too, such as those of the railway companies before 1948, and probate records from the chief church court prior to 1858.

A tight and efficient control of administration, finance and justice ultimately leads to an expanding bureaucracy and invariably requires accurate and careful record-keeping. The records then need to be made easy to find and refer to. Our website, **www.nationalarchives.gov.uk**, contains a wealth of online Research Guides to help you decide which items to choose and make the most of your time with us. More than two-thirds of our visitors come to research their family history, so these guides are designed for people just like you.

Only a tiny fraction of the records that were originally created centrally are selected for permanent preservation, on the grounds of their lasting historical interest and value. We currently care for about ten million original documents, each with its own unique catalogue reference. You can trawl our extensive online catalogues at **www.nationalarchives.gov.uk/catalogue** for references to almost all our material, a growing amount of which can be searched by personal-name. You can thus do a lot at home before you wend your way to Kew. When you are ready, you can then use our website to register for a reader's ticket and to place an advance order for specific original documents which will await your arrival. You can call us at 020 8876 3444 if you are unsure what we hold, or contact us online at **www.national archives.gov.uk/contact/**. Read this book too! You will then come fully prepared, having planned ahead exactly what it is you are after, and how and where you are most likely to find it, and will thus avoid going home disappointed.

Some of our archives have been indexed and digital images of them made available at **www.nationalarchives.gov.uk/documentsonline**, including wills which were proved in the chief church court before 1858, and some military and Royal Naval sources. Many items are available on microfilm in the National Archives, and copies of some of these can be inspected in the Family Records Centre, our central London reading room. This was opened in March 1997, and is combined with the public search room of the General Register Office for England and Wales. Copies of a number of our microfilmed records are also available for hire for a small fee in family history centres of the Church of Jesus Christ of Latter-day Saints throughout the world.

On 2 April 2003 we were joined by the Historical Manuscripts Commission and renamed as the National Archives. We thus now provide a one-stop shop for information about both official and private archives relating to any aspect of British history, because the Historical Manuscripts Commission (renamed as the National Advisory Service) is the conduit for details about historical collections and manuscripts and their whereabouts outside the National Archives via the National Register of Archives at **www.nationalarchives.gov.uk/nra**. It also hosts the Manorial Documents Register at **www.nationalarchives.gov.uk/mdr** and serves as the archival gateway to United Kingdom and international record repositories with substantial manuscript collections noted in the National Register of Archives indexes (ARCHON) at **www.nationalarchives.gov.uk/archon**.

You can gain direct access to the online catalogues to more than 8.5 million archives deposited in over 390 local record offices and other repositories in England by visiting Access to Archives (A2A) at **www.nationalarchives. gov.uk/a2a**, which was launched in 2001. Not every catalogue, nor even every local repository, is yet included, but it is a wonderful time-saving resource for planning your research, when the material you want to examine is held elsewhere than in the National Archives.

In this book, I have listed the sorts of archives you will find specially valuable, choosing only those series of documents most likely to furnish information about birth, marriage, death, family relationships and biographical profiles of the people mentioned in them. I have then described their contents, and how you can most easily and quickly find, help yourself to or order the ones you want. In each section I have cited key books and Research Guides to help you to expand your knowledge about each topic. The accompanying illustrations show examples of what you can expect to find in some of our key documents. The book ends with a list of further reading and useful addresses mentioned in the text.

This introductory dip-book cannot hope to tell you everything about our archives and their genealogical potential, but I hope you will enjoy reading it as much as I enjoyed its creation. For a more in-depth analysis, you can then go on to study the other books mentioned in the text.

Now read on.

1 INTRODUCTION TO THE NATIONAL ARCHIVES

Should you be at Kew or the Family Records Centre?

First, collect and sort out all the information you possess about your family past and present, and then draw up a pedigree chart showing the names of your known kinsfolk, generation by generation, and how they are all linked to you. Include their dates and places of birth, marriage and death. You can see from this chart where the gaps are and decide which ones to try and fill first.

Possibly the better place for starting your more recent English and Welsh family history research might be the Family Records Centre in Islington, London. No original documents are stored here, but you will find filmed copies and indexed digital images of some of our essential genealogical sources. There is free access to many other helpful online resources and CD-ROM databases too. You do not need a reader's ticket to use the Family Records Centre, and most items are self-service. The website address is **www.familyrecords.gov.uk/frc**. This is linked to **www.family records.gov.uk**, a portal providing access to the websites of a consortium of partners including the English and Welsh and the Scottish General Register Offices, the National Archives at Kew, the National Archives of Scotland, the Public Record Office of Northern Ireland, the National Library of Wales and other important institutions in the United Kingdom.

What you often can do is explore the Family Records Centre copies of and indexes to core material to construct at least a rudimentary family tree, and then visit the National Archives, at Kew, or other repositories, to bulk out the story. For a full description of the available resources, read my *The Family Records Centre, a User's Guide*, and visit **www.familyrecords. gov.uk/frc**.

Depending on what you know already, you may find it more appropriate to start at Kew. Look at the A to Z section of this book for guidance about this. There are likely to be other archive offices, libraries and institutions that will require your attention too.

The National Archives, Ruskin Avenue, Kew, Richmond, Surrey TW9 4DU.

TELEPHONE: 020 8876 3444

FAX: 020 8878 8905

EMAIL: *www.nationalarchives.gov.uk/contact/form*

WEBSITE: *www.nationalarchives.gov.uk*

OPENING HOURS:

    Monday, Wednesday and Friday 9 am to 5 pm

    Tuesday 10 am to 7 pm

    Thursday 9 am to 7 pm

    Saturday 9.30 am to 5 pm

DOCUMENT ORDERING ON SITE:

    Monday, Wednesday, Friday 9.30 am to 4.15 pm

    Tuesday 10 am to 4.45 pm

    Thursday 9.30 am to 4.45 pm

    Saturday 9.30 am to 3.15 pm

It is about 10 minutes' walk from the underground station at Kew Gardens, and about 20 minutes' walk from Kew Bridge railway station. The R68 bus from Richmond Station terminates outside Kew Retail Park, about 50 metres from the precincts of the National Archives. A map is available at **www.nationalarchives.gov.uk/visit/where.htm**. There is good free car parking on site.

We have a public restaurant, coffee bar, bookshop and cyber café.

Things you need to know

Entry to our public search areas is by reader's ticket. Register online for a ticket at **www.nationalarchives.gov.uk/registration** and then collect your ticket from our main reception desk. You will need to bring a UK driving licence, cheque guarantee card, debit card or credit card, or, if you are not a UK citizen, your passport or national ID card.

Children under 14 must be accompanied by an adult who has a reader's ticket. The adult will be asked to sign a declaration taking responsibility for the child whilst on the premises.

You will need to use your reader's ticket every time you visit us and when ordering original documents. It is renewable every three years.

There is no charge for doing your own research.

There is no need to book a seat.

Most of our records relate to England and Wales.

You can buy or photograph copies of many records.

In most cases, records are not transferred until they are 30 years old. Under the Freedom of Information Act 2000 you can now write to us, email or fax us to ask to see government records created more recently. Some sensitive records are closed for longer periods, but you can request a review of this.

Things to do before your trip to Kew

- Be specific and stick to known facts about your family's past.
- Double-check your sources to avoid any gaps or conflicts of information.
- Write down exactly who and what you are going to investigate – and don't be too ambitious.
- Make a list of the sources most likely to yield the answers you need.
- Check what these sources contain. You may find you need to add new research items, and cross out one or two.
- Prioritize the list. It will be your research guide on what has to be done, and should be regularly reviewed as you go along.
- Where are these sources? Consult **www.nationalarchives.gov.uk/ catalogue** or guides to record office holdings, or give us a call at 020 8876 3444. It is better to ask first before making a wasted journey to the wrong place.

Do you need to visit the National Archives, or can you search copies elsewhere? Some of our most popular records for family historians are now indexed and digital images and transcripts of them are on the internet. Visit **www.nationalarchives.gov.uk/census**, **www.nationalarchives.gov.uk/ documentsonline**, **www.familyrecords.gov.uk**, http://ancestry.co.uk, **www.1837online.com**, **www.originsnetwork.com** and **www.national archivist.com** to see what you can search online. You will have to pay to use some of these websites. Always read the opening screen to find out exactly what is included and excluded.

Indexed digital images of the following records are available at **www.national archives.gov.uk/documentsonline**:

- Registered copies of wills proved in the Prerogative Court of Canterbury between 1384 and 1858. There are more than one million of these, searchable by personal-name, place, occupation and date range;
- Death Duty register entries relating to probate courts other than the Prerogative Court of Canterbury, between 1796 and 1811. You can search the indexes by name, occupation or status, parish and county of death, and probate date for more than 66,000 liable estates;
- First World War campaign medal index cards for British Army and Royal Flying Corps personnel;
- Second World War medals claimed by and issued to merchant seamen between 1946 and 2002;
- Service registers of over 500,000 ratings who joined the Royal Navy as regular seamen between 1873 and 1923;
- Selected First World War British Army diaries between 1914 and 1922, which are searchable by battalion.

There are handy search tips to help you get the best results from each of these, and I have referred to this website where relevant in this book.

You can access the above indexes and digital images free of charge both in the National Archives and in the Family Records Centre, in London, but you will have to pay for any copies, and you cannot email or save copies to disk. If you use this website elsewhere, there is a flat fee to view each document. Look out for more indexed digitised images of our records at this website.

A number of our records are also available on microform. If you live a long distance away from Kew, consider paying the small monthly or three-monthly fee to hire in copies at a family history centre near you. The centres are run by members of the Church of Jesus Christ of Latter-day Saints. Visit **www.familysearch.org** to find out their whereabouts, and to study the online library catalogue of books, microfilms, microfiche and CD-ROMs you can borrow.

The excellent series of Gibson guides to local and family history sources, published by the Federation of Family History Societies (FFHS) and regularly updated, tell you about local copies and indexes to some of our holdings, as well as providing a thorough county-by-county survey of the existence and whereabouts of known records of a particular type. County record offices and local reference libraries will have good family and local history collections and copies too.

**How are the
records arranged?**

Our documents are arranged in exactly the same way as they were when they were deposited in the National Archives by the relevant government bodies. Every book, box, bundle, file or loose document has its own unique reference, so that it can be quickly and easily retrieved and replaced, quoted and found again.

When working documents become archives, the original references are converted to archival ones. A catalogue is compiled as a finding aid to each group of records, listing archive-by-archive reference, a brief description of its date coverage and its content. We employ a three-part reference scheme (letter code, series number and piece number). The coded letters represent the government department or body depositing its archives. Each group of archives within a departmental letter code is assigned a series number, and then every book, bundle, box, file or loose document within that series is given a unique sequential piece number. Sometimes there will be a sub-number too, as with some maps, so instead of the document reference being in three parts there will be four.

The individual series catalogues to our archives are available online at **www. nationalarchives.gov.uk/catalogue**. This seamless online catalogue has pulled together almost ten million searchable descriptions of our holdings.

There are no pictures of our documents in the catalogue. For some of these, you can view the indexed digital images at **www.nationalarchives.gov.uk/ documentsonline**, our themed online exhibitions at **www.national archives.gov.uk/exhibitions**, and **www.movinghere.org.uk**, which focuses on immigrants to England from the Caribbean, Ireland, South Asia and Jewish communities in the last 200 years.

Every archive repository adopts its own cataloguing system. Many of the catalogues are now uploaded onto the internet. You can access a lot of them at **www.nationalarchives.gov.uk/a2a** or by visiting **www.national archives.gov.uk/archon** and clicking on the link to the website of the record office you want.

Our home page at *www.nationalarchives.gov.uk*

How can you get to the records in the National Archives?

Start by opening up our home page at **www.nationalarchives.gov.uk**. You will see a series of tab headings along the toolbar at the top. If you point the mouse arrow over any of these you will see a list (menu) of contents under each heading. By pointing and clicking the mouse arrow over any of these you will be taken directly to that part of our website.

If you are new to this site, click on that tab to reach the Help section, where a list of Frequently Asked Questions should resolve many of your initial queries about us. There is a link to our online Records Research Guides. Use this to find the Guide you need. Read through the text, and when you've decided there is a set of records you want to search, click on the underlined letter code and series number. This will reveal 'Quick reference' and 'Full details' summaries. Click on 'Browse from here' to search the catalogue itself. You can also reach the Guides by pointing the mouse arrow over the 'Research, education and online exhibitions' tab and clicking on 'Research guides'.

As you read down the catalogue entries, find out more about their content by clicking on the underlined descriptions. You can also browse the catalogue starting from a particular document reference.

Search the catalogue

Alternatively you might want to search the catalogue by placing the mouse arrow over 'Search the archives' and clicking on 'the catalogue' at our home page, and then the magnifying glass icon at the top right of the screen.

You must complete the first of the three search boxes on the screen with a keyword or phrase; the other two boxes (year range, and department or

The three search boxes

series code) are optional. Try to avoid long phrases. A search for a phrase will only find entries that have words in next to each other and in exactly the same order, so to retrieve several words placed anywhere in the catalogue descriptions, link your keywords with 'AND' between each of them. To search for exact spellings put the word or phrase inside double quotation marks. When you key in a name, subject, place and dates in the search boxes, the computer will list every matching catalogue entry. If you want to search for acronyms, leave out the final full stop or omit the punctuation marks altogether. Now click on 'Search'. Click on 'Search tips' for other helpful hints.

The screen will tell you how many matching entries were found in our catalogues, and whether there are any relevant Research Guides. You can select which Guides you want to read from the scroll list underneath. The catalogue references are arranged alphabetically by letter code and reference number, and describe the title/scope and content of each document, and its covering dates. If you click on the underlined entry in the second column (title/scope and content) a 'Quick reference' box will reveal the covering dates, scope and content, access conditions, closure status, where the document is held, and any restrictions on its usage.

If there are a lot of results, then the departmental letter codes arranged in descending order of total entries, their titles/scope and content, and number of catalogue entries will appear. Click on this number for a screen display of precise document references within each letter code. The number of displayed hits is restricted to 3,000.

You can go directly to the catalogues of the tax lists before 1688 at **www. nationalarchives.gov.uk/e179** and some of our Equity Pleadings at **www.nationalarchives.gov.uk/equity.**

As well as being accessible remotely, our computerized catalogues can be consulted on site at Kew and in the Family Records Centre.

We have bound copies of the individual catalogues, giving identical information to what appears online. We also have some supplementary finding aids available at Kew, which have not yet been uploaded onto our website.

Problems?

- Sadly, our archives are not fully indexed by personal-name, but a number of them are. Try keying in the name or place in which you are interested.
- If there are more than 3,000 matches, click on the 'Refine search' tab on the right of the screen and try another relevant keyword to reduce the number.
- If a keyword is not found in a catalogue, this doesn't necessarily mean we don't hold what you want, because the descriptions can be very short or cryptic and don't tell you everything. Try different wording or key in the place-name and period when your ancestor was known to be there.
- The screen tells you there are no catalogue entries for a surname. Some series are arranged in surname ranges, rather than listing every surname. Try the first three or four characters of the surname, followed by a wild-card (*), for instance, Garf* instead of Garfunkel. This will give you the document reference including that part of the alphabet.
- Apostrophes are treated as punctuation, so leave a space instead. For instance, O Brien finds O'Brien, Bo ness finds Bo'ness, O'Brien finds Obrien. *Brien finds the most variations, because it includes any word ending with Brien.
- If you suspect that a person should be in a specific document which doesn't respond to your keyword request, order it up anyway.
- If you read the online 'Full details' about a likely-looking series, this may help too, or suggest other series you might explore.

If you have already searched the online catalogues at home, you will have formed an idea of the size of your task. You can print out a copy of the entries, and then tick them off as you work your way down the list of the relevant ones, save your catalogue search results to refer to whilst in the National Archives, or make a note of the full references to any documents you want to inspect.

Can you order documents in advance?

Yes you can. If you do this within our document ordering hours, the documents can be delivered on the same day. You can go straight from any online catalogue entry to 'Request this'. If you already have document references then go to **www.nationalarchives.gov.uk/advanceorders** to complete the online application form, or phone us at 020 8392 5200. We will need your name, reader's ticket number if you already have one, the date of your visit, full document references, and daytime phone number.

Some documents are not on site. Any such documents requested before 11.00 am will take three working days for delivery to Kew.

What if you can't visit in person?

We don't offer a full research service, but we can deal with general and catalogue enquiries by post, phone, fax or email. We offer a pre-paid postal service for searches conducted under the Freedom of Information Act 2000. For more information visit **www.nationalarchives.gov.uk/foi/ research.htm**.

If you have precise document references, you can order copies in a variety of formats (paper, microform, CD-ROM or DVD). Complete one of the online application forms by clicking on **www.nationalarchives.gov.uk/ recordcopying/**. You can also place your copying request by post.

You may prefer to hire the services of a professional searcher to identify and examine documents for you. You can find a list of names and addresses of such people at **www.nationalarchives.gov.uk/irlist**.

What else do you need to know?

Don't be frightened. The first visit to any new place can be very intimidating, so the more you can do before you come, the more confident you will feel. If, having read this book, you are still unsure about what to do or what we hold, give us a call at 020 8876 3444. We want you to enjoy the research experience and visit us again.

What to bring

Arm yourself with
- Your reader's ticket, or ID if you haven't already got one.
- Pencils (pens are not allowed). Erasers and pencil sharpeners are forbidden as they might cause damage to our documents.
- A notebook or bound file paper pad (no more than ten loose sheets are allowed in the public search areas), or a typewriter, laptop computer, tape recorder or Dictaphone to use in the special designated areas.
- A digital camera if you want to photograph original documents.
- Your checklist of sources to search on each visit.
- Any document references you have already ordered or want to order as soon as you arrive.
- A sketch family tree to remind you what stage you have reached and who and what you are looking for.
- Cash, cheque book or credit card for purchasing document copies.
- Cash for any drinks or other refreshments.

Don't bring too much stuff – most of it will probably spend the day in the locker.

Dress comfortably.

Be prepared

The National Archives is not near any other family history venue. Once you have arrived, plan to stay until closing time to make the most of our in-house facilities, and take regular breaks to clear your head.

Facilities for people with special needs

The entrance to the National Archives is 100 metres from our car park, and a 10-minute walk from Kew Gardens Underground Station. We can call a cab for you when you leave the premises. We have six marked bays at the rear of the building for cars used by disabled people with blue badges. We also have two wheelchairs available. Should you require a wheelchair or have any other needs, do contact us in advance, by calling 020 8876 3444 or by emailing **your-views@nationalarchives.gov.uk**. The National Archives is very user-friendly: there are lifts to all the public search areas, and toilets for holders and non-holders of RADAR keys on each floor. We have designated areas in the Research Enquiries Room for computer users in wheelchairs and there are special keyboards and mice for people with manual dexterity difficulties. We have staff trained in sign language to help out with any hearing difficulties, and induction loops for people with hearing aids. We have no Braille versions of our records, but we can lend you a magnifying glass in the public search areas, or you can purchase a magnification sheet from our bookshop; some of our microfilm and microfiche readers are equipped with extra magnification and focus controls, and there is an enhanced reader screen in the Library and Resource Centre to enlarge the print in our books and periodicals. We also have a microfilm reader which has been adapted for use by people with manual dexterity problems.

Food and drink

The cafeteria is open from 9am to 4pm on Monday, Wednesday, Friday and Saturday and from 9am to 5.30pm on Tuesday and Thursday. It serves breakfast and morning snacks and drinks until 11.30am and then hot and cold lunches. The coffee bar is open from 9am until 3pm on Monday, Wednesday and Friday, and from 9am to 3.30pm on Tuesday and Thursday. There are hot and cold drink dispensers and a water point in the same area. You can eat your own sandwiches or snacks in the cafeteria or in our grounds. No food or drink is permitted in the public search areas or reference rooms.

Closure dates

Make sure you know when we are closed to the public. These include all Bank Holidays (including the Saturday before), with special arrangements at Christmas and for annual stocktaking, normally early December. These are announced at our website, **www.nationalarchives.gov.uk/visit/times. htm**, and on site.

Research Guides and 'How to ...' leaflets

Our Research Guides cover about 15,000 different series of archives from 375 branches of central government. They are available, free of charge, both online and in the Research Enquiries Room.

'How to...' interactive leaflets and panels are available in the Microfilm Reading Room to help you wend your way through the various catalogues. They cover:

• Domestic sources (indexes to births, marriages and deaths, overseas births, marriages and deaths, the International Genealogical Index, nonconformist registers, apprenticeship tax registers, wills, Death Duty registers);
• First World War army family history;
• Army service records and medals;
• Royal Navy service and medals;
• Merchant Navy service and records;
• Royal Air Force service and medals.

Do help yourself to the relevant leaflets, as these will make your task so much easier.

Throughout the building, computer terminals enable you to access and search all our catalogues simultaneously and quickly online, and then order your chosen pieces. Because of this, the layout and navigation round our catalogues is slightly different to our website version, but you will still get the same results. Just follow the instructions on the screen. You can also use the computer terminals to view indexed digital images of some of our material at **www.nationalarchives.gov.uk/documentsonline**. This service is free in the National Archives, but you will have to pay if you want printouts.

The public screens in all our search areas allow you to access many designated 'Useful Websites' and CD-ROM databases via our Online Publications and Electronic Resources Archive.

When you order your first documents for the day, the screen will ask you some simple questions:

• Are you ordering documents that are mostly dated pre-1680 or are maps, rolls or documents that you know to be large? If the answer is 'Yes' then a seat will be automatically allocated to you in the Map and Large Document Room. If the answer is 'No':

• Will you be using a laptop computer, camera or Dictaphone? If the answer is 'Yes', there is a specially designated area in the Document Reading Room. If you are using a camera, register with the Record Copying team in the Document Reading Room. If the answer is 'No':

• Choose and reserve a seat in the Document Reading Room by clicking on the on-screen seating plan.

• Now order each of your three documents, by completing the boxes for the departmental letter code, series number and piece number.

• If you have just identified three document references using the 'Search the catalogue' facility, click on 'Request this' for each one in turn.

You can request up to 21 documents per day, but you can help yourself to as many microfilms or microfiche as you like, one at a time.

Original documents usually take approximately half an hour to arrive in the reading rooms. You can check on progress during this period by swiping your reader's ticket at any of the Current Order Status screens throughout the building.

Our Information Points are there to help. Treat them as human signposts to where you should be.

We welcome constructive comments about your visit, especially if there is anything we can do to improve the quality of our service. We receive many compliments on how user-friendly the National Archives is, but we need to know if you feel you have a complaint about our service, so we can swiftly put things right.

What do I do? A step-by-step reminder

1 Have your reader's ticket with you at all times.
2 Consult your checklist of sources to tackle, then read the relevant section in this book to refresh your memory.

3 **Deposit your belongings in the cloakroom and locker.** Remember the rule of pencils, notebook, file paper pad, 10 loose sheets of paper, laptop, Dictaphone and camera, magnifying glass or magnifying sheet if required, plus cash for photocopies.

4 **Swipe your reader's ticket through the security barrier, and go up to the Research Enquiries Room.** If you have your document references, choose a seat by clicking on 'Order Documents', and then order up your first three.

5 **If you haven't already got your document references, search our catalogues.** Don't forget to click on 'Access' once you have found a document reference to find out if you can help yourself to a microfilm or microfiche copy in our Microfilm Reading Room, or from the open shelves, if you will need to order it as an original document, or if it is still closed to the public.

6 **Order your document.** When you are ready, click on 'Request this' and follow the prompts on the computer screen.

Help!

• *Your reference isn't valid.* Have you checked that you have inserted the letter code, series number and piece number in the correct boxes? Have you ordered more than one piece number within that series at one go? If the document reference is in four parts, have you keyed this information in the right boxes? If you get stuck, ask for help.

• *The document isn't available.* The document may already be in use by another reader. Check with staff. The document may have been requested by a member of staff. It should be possible to retrieve it for you to inspect. The document might be awaiting copying. It may not be possible to rescue this for you, though staff will do their best. The document might have been withdrawn for conservation or repairs, or borrowed back by a government department. You may have to wait some time for this.

7 **Collect your documents and get busy.** Your orders are delivered to your seat-numbered locker in the Document Reading Room or the production counter in the Map and Large Document Room. The rule is, three volumes, or one file or one loose document at your table at a time.

Once your documents have been collected, you can order the next batch of three. There is a maximum of 21 items per day.

When using a box of loose papers, make sure you keep them in the same order as you found them.

Use the foam wedges provided in both search rooms to support heavy or fragile books, and the leather and beaded weights for holding down large or unwieldy documents and rolls.

If the handwriting of a particular document is very faded, ask if you can study it under an ultra-violet lamp.

You can take notes from all our archives, using a pencil and paper, typewriter, laptop computer, tape recorder or Dictaphone.

If you have problems understanding the documents you have several courses of action. Staff will help you decipher or understand the odd word, or explain some archaic administrative or legal terminology. They cannot do all the spadework for you, but they can point you in the direction of further help. For more information, see pp. 18–19.

A lot of early documents which were written in Latin have been translated and published. Check *Text and Calendars: An Analytical Guide to Serial Publications*, compiled by E.L.C. Mullins, and **www.rhs.ac.uk**.

You may prefer to have a copy of a document (see below). If this is large copying might be costly, so consider employing a professional independent researcher.

8 **Buy or make your own copies.** You can make your own photocopies of microforms in the Microfilm Reading Room and from the websites and databases in our Library. Remember to write the full document references on the back of any copies if they are not given on the document itself.

You can photograph many of our original documents yourself, but you will need permission to do this. We only permit digital cameras.

Some practical advice

- Plan ahead. Use our online services as much as you can, especially our online catalogues and advance ordering forms, at **www.nationalarchives. gov.uk/catalogue**. Order your first batch of documents ahead of your visit.
- Call us at 020 8876 3444 if you are unsure whether we have the sources you want, or contact us at **www.nationalarchives.gov.uk/contact/**.
- Read our online Research Guides at **www.nationalarchives.gov.uk/ gettingstarted/guides.htm**.
- Use this book!
- Be realistic. Don't push yourself too hard on one trip.
- Spread your research over two consecutive days, if you can, one of which is a late night. Ask for documents you have not finished with to be kept out for you to use the next day.
- Use our Research Guides and interactive 'How to…' leaflets when on site.
- Maximize your time. While you are waiting for items, do some research in the Microfilm Reading Room, or browse round our Library and Resource Centre. You could also be looking for further document references using our online catalogues, Research Guides and supplementary finding aids.
- Always write down full references to every document you search or copy, and the titles of every book, periodical, CD-ROM database and website you have examined – even if the results were negative.
- Take regular breaks. Some documents are very long-winded, repetitive and full of legal jargon, so it is easy to become fazed by them.
- The step-by-step approach works best. Regularly review your search checklist, and add new facts to your family tree as you go along. This prevents you becoming overwhelmed by the experience and drowned in paperwork.
- Ask us for guidance if you get stuck. We're here to help.

2 VITAL RECORDS HELD ELSEWHERE

Here is some information about material we don't hold at Kew or in the Family Records Centre, but about which we are frequently asked.

Sources about Scots and Irish ancestors

At **www.scotlandspeople.gov.uk** you can pay to view indexed digital images of the registrations of births 1855–1904, marriages 1855–1929, and deaths 1855–1954 in Scotland, plus a variety of indexed returns relating to Scots' births, marriages and deaths overseas. You can also call up indexed digital images of the 1871, 1881, 1891 and 1901 census returns of Scotland, though at present only the indexes to the births, baptisms and banns and marriages which took place in the Church of Scotland between 1553 and 1854 are accessible online. Extracts from these Old Parochial Registers are similarly searchable at **www.familysearch.org**.

Indexes to more than 520,000 wills and testaments (probate documents) of Scots confirmed between 1513 and 1901 are freely available at **www. scotlandspeople.gov.uk**. You will have to pay a small fee to inspect digital images of the documents themselves.

Records about many Scots who served in the British Army, Royal Navy, Royal Marines, Royal Air Force and Merchant Navy are in the National Archives.

For copies of Irish non-Roman Catholic marriage registrations from 1 April 1845, and for all birth, marriage and death registrations for the whole of Ireland 1864–1921, and then for the Republic of Ireland to date, apply to the General Register Office of Ireland, in Dublin, or online at **www. groireland.ie**. Microfilm copies of all the indexes to the above are available for hire in family history centres. Brief details of births registered before 1875 and of non-Catholic marriages between 1845 and 1864 are included in the International Genealogical Index (see page 24). For such events registered in Northern Ireland from 1 January 1922 onwards, contact the General Register Office (Northern Ireland) in Belfast, or use the online certificate ordering service at **www.groni.gov.uk**.

Many Irish documents of particular interest to family historians were burnt in 1922. These included thousands of parish registers of baptism, marriage and burial, and wills before 1903, and almost all the census returns before 1901. Surviving census returns, transcripts of them, and other records are kept in the National Archives of Ireland, in Dublin. Admission is by reader's ticket. The 1901 census returns have been microfilmed, and copies can be hired in family history centres. You can also search the original census returns for 2 April 1911 here too. Filmed copies of the 1901 census returns for the six Northern Irish counties are held in the Public Record Office of Northern Ireland (PRONI), in Belfast. You will need a reader's ticket to search these. There are numerous personal-name indexes to the Irish censuses taken between 1851 and 1911 available online; these are listed by county and then by place at **www.census-online.com/links/Ireland**. Personal-name indexes to the 1831 and 1841 Irish census returns are available on CD-ROM.

Look at **www.nationalarchives.ie** for details of online databases, which include indexes to Irish wills proved between 1484 and 1858, to Griffith's Primary Valuation of Ireland, undertaken on the ownership and tenancy of every property, townland by townland within each county from 1848 until 1864, and to Irish transportations of convicted felons to Australia from 1780 to 1868. There are accompanying explanatory notes about these resources. You can search the earlier Tithe Applotment Books, 1823–38 on CD-ROM. The PRONI website at **www.proni.gov.uk** contains personal-name indexes to a variety of digital images of records about freeholders and voters in the northern counties. Read the accompanying online leaflets. A number of indexed digital images of Irish records can also be searched at **www.origins network.com** using a subscription service. Those available so far include the 1851 census returns of the city of Dublin, Griffith's Primary Valuation of Ireland and the Irish Wills Index. Copies of the latter two databases are available in our Online Publications and Electronic Resources Archive, at Kew, and at the Family Records Centre. Visit **http://ancestry.co.uk** for details about Irish immigrants arriving at the port of New York during the Potato Famine, 1846–51, and **www.census-online.com/links/Ireland** for passenger and immigrants' lists of Irish people sailing to America, 1846–86, and for details about Scots-Irish settlers in America between the 1500s and 1800s. At the latter website you can also find a list of databases on CD-ROM relating to Irish immigrants to America.

Personnel records relating to men serving in the Royal Irish Constabulary before 1922 are in the National Archives. Extracted profiles about constabularymen between 1816 and 1921 are also searchable by personal-name at **http://ancestry.co.uk**. We have much material about the careers of Irish servicemen in the British armed forces and Merchant Navy; see the A to Z section of this book for more details.

Parish registers of baptism, marriage and burial

Before 1 July 1837, when centralized registration of births and deaths began in England and Wales, generally only the dates of baptism rather than birth and of burial instead of death were recorded. Be careful that you don't confuse a date of birth with a date of baptism, which might take place immediately after birth or, at the other extreme, be delayed for years. Burial, on the other hand, occurred fairly swiftly, within a matter of days or at most a couple of weeks.

Since 1538, the clergy of each Anglican parish church have been required to keep a written account of all baptism, marriage and burial services performed there. The extant register books will help you fix the basic structure of your family's history. When they are full, most parish registers are deposited for safekeeping in county record offices. To find their start-dates, present whereabouts and any indexes or copies of them, look at *The Phillimore Atlas and Index of Parish Registers*, edited by C.R. Humphery-Smith, or phone the relevant county record office, whose contact details can be located at **www.nationalarchives.gov.uk/ archon/**.

Extracts from the baptism and marriage registers of many parishes have been included in the International Genealogical Index, compiled by the Church of Jesus Christ of Latter-day Saints from vital records worldwide. You can trawl the most recent edition online at **www.familysearch.org**. There is an accompanying list of places, periods and events covered. No living people are recorded. The earliest, microfiche, edition dates from 1968, when it was known as the Computer File Index, and every new updated version has added extra entries. Starting in 1992, the International Genealogical Index began to mix these 'controlled extraction program' entries taken from vital records with information supplied in family group sheets of compiled records submitted by patrons of the Church, and this has led to index entries overlapping, duplicating or conflicting with each other. Such submissions have not been authenticated against original sources.

The British Isles Vital Records Index, first issued in 1998 and updated in 2002, is available online in the Family Records Centre and as part of our Online Publications and Electronic Resources Archive in the National Archives at Kew. This index has reverted to the original controlled extraction program.

As well as baptism and marriage entries from Anglican registers, embedded in the International Genealogical Index are extracts from the authenticated birth and baptism registers deposited by dissenters' chapels with the Registrar General of England and Wales after 1837, and now in the National Archives. For more information about these records see **NON-CONFORMISTS**. However, lots of chapels never surrendered their registers centrally, so you may need to contact the appropriate local record office to trace their coverage and present whereabouts; finding track of any extant registers might be difficult. Try the relevant county volume of the *National Index of Parish Registers*, published by the Society of Genealogists. Details of any known copies or indexes will be mentioned. There is a separate listing, edited by D. Ifans, of Welsh chapel registers, many of which are in the National Library of Wales in Aberystwyth.

The British Isles Vital Records Index contains extracts from 80 per cent of the duplicate birth certificates presented by nonconformists to Dr Williams's Registry in London for registration between 1742 and 1837, along with similar extracts from the Wesleyan Methodist Metropolitan Registry from 1818 until 1840. The actual registers and duplicate certificates are in the National Archives, at Kew. See **NONCONFORMISTS**.

Both the International Genealogical Index and the British Isles Vital Records Index should be used solely as finding aids to original register entries, rather than as a source in themselves. They are not complete transcriptions and do not extend over every parish, nor over the entire period or all events recorded by the registers mined to compile the indexes. Always double-check the register books anyway, to make sure there has been no error and to get a feel for who else was in the community at the same time as your ancestors, and what other surnames and forenames made up the contemporary pool.

The Federation of Family History Societies is running an ongoing project to make parish register indexes, assembled by member societies, available online using a pay-per-view service at **www.familyhistoryonline.net**. The Federation is also supervising a nationwide marriage index for the period 1754 to 1837, which will eventually be uploaded too. For abbreviated entries of marriages in many English counties between 1538 and 1840 and which were published before 1952, search the Boyd Index at **www.origins network.com**. There is a very useful database at **http://ancestry.co.uk** containing Pallot's Marriage Index of more than four million marriage (and a number of baptism) entries from London and other church registers between 1780 and 1837. If you have lost track of your forebears or cannot locate their marriages, try this one, as you will be surprised how many people ventured to the capital city to get married. The database lists the parishes and dates covered, which you can also glean from *The Phillimore Atlas and Index of Parish Registers*. The index is also available on CD-ROM.

Few burials are included in either the International Genealogical Index or the British Isles Vital Records Index. However, the Federation of Family History Societies has in progress a National Burial Index containing extracts from the registers of churches, chapels and cemeteries throughout England and Wales. Two CD-ROM editions have appeared so far, in 2001 and 2004, available as online databases in the Family Records Centre, in London, and through our Online Publications and Electronic Resources Archive at Kew; many local reference libraries, record offices and family history centres also have copies. Each edition contains a complete listing of places and dates covered. The index is especially good for the years from 1812 leading up to the commencement of civil registration of deaths in 1837. Try also Boyd's London Burials Index for the period 1538 to 1853, at **www.originsnetwork.com**. This largely relates to male inhumations, but includes the names of many dissenters interred in Bunhill Fields. Copies of the index are available on microfiche in the Family Records Centre and the Corporation of London Guildhall Library, whilst the bound index volumes are lodged in the library of the Society of Genealogists in London.

Wills proved locally in England and Wales before 1858

Up to 9 January 1858, wills were proved in church or other probate courts; see **WILLS AND OTHER PROBATE RECORDS**. The National Archives holds probate material only for the Prerogative Court of Canterbury. You can discover the whereabouts of indexes, copies, registered and original wills and administration grants by consulting *Probate Jurisdictions: Where to Look for Wills* by J. Gibson and E. Churchill. Some indexes have been uploaded on to the internet.

Wills proved in England and Wales from 1858 onwards

Probates granted in the Principal Probate Registry (PPR) and civil district probate registries (DPRs) of England and Wales from 11 January 1858 to date can be read for a fee in the Probate Searchroom, in the Principal Registry of the Family Division, in London, or in one of the local 12 district probate registries or 18 sub-registries; contact details are in *The Family and Local History Handbook* by R. Blatchford, and at **www. hmcourts-service.gov.uk/cms/wills.htm**. The annual bound-up alphabetical calendars to wills and grants of letters of administration in the Principal Probate Registry run to 1972, then there are yearly microfiche calendars until 1995, with computerized indexes from 1996 onwards. Most civil district probate registries have calendars covering at least the last 50 years: more details are in *Probate Jurisdictions: Where to Look for Wills*. Microfiche copies of the indexes to 1943 are available in the Family Records Centre, the National Archives, family history centres and many reference libraries and local record offices.

Alternatively, a four-year search can be undertaken for you. Write to the Chief Clerk, Postal Searches and Copies Department, at the Probate Sub-Registry, York, giving full details of the person's name, last known address, and exact or approximate date of death. The flat fee includes any resulting document copy. The indexed entries about administration grants are very full, dispensing with the need to purchase a copy if all you want is to extract genealogical information about the entitled next of kin.

As dates of death are given in the calendars they can serve as a substitute for death certificates. However, not everyone made a will, so this route is not foolproof.

Electoral registers

Originally only freeholders owning landed estates worth over 40 shillings a year were entitled to elect parliamentary representatives. The franchise was extended in 1832, and from 1884 almost every male over the age of 21 could cast a ballot. Women aged more than 30 became enfranchised in 1918, total equality coming in 1928. Since 1969, everyone has been able to vote once they reach the age of 18, with certain exceptions.

A register of voters is compiled and published each year, based on the information supplied every October by householders, but the electoral registers are not easy to use as a genealogical source. They do not give family relationships, but merely the first name, initials for any other forenames, and the surname of each resident at a particular address. From 1951, young adults reaching the minimum age during the forthcoming year have been included, and since 1971, their actual birthdates. The National Archives holds only a few printed copies, dating from the 1870s. These are listed in our online library catalogue at **www.library.nationalarchives.gov.uk** and in *Tracing your Ancestors in the Public Record Office* by A. Bevan.

The British Library in London has a complete set of annual electoral registers for the United Kingdom published in 1937, in 1938 and from 1947 onwards. To find out what other earlier registers are kept there, consult *Parliamentary Constituencies and Their Registers since 1832* by R.H.A. Cheffins, or try the Library's integrated catalogue at **http://catalogue.bl.uk**. Copies of old and recent local voters' lists can often be located in county record offices and reference libraries. You can trawl the most recent edition on CD-ROM in the Family Records Centre. The current and previous year's United Kingdom electoral rolls are accessible at **www.tracesmart.co.uk** too. There is a charge for viewing the full details of any entry.

Directories of names

London and provincial directories of names and places of residence of members of the nobility, gentry, of the middle class, professional people, farmers, hoteliers, innkeepers, craftsmen and traders began to be published in the late 17th century, as commercial guides. A number of specialist publishers set themselves up, generally concentrating on different parts of the country and relying on local agents to collect the requisite information, which was supposedly regularly updated. Sometimes, though, the editors lifted information from others' directories, or repeated the contents of the previous edition without alteration, so they are not always complete or accurate. They did not include every household, either, so factory and farm-workers and other employees will not be mentioned.

By the early 19th century, London and local directories began to be published every year, and the number of publishers decreased. By the mid-19th century the volumes had become very comprehensive. The London editions contained a commercial section listing alphabetically house-holders' names, their addresses and their occupation or profession; a court directory; an official directory giving the names and addresses of people in government and legal offices; an alphabetical street directory of the names of householders; an alphabetical trade and professional directory; a list of law officers including London and the provinces; a parliamentary directory; a city, clerical and parochial directory; and finally, a bankers' directory. Since many tradesmen lived above their workshops, their given business addresses were also their homes, which make directories a useful source when searching the ten-yearly census returns from 1841 up to 1901.

Provincial directories might focus on one county, combine several contiguous counties, or confine themselves to a city and its outskirts. Generally the county directories were arranged under administrative division, and then alphabetically by their constituent towns, villages and hamlets. Following a brief economic and social summary for each place came an alphabetical list of the names and addresses of private residents, professional and trades-people, innkeepers and farmers.

You can find out when and by whom county and city directories were pub-lished by studying *British Directories: A Bibliography and Guide to Direc-tories published in England and Wales (1850–1950) and Scotland (1773–1950)* by G. Shaw and A. Tipper, and *The Directories of London, 1677–1977* by P.J. Atkins. There are only a few copies of county and city directories in the National Archives. Search our library catalogue online at **www.library. nationalarchives.gov.uk** to check on what we hold. The Corporation of London Guildhall Library has an excellent collection of London and provincial directories, and no reader's ticket is required to use these facilities. It is always worth trying the catalogues of county and borough record offices and reference libraries.

A series of digital copies of at least one local or trade directory for each county and city in England and Wales during the 1850s, 1890s and 1910s is being uploaded at **www.historicaldirectories.org**. Facsimiles of many directories have been made available on microfiche, and on CD-ROM. Some of these can be searched at the Family Records Centre.

If your ancestor was engaged in one of the professions then check a contem-porary published directory of its members or fellows. Some directories give biographical profiles outlining the education, academic training, careers and current addresses of members, and there may be a special section for deaths and obituaries of members. Consult the *Directory of British Associations and Associations in Ireland*, widely available in local reference libraries. Generally, professional associations will have a website too.

Visit **www.nationalarchivist.com** to view digital images of historical direc-tories of members of a number of the professions, officers in the British Army, trades and of the nobility and gentry. The National Archives has good runs of annual *Law Lists* of attorneys, solicitors and barristers from 1799 until 1976, *Medical Directories* of general practitioners, surgeons and consultants from 1895 to 1987, *Clergy Lists* between 1842 and 1917, and *Crockford's Clerical Directory: A Directory of the Clergy of the Church of*

England, the Church in Wales, the Scottish Episcopal Church, and the Church of Ireland from 1888 onwards, as well as complete sets of *Who's Who* from its inception in 1849, and *Who Was Who* from 1897 onwards. A cumulative index to both publications from 1897 up to 1996 is available on CD-ROM in the Family Records Centre. Published peerages and handbooks to the titled, landed and official classes, and the *Dictionary of National Biography* are widely available in local reference libraries, and some are available online. The Guildhall Library has an extensive collection of professional directories and guides to the nobility and gentry.

Newspapers

Enticing though they may seem, unless they are indexed in some way or you know the exact date of an article or report, national and provincial newspapers can pose a nightmare for the family historian. As well as providing items of news and events, they can be gleaned for advertisements, estate agents' particulars, auctioneers' details, announcements of births, marriages and deaths, and obituaries and funeral reports. The obituaries and funeral notices often contain nuggets of family information and anecdotes available nowhere else.

If you glance through the yearly *Willing's Press Guide* you can find out about national, international and provincial papers and magazines.

The National Archives has microfilm copies of *The Times* from 1785 up to 2001, which are indexed between 1790 and 1980 on CD-ROM. You can also access free digital copies of back numbers of this newspaper prior to 1985 in the National Archives and in the Family Records Centre. Later issues (including *The Sunday Times*), can be inspected at **www.newsint-archive. co.uk** using a subscription service. Both of these are an excellent resource for birth, marriage and death announcements, and for obituaries, particularly those which might be published some time after the events themselves. You can also search for details of court cases, divorce proceedings, formal changes of name, bankruptcies, and the news of the day.

We also hold the twice-weekly editions of the government-authorized *London Gazette* from 1665 onwards. Most issues up to 1986 are on microform, and later editions are in our Library and Resource Centre at Kew. From 1795, there are integral subject indexes. You can search copies of these on our open shelves in the Microfilm Reading Room for 1914–20 and 1939–48, and an index for the period between 1830 and 1883 is available in the Research Enquiries Room. Digital copies of back-issues of the *London Gazette* and *Edinburgh Gazette* from 1900 to 1979 and *Belfast Gazette* from 1921 to 1939 are freely accessible online at **www.gazettes-online.co.uk/ index**. It is planned to make digital copies of all 20th-century issues available in this way. There is a special section for searches devoted to back numbers for the First World War (1914–20) and Second World War (1939–48).

To consult back-issues of other national and local newspapers and journals you may have to resort to the Newspaper Library, which is part of the British Library, in Colindale, London, for which you will need a reader's ticket. You can consult the online catalogue to more than 52,000 newspaper titles and periodicals at **www.bl.uk/catalogues/newspapers**. The collection includes all the national newspapers published in the United Kingdom since 1801, plus most provincial issues since the 18th century, and some dating from a century earlier in European languages worldwide. Many local record offices and reference libraries hold copies of newspapers and journals for their own areas, and some have been indexed.

Manorial records

Until copyhold tenure was abolished in 1925, most land in England and Wales was held from lords of manors in return for rent, dues or services. To learn which manors controlled landownership and occupancy in the parishes where your ancestors lived, inspect a local trade directory from the late 19th century, or look in the Manorial Documents Register of the National Advisory Service in the National Archives. The parish index will inform you of the names of the relevant manors. There is a corresponding manorial index to tell you what records are known to survive and their whereabouts. These cross-referenced indexes are gradually being uploaded on to **www.nationalarchives.gov.uk/mdr**.

Manorial records are useful for family historians because they sometimes long predate parish registers, the earliest stretching back to the early 13th century. Their major drawback is that they were written in Latin, although English was used between 1653 and 1660, and after 1733. Rarely are the records complete or continuous, but from the rolls and books reporting the minutes of the meetings of the twice-yearly general court baron of the lord of the manor or his steward you can discover when tenants' lands changed hands, where the property was situated, its size and the annual rental.

The meeting of the manorial court baron was normally combined with the court leet, and this dealt with infringements such as straying cattle, blocked ditches and non-appearance of tenants at the court without a good reason. The court relied on tenants informing on each other's conduct and misbehaviour. Once a year, the court leet appointed manorial officers such as the ale-tasters, the constables to keep law and order, the pindar to supervise the pound for stray animals, and the hayward, who looked after the hedges. A lot of these job titles evolved into surnames. Other important manorial records are the six-monthly rent books and rolls, which note the name of every tenant, their property and rent due or received.

Records of manors held by the Crown are in the National Archives (see p. 122). Many manorial documents were eventually deposited by lords of manors in county record offices, though some still remain in private hands;

check the manorial index of the Manorial Documents Register of the National Advisory Service, in the National Archives.

County records

The administrative and judicial business archives of local government are kept in county and borough record offices. These include petty and quarter sessions rolls and books, lists of people liable for jury service, parish musters of men prepared for balloting into the local militia, reports of coroners' inquests, Old Poor Law examination and settlement papers and removal orders, New Poor Law Union workhouse, infirmary and other records, smallpox vaccination records, local tax and rating returns, poll books and electoral registers, local maps and plans, licence applications, parish registers and other parochial records, manorial material, wills, school registers and records, local newspapers, photographs, books about the area and its history, deposited family, estate and business papers, and hospital records.

Online catalogues to a number of these archives are available at **www.nationalarchives.gov.uk/a2a**. You can find the websites of many record offices and institutions with manuscript collections by visiting **www.nationalarchives.gov.uk/archon** and selecting the county, country or title you want to pursue. Try also the website of the National Register of Archives, at **www.nationalarchives.gov.uk/nra**, which is a database containing details about the dates and whereabouts of family and business papers. For hospital records within a specific town in England and Wales, use **www.nationalarchives.gov.uk/hospitalrecords**. Try **www.nationalarchives.gov.uk/archon** for any updated information about records of specific hospitals.

Many record offices operate a paid genealogical research service if you are unable to get there yourself, but you may prefer to hire a resident family historian for a fee. Record offices sometimes have lists of researchers and record agents. You can also find out about them from the local family history society, by personal recommendation or by advertisement in the genealogical press. The Association of Genealogists and Researchers in Archives (AGRA) maintains a list of members, their specialisms and contact details. The website address of this professional body is **www.agra.org.uk**.

3 THE RECORDS A TO Z

Apprenticeship records

From the Middle Ages, in order to acquire the necessary skills of a particular trade, craft or profession, a young person was bound to a master for an agreed number of years. The terms and conditions of apprenticeship were set out in dated deeds of indenture, signed by the parent or guardian and the master, each of whom kept a copy.

In Great Britain between 1710 and 1811, Stamp Duty was payable on apprenticeship indentures, based on the premium (lump sum) paid for the training and upkeep of the boy or girl. It fell due within two months of signature for apprenticeships within 50 miles of London, and within six months for those elsewhere. Payment could, however, be deferred for up to a year after completion of the apprenticeship. Parish and charity apprenticeships were exempt. If someone was apprenticed to another member of the family, as often happened, although no money changed hands, duty was still assessed on the estimated value of the apprenticeship.

If an apprentice was passed on to another master and a further premium paid, it too became dutiable.

What will you find? The microfilmed apprenticeship registers are in series IR 1. There are separate City or Town Registers for apprenticeship indentures stamped in London from October 1711 until January 1811, and Country Registers for indentures stamped locally between May 1710 and September 1808. The entries are numbered consecutively and are arranged chronologically by date of stamping on each day of the week. The enrolments in the Country Registers are organized in regional blocks because the batches of indentures sent to London by the local agents were written up together.

Every entry should record the date of payment, name, place and county of residence and occupation of the master, the apprentice's name, date of the indenture, term of years for which he or she was bound or the period remaining if it was an assignment to another master, the premium paid, and amount of duty. To 1752, the entries should also include the name, domicile and status or occupation of the apprentice's parent or guardian.

Since boys and girls were usually bound out between the ages of 12 and 14, the given details about their places of abode lend a forceful clue to their birthplaces. Apprenticeship was often entrusted to relatives or natives of the same place but living elsewhere, so by probing into the masters' family backgrounds, especially after 1752, you may incidentally discover the home parishes of their apprentices.

The Apprenticeship registers contain many thousands of entries. You can search indexes to the names of taxed apprenticeships 1710–62 and 1763–74 on microfiche. The indexes are also searchable online at **www.origins network.com**. There is an index of masters, 1710–74, also available on microfiche, linked by page numbers to the indexes of apprentices, enabling you to discover who any individual trained, where they came from, and which former apprentices themselves became masters.

For later entries you will need to trawl through the actual apprenticeship registers for both City (Town) and Country.

- The Duty proved extremely difficult to enforce, and it seems that there was widespread evasion, so you may be unlucky.
- If he/she was likely to be bound out at parish expense you could try the parochial overseers of the poor accounts for any record of money paid to a local farmer or householder willing to employ such a young boy or girl as cheap labour. This was generally done when the child was about 7 or 8 and apprenticeship continued up to 21. The parish copies of the signed indentures may survive. They will identify the names of the overseers, the person taking on the child, the youngster and perhaps even a parent, and will outline the terms and conditions and date when apprenticeship was to begin. This material is now mainly on deposit in county record offices.
- Breaches of apprenticeship were pursued in the county quarter sessions, so these records may help too. Many of the catalogues to county quarter sessions records are now accessible online at **www.national archives.gov. uk/a2a**. You can also find their whereabouts from *Quarter Sessions Records for Family Historians: A Select List*, by J. Gibson.
- City or borough apprentices can be tracked down in the binding-out and freedom registers of the Corporation, individual livery company, guild or burgess books. These are held in the relevant city or borough record office, and some have been indexed and published. Many of the City of London livery company records are in the Guildhall Library. Online indexes to a number of these can be inspected at **www.origins network.com**. For details of City of London livery companies whose records are not on deposit in Guildhall Library, visit **www.history.ac.uk/ gh/livintro.htm**.
- If your ancestor did not undergo any formal apprenticeship, there is unlikely to be any written record of it. The Duty was confined to trades, crafts and professions rather than domestic or agricultural work. A statute of 1563 made mandatory apprenticeship only to existing trades and crafts, particularly in the area in and around the City of London.
- Your ancestor was apprenticed after the Duty was abolished. As private documents, apprenticeship indentures occasionally surface among family and business records of the parties concerned. It is worth contacting the company, firm or business to which the person was apprenticed, if it still exists. Try keying-in the business title at **www.nationalarchives. gov.uk/nra**.

**Other apprentice-
ship records in
the National
Archives**

Wills of masters frequently mention their apprentices as beneficiaries. See
WILLS AND OTHER PROBATE RECORDS.

From 1729, a person wishing to become an attorney or solicitor was required
to undergo a period of training (known as articles of clerkship) for five
years with a fully qualified practitioner. In 1749, an Act of Parliament
decreed that a statement should be filed with the relevant court confirming
that the articles had actually been carried out.

We hold copies of many articles of clerkship, affidavits of due execution,
enrolments of admission and oaths of allegiance of lawyers in England. For
attorneys and solicitors in the Courts of Great Sessions in Wales, contact
the National Library of Wales in Aberystwyth, visit its website at **www.
llgc.org.uk**, and consult *A Guide to the Records of Great Sessions in Wales*
by G. Parry. The dated articles of clerkship provide the name, address,
status or occupation of the parent or guardian, the name and address of the
attorney or solicitor, and the name of the clerk, the terms and conditions of
the clerkship, and how much was paid; they were then signed. Articles of
clerkship in the Court of Common Pleas between 1730 and 1838 are in series
CP 5. There is a personal-name index to the numbered deeds attached to
our bound catalogue for this series. The dated sworn affidavits of due execution give details of the name and address of the attorney, the parties to
the articles, the court in which the clerk was now qualified to practise, plus
his address, the date of the original agreement, the term of years and start-
date, and the signatures of the witnesses to the articles. These likewise may
give family relationships and clerks' ages. Affidavits of due execution of
articles of clerkship filed in the Court of King's Bench between 1775 and
1817 are in series KB 105, from 1817 to 1834 in series KB 106, from 1834 to 1875
in series KB 107, and affidavits relating to people who were not admitted
between 1831 and 1848 are in series KB 109. There are personal-name indexes to the affidavits between 1749 and 1845 in series KB 170; this also includes
indexes to the registers of articles from 1749 until 1777, which no longer survive. Affidavits of due execution filed in the Court of Exchequer of Pleas
from 1833 until 1855 can be found in E 4/3. Copies of articles of clerkship
from 1729 to 1800, and affidavits filed in the Palatinate Court of Chester
from 1728 to 1830, are in series CHES 36, affidavits filed in the Palatinate
Court of Durham between 1660 and 1843 are in series DURH 9, and copies
of articles and affidavits 1749–1814 in the Palatinate Court of Lancaster are
in series PL 23. You can find copies of articles of clerkship filed in the
equity Court of Chancery from 1801 up to 1831 in C 217/184 and 185, and
affidavits of due execution of articles of clerkship from 1730 until 1836 in
C 217/23–40, and for the period 1800–39 in C 217/183, 186 and 187, the last
two of which also include copies of articles of clerkship 1800–39 and
1823–36 respectively. Only specimens of affidavits enrolled after 1875 have
been preserved, in series J 89.

Soldiers' children: the admission and discharge registers of orphaned or
unclaimed boys and girls in the Royal Military Asylum (called the Duke of
York's Military School from 1892), 1803–1956, include those who were
apprenticed, in WO 143/17–25. There is an apprenticeship book, 1806–48, in
WO 143/52, and a list of apprentices, 1806–35, who enlisted in the

Army but were returned to their masters to complete their training, in WO 25/2962.

Seamen's children: registers of child apprentices from the Royal Naval School (Greenwich Hospital School), 1808–38, are in ADM 73/421–48.

Registers of apprentices protected from impressment into the Royal Navy, 1740–59, 1761–2 and 1795–1806, are in series ADM 7.

Merchant Navy apprentices: under an Act of 1823, ships over 80 tons had to carry apprentices and their names were enrolled. Compulsory apprenticeship was abolished in 1849. Indexes of their names, ages, dates and periods of indenture, together with the names of their masters, 1824–1953, are in series BT 150. Five-yearly samples of the original indentures 1845–1950 are in series BT 151, and 1895–1935 in series BT 152.

To find out more, read our Research Guides:
Apprenticeship Records as Sources for Genealogy
Lawyers: Records of Attorneys and Solicitors; and
City Livery Companies and Related Organisations, a Guide to their Archives in Guildhall Library

Army service records

There was no regular standing army in England until 1642. Prior to this, county militia, made up of able-bodied men between certain ages, served as a local defence force, and later as a standby (see p. 52 on surviving records).

In 1660, a small standing army was established under a Secretary at War. From 1855, the War Office took charge. Until 1855 too, a Board of Ordnance was responsible for supplying arms and fortresses, for gunners (the Royal Artillery), and for engineers (the Royal Engineers), who, before the early 18th century were usually civilians.

The British Army was made up of regiments: Guards or Household troops (Horse and Foot); Cavalry (originally Horse and Dragoons); Infantry (Foot and Line); and Corps (Royal Artillery and Royal Engineers), each comprising 600 to 1,000 men. A typical regiment consisted of two battalions, one stationed abroad and the other at home from which men were sent to replace the overseas stations. The local militia formed the third battalion. Up to 1772, members of the Royal Engineers were officers, employing casual labour, after which a special Corps of Royal Military Artificers was set up, comprised solely of other ranks. In 1811, this became the Royal Corps of Sappers and Miners, with both officers and men, and in 1856 it was amalgamated with the Royal Engineers.

In 1751 the Army was reorganized and each regiment assigned a number in order of seniority. This continued until 1881, but the numbers were still used much later. At this point, many of the regiments were merged and linked to specific counties.

There is a wide range of sources for military genealogy. Look out for *Army Records for Family Historians* by S. Fowler and W. Spencer. We have a copy of *Armies of the Crown: The Bibliography of their Regimental Histories, Great Britain, the Empire and Commonwealth* and in our Online Publications and Electronic Resources Archive. Visit our exhibition of British Battles, from the Crimea to Korea, at **www.nationalarchives.gov.uk/battles**.

17TH CENTURY TO 1913

If you can discover your ancestor's dates of service, his regiment or a campaign in which he fought, this will make your task simpler. As many of the records are arranged by regiment it will help to know to which one your ancestor belonged.

Was your ancestor a commissioned officer? If so turn to p. 41.

Was your ancestor a non-commissioned officer or other rank? See below.

Don't know? Search the printed *Army Lists*. These were published annually from 1754 to 1879, and then four times a year (in January, April, July and October) until 1950. There are copies of these and later *Lists* on the open shelves in the Microfilm Reading Room. Many are available in local libraries too. Look at a volume covering a year when you know your forebear was in the British Army. From 1766, there is a personal-name index at the back, although the names of commissioned officers in the Artillery and Engineers are only indexed from 1803. There are additional indexed, amended *Lists* between 1754 and 1879 in series WO 65. Look up the page reference for details of his regiment, current rank and date of his present commission. If his name doesn't appear and you have tried *Lists* for several years without success, consult the records about non-commissioned officers and men.

Other ranks

'Other ranks' includes privates in the Infantry, troopers in the Cavalry, trumpeters and drummers, gunners and sappers, serving under corporals and sergeants, who were non-commissioned officers. There are records about regular soldiers from the early 18th century onwards. Before 1871, men at 18 could enlist voluntarily and for life, which was usually treated as 21 years. Boys under 18 could join too, but their reckonable service only commenced at 18. They served until they were disabled or into old age. Starting in 1871, they could opt for a 12-year short-service engagement, the last six of which were spent on reserve. Re-engagement was permitted for up to a maximum of 21 years' service in all. After 1810, soldiers were able to buy themselves out of the Army early.

What will you find? The service records of army out-pensioners of the Royal Hospital Chelsea, 1760–1913, are in series WO 97 and other discharge documents of pensioners, 1782–1887, are in WO 121/1–136, both of which include men in invalid and veteran battalions on garrison duty. The individual personnel papers are arranged according to date of discharge. From 1883 up to 1913, you should be able to trace the careers of men on short-term engagements too. The signed papers contain details of regimental number and regiment,

WO 97/1453: Attestation and discharge of Corporal John Lyons, a soldier for over 20 years. In 1857, he was one of the first recipients of the Victoria Cross for his outstanding gallantry at Sebastopol, during the Crimean War.

date and place of enlistment, age and occupation on joining, birthplace, a full physical description, a summary of his army career including dates of service in and transfers from other regiments, ranks attained, any promotions, courts martial and demotions, good conduct pay, awards of campaign or gallantry medals, a medical sheet, and the date and place of discharge and on what grounds. The pensioner's date of death may be recorded too. From 1855 the intended place of residence was set out, and from 1883 the name and relationship of the next of kin.

Series WO 97 is on microfilm up to 1854 (you can hire a copy in family history centres) but later records have to be ordered up as original documents.

Service records of men in the Royal Artillery discharged between 1791 and 1855, and in the Royal Horse Artillery from 1803 to 1863, are in series WO 69, and thereafter in series WO 97. The records in series WO 69 are arranged under the unit in which a soldier last served, and include the attestation papers, name, age, a physical description, birthplace, trade, dates of service and any promotions, with the dates of marriage and death. Series WO 97 also yields details of artillerymen going to pension from 1760 to 1854. Royal Engineers' service records are in WO 97. Description Books relating to

Royal Engineers between 1787 and 1807 are in WO 54/313–16, and include information about Sappers and Miners. The entry books of discharges, casualties and transfers of Artillery and Engineer (Sappers and Miners) soldiers from 1740 to 1859 are in WO 54/317–37.

The service records of non-commissioned officers and other ranks in the Life Guards, Royal Horse Guards and Household Battalion from 1799 until 1920 are traceable in series WO 400.

Finding aids

You can search the online index to the names of soldiers discharged to pension between 1760 and 1854, using our online catalogue to series WO 97, and for those discharged between 1782 and 1887 in WO 121/1–136. Just key in the surname and forenames, the approximate year of birth if you know it, and the series number WO 97 and/or WO 121.

The screen will display the document reference, the name, any aliases, the place and county of birth, the regiment in which he last served, age at discharge and length of service, and the dates of service (WO 97) or the year of discharge (WO 121), plus the microfilm image number (WO 121).

There is no personal-name index to service documents in series WO 97 of soldiers discharged to pension between 1855 and 1882. Up to 1872, they are arranged by regiment or unit, then alphabetically by soldier's name. You will need to order the box of original documents covering those surnames in your part of the alphabet, in series WO 97. From 1873 to 1882, the documents are catalogued by type: Cavalry, Artillery, Engineers, Foot Guards, Infantry and Miscellaneous Corps, and then alphabetically by surname range. The service papers of men discharged between 1883 and 1900, and 1900 and 1913 are listed alphabetically by surname range regardless of regiment or unit.

For service records of artillerymen in series WO 69, you will need to search the indexes and posting books in WO 69/779–82, 801–39 to identify the last unit in which a man served, before looking at the papers themselves.

What if you can't find your ancestor?

• The service papers might have been misfiled. If you haven't already done so, search through the entire contents of the document box. If this fails, then try the boxes of mis-sorts in WO 97/6355–83 for discharges to pension between 1843 and 1899, and WO 97/6323–54 for discharges between 1900 and 1913. Again, these are listed alphabetically by surname range, regardless of regiment or unit.

• You might have been looking at papers for the wrong regiment. Lots of soldiers switched regiments during the course of their careers. The pensioners' papers are filed under the last regiment in which they served before discharge. Taking a date when your ancestor belonged to a particular regiment, study the three-monthly muster books for that regiment in series WO 10 (Artillery, 1710–1878), WO 11 (Engineers, 1816–78), WO 12 (general, including Invalid and Veteran battalions, 1732–1878) or WO 16 (all, 1877–98) to find out when and why he left. Try the 'Topic Index' part of our online catalogue for the growing list of references to musters of individual regiments in series WO 10, WO 11 and WO 12 which are being uploaded. The volumes are arranged alphabetically within each rank. When his name disappears from the muster, look at the list of non-effectives at the end for the date and reason for leaving, his birthplace, trade and date of enlistment.

• Your ancestor might not have received a pension. If you know the regiment, inspect the muster books for his period of service. The musters set out each soldier's regimental number, dates between which he was paid, dates of any awards of good conduct pay, reasons for any absences, and any additional remarks such as dates and places of hospitalization or death in service. If he joined or left the regiment during that three-month period the accrued months, weeks and days of service will be noted. For new recruits, search the list of their names at the end of the muster. This will tell you when and where the soldier enlisted or transferred from another regiment, his age and former occupation. From 1868, a special list at the end of each muster gave the names of soldiers' wives and when placed on the married establishment, together with the number, sex, ages, but not the names, of their children. Deserters can be traced in the regimental musters, like casualties, as well as in series WO 25 between 1811 and 1852, and in series HO 75 from 1828 to 1845.

• Your ancestor might have died in service. Besides the lists of non-effectives described above, you could examine the monthly and quarterly casualty returns from 1809 until about 1875, in series WO 25. These are arranged by regiment. They also record details about absentees, deserters and discharged men. Each soldier's name is given, plus his last rank, birthplace, former trade, date, place and nature of the casualty, together with details about his debts or credits, and the name of the next of kin or chief creditor. Try the pension records in series PIN 71, which includes disabled soldiers' and widows' pension applications made between 1880 and 1914. The date range given against each person's name in the catalogue relates to the date of enlistment and when the pension was stopped.

• He might have been in one of the Indian Army regiments. Records of soldiers recruited by the Madras, Bengal and Bombay Native Regiments are kept in the Asia, Pacific and Africa Collections, in the British Library in London.

• Your ancestor might have assumed a different identity. The Army promised a uniform, regular food and pay, adventure, excitement, and a means of escape from destitution, unemployment, creditors, family and the law. You may be lucky enough to trace such a person's army service record, but not his birth or baptism, because his personal details were falsified, including his age and birthplace. Where a soldier resorted to aliases, these will be disclosed by the WO 97 and WO 121 online databases. The mis-sorts of soldiers' papers from 1843 to 1913, in series WO 97, include those relating to men who enlisted under assumed names and later confessed their real identities. The papers are arranged under their true names.

• Your ancestor might have served in the First World War. His service papers were likely to have been removed and kept with those of his later service for pension purposes. See the section on army service records of the First World War and later (p. 43).

Microfiche copies of the General Register Office indexes to regimental registers of births and baptisms of families of army personnel stationed at home and abroad, 1761–1924, will tell you the regiment, place and year the events occurred. The indexes to army chaplains' overseas returns (Army Returns) of births and marriages, 1796–1955, and deaths, 1796–1950, will reveal only the station and year. There are separate indexes listing deaths of members of the Natal and South African Field Forces during the Boer War (1899–1902), also on microfiche. The indexes are available at **www.1837 online.com/Trace2web/LogonServlet**.

If you know where your soldier was stationed, consult *In Search of the 'Forlorn Hope': A Comprehensive Guide to Locating British Regiments and their Records,* by J.M. Kitzmiller. This will tell you which regiments were where at what date. Then you can burrow your way through the muster books of each regiment in series WO 10–WO 12 or in series WO 16 to locate your ancestor by process of elimination.

If you know where your soldier lived in retirement, you could try the pension registers covering that district between 1842 and 1883, in series WO 22, or between 1702 and 1917, in series WO 23. The latter includes former members of colonial regiments, pensioners settled in the colonies, and former soldiers in the East India Company service (1814–75). These list names of recipients in alphabetical order, plus their last rank and regiment at the time of discharge. Names of pensioners in India, Canada and South Africa recorded in WO 120/35, 69 and 70, can be found in *British Army Pensioners Abroad, 1772–1899,* by N.K. Crowder. Admission books relating to pensions awarded for length of service, 1823–1913, in series WO 117, are arranged in date order. From 1857, they contain details of regiment, last rank, age at discharge, years of service, pension rate, duration of any time spent overseas which would boost the pension, a regimental surgeon's report, a character reference, cause of any disability, a physical description, birthplace and usual trade. From 1874, they record the intended place of residence, date of discharge and number of good conduct badges received. Similar information about pensioners discharged because of disablement 1715–1913 is contained in series WO 116, and for men discharged from the Royal Hospital in Kilmainham, outside Dublin, Ireland, 1704–1922, in series WO 118. A selection of war pension files relating to applications made by disabled soldiers or their widows, relating to service prior to 1914, are in series PIN 71. The entries cover the period 1854–1979, and the names of applicants in this series are searchable online. The conduct sheets include details of age, birthplace, parents' names and those of any siblings, religious denomination, a physical description and marital status.

For details about military wills, see p. 182.

Medals

The medal rolls marking campaigns between 1793 and 1949 are in series WO 100. They are available on microfilm in our Microfilm Reading Room, or you can hire a copy from a family history centre. The first campaign medal to be awarded to all ranks was the Waterloo Medal, issued in 1816. The Military General Service Medal for survivors of battles during the wars with France to 1814 was retrospectively given only to those still alive in 1847. Search the online catalogue for the campaign in which you are interested. In the bound copy of the catalogue, the medals are listed by campaign, in date order, and then by regiment.

Awards of the Victoria Cross for acts of outstanding bravery, 1856–1957, are enshrined in series WO 98, and from the time of the Crimean War (1854–6) up to 1914 in series WO 32, codes 50D and 50M. We also hold material relating to other gallantry awards. Long-service (18 years) and good conduct medals were introduced in 1831, and you can examine the lists of recipients up to 1953 in series WO 102.

To find out more, read our Research Guides:
British Army: Useful Sources for Tracing Soldiers
Medieval and Early Modern Soldiers
Civil War Soldiers, 1642–1660
British Army Soldiers' Discharge Papers, 1760–1913
British Army Muster Rolls and Pay Lists, c 1730–1898
British Army Courts Martial, 17th–20th Centuries
British Army Soldiers' Pensions, 1702–1913
Medals: British Armed Services: Campaign Medals, and Other Service Medals
Medals: British Armed Services: Gallantry
Medals: British Armed Services: Gallantry, Further Information.

Army officers before 1914

A commissioned army officer's career outline can be gleaned from the printed *Army Lists*, published every year from 1754. An almost complete set of these is in the Microfilm Reading Room, and many reference libraries have copies too. Look in the personal-name index at the back for entries after 1766 for the page reference, on which you will discover the officer's current rank and date when commissioned. The *Lists* encompass officers on full and on half-pay. Annotated *Army Lists* from 1754 to 1879 are in series WO 65. The quarterly *Army Lists*, from 1879, provide birth dates and promotions and a seniority list arranged by rank. After April 1881, they record war service too, though from 1909 until 1922 these appear only in the January issue.

Up to the end of October 1871, commissions in the Army were bought and sold, except in the Royal Artillery, Engineers and Ordnance, where promotion was based on merit.

What will you find?

You can search the applications and supporting testimonials for commissions in Commander-in-Chief's Memoranda, 1793–1870, in series WO 31. These loose papers are filed chronologically in bundles, according to the date of appointment, and then in regimental order, so are fairly easy to worm your way through. Once you have located the date of the commission from the *Army List*, search the online catalogue or bound copy of it for the bundles covering the two weeks up to and including the date of the commission for the right reference. You will then need to order them as an original document. As well as revealing the reason and background to the sale and vacancy, and how much the commission cost, the application papers often provide valuable insight into regimental loyalty spanning several generations of a family, the testimonials and correspondence describing the character and education of the applicant.

Returns of officers'
services

The first official records to include biographical information about army officers were the returns of service relating to commissioned officers retired on full or half-pay, made in 1828, in series WO 25. The volumes are now available on microfilm, and are arranged alphabetically by name. The signed and dated returns give the age of each officer when first commissioned, his date and place of marriage, wife's name, and details of children's births and places of baptism, as well as a dated summary of his military career. In 1829, and from 1870 to 1872, similar returns were compiled for commissioned officers on the active list, to which were added their dates and places of birth. There are some returns dating from earlier than 1870, and a few after 1872. These returns are arranged by regiment. A return of services of retired officers was undertaken in 1847, and arranged alphabetically. Other regimental service records between 1755 and 1915 may be found in series WO 76, and for Artillery officers from 1771 to 1870 and Engineers from 1796 to 1922, see series WO 25. Series WO 76 is on microfilm too. Copies of these microfilms can be hired in family history centres.

Registers of service of every commissioned officer at 1 November 1871 are in series WO 74. These too are arranged by regiment.

Finding aids

There is an incomplete card index of officers' names in the Microfilm Reading Room. This will give you the WO 25 and/or WO 76 film numbers and page references for any surviving service returns.

What if you
can't find your
ancestor?

• He wasn't a commissioned officer. Try the records relating to non-commissioned officers and other ranks.
• He was in the Indian Army. Try the Asia, Pacific and Africa Collections, in the British Library. The printed *Army Lists* include the names of officers commissioned in the native Indian regiments.
• You've searched the wrong period. Search the *Army Lists* for other years.

Other records
about army
officers in the
National Archives

Details about officers commissioned prior to 1727 can be found in *English Army Lists and Commission Registers, 1661–1714*, and *George I's Army, 1714–1727*, both by C. Dalton. A few manuscript lists of commissioned officers between 1702 and 1823 are in series WO 64, to which there is a manuscript index between 1704 and 1765. Look also in *List of Officers in the Royal Regiment of Artillery, 1716–June 1914, Roll of Officers of the Corps of Royal Engineers from 1660 to 1898* and *Commissioned Officers in the Medical Services of the British Army, 1660–1960*, by A. Peterkin, W. Johnston and R. Drew.

Baptism certificates had to be produced by candidates for government service, as membership of the Established Church of England implied loyalty to the British Crown. There are lots of such certificates of army officers in WO 23/8903–20 (code 21A) for the period 1777 to 1868, and from 1755 to 1908 in series WO 42. The documents in the latter series are mostly arranged alphabetically between 1776 and 1881. Marriages reported by commissioned officers between 1830 and 1882 are included in WO 25/3239–45.

Army officers became entitled to a retirement pension in November 1871. Previously, they sold their commissions or went onto half-pay. Half-pay was introduced in 1641 for officers of reduced or disbanded regiments, and eventually evolved into a retainer fee for as long as the commission was held. From 1812, it was payable to officers deemed unfit for further service. Ledgers containing details of half-pay, 1737–1921, are in series PMG 4, and until 1841 they are arranged by regiment. Thereafter the entries run alphabetically by surname of officer. They record the final rank and last regiment, total annual pension, its date of commencement and when the four equal instalments were paid out each year, the eventual date of death, and to whom pension arrears were to be sent according to the officer's will or as part of the administration of his estate, and any family relationship between them. From 1837, addresses of both the officer and recipient of arrears are given too, and later still the officer's date of birth is included. A few officers were entitled to retire on full pay: series PMG 3 consists of ledgers of payments made to them between 1813 and 1896. Pensions awarded to wounded officers, 1812–97, are recorded in series WO 23, and ledgers of payments from 1814 to 1920 are in series PMG 9.

Applications for widows' pensions, 1755–1908, can be found in series WO 42, which includes supporting proofs of marriage and births of children, as well as details of burial and wills left by deceased commissioned officers.

Microfiche copies of the General Register Office indexes to regimental registers of births and baptisms of families of army officers stationed at home and abroad, 1761–1924, reveal their regiments, places and years the events happened. You should also consult the Army Returns (see p. 42). The indexes are also available at **www.1837online.com/Trace2web/ LogonServlet**.

For military wills, see p. 182.

To find out more, read our Research Guides:
British Army Lists
British Army: Officers' Commissions
British Army Officers' Records 1660–1913
Medals: British Armed Services: Campaign Medals, and Other Service Medals
Medals: British Armed Services: Gallantry
Medals: British Armed Services: Gallantry, Further Information.

ARMY SERVICE RECORDS OF THE FIRST WORLD WAR AND LATER

In 1914, there were 133,514 officers and men in the British Army. By 1918, a further 7,712,772 men and women had enlisted, almost a third of them volunteering before conscription.

The minimum joining age was 18, and 19 for service abroad, but more than a quarter of a million under-age boys had enlisted before 1916. Many lied about their true ages and gave assumed names to avoid detection by their parents. Because of heavy losses at the Front, by the close of 1915 voluntary enlistment had seriously withered. Phased-in conscription was introduced for single men between the ages of 19 and 35 in January 1916, extended to married men in April the same year, and all males within the prescribed age groups had to register and show proof of age.

Only about 40 per cent of army service papers survive for non-commissioned officers and other ranks who left the Army or died before 1921, and less than 86 per cent of service records of commissioned officers who left the Army or died before 1 April 1922. This is because they were severely damaged by fire in 1940. The service records of the Foot Guards (the Coldstream/ Grenadier/Irish/Scots/Welsh) have been retained by their regimental head-quarters, in Wellington Barracks, London. For career details about officers and men in the British Army whose service ran after the above dates, contact the Army Personnel Centre in Glasgow. However, this is only released to the person him or herself, to someone with his or her written permission, or to the next of kin, and a fee is payable. You will need to spec-ify your exact relationship to the person. For service details of members of the colonial regiments, you will have to contact the national archives of the relevant country, though those relating to members of the Indian Army are in the Asia, Pacific and Africa Collections in the British Library in London.

Read _Army Service Records of the First World War_ by W. Spencer, for a full des-cription of our holdings. Visit our online exhibitions at **www.national archives.gov.uk/pathways/firstworldwar** and at **www.nationalarchives. gov.uk/battles**, which includes digital images of documents and text about D-Day, 1944, and the Korean War.

What will you find? Was your ancestor a commissioned officer, non-commissioned officer or other rank? If he was a commissioned officer see p. 48. If not, then read on. If you are unsure, check the personal-name indexes at the back of the print-ed _Army Lists_ for the war years to locate the page references to entries for commissioned officers, arranged by regiment, rank and seniority of com-mission.

Soldiers' services, 1914–20

You can search microfilmed copies of extant 'burnt' and fragments of sur-viving documents in series WO 363. Copies of the microfilms can be hired in family history centres. They are arranged alphabetically by the surnames and personal-names of non-commissioned officers and other ranks. The filmed copies may range from a few scraps of charred paper to an entire personnel file. The various forms record the soldier's name, rank, regiment, battalion and regimental number, his age and birthplace, occupation on joining up, a physical description, any former military service, the date and place of enlistment, followed by details of war service (including any courts martial), awards of campaign or gallantry medals, a conduct sheet, and a medical history sheet. You can also find out the name and address of his next of kin, parents or grandparents, the name and address of his wife and dates of birth of legitimate children, and the names and ages of brothers

WO 363/V60, f1049: Richard Verner's Army service papers include a statement listing his surviving relatives. He was killed with his brother Adrian on the first day of the Battle of the Somme, in 1916.

and sisters. If the soldier was killed or died in service this was written into the documentation. The discharge form gave the man's intended address on leaving the Army, the reason for his discharge and a character reference.

If your relative was in the Household Cavalry, try series WO 400, which runs up to 1920. If he served in one of the Foot Guards, then contact the Guards Regimental Headquarters.

The Forms of Enrolment between 1917 and 1920 of women joining the Women's Army Auxiliary Corps (WAAC), set up in 1917, are in series WO 398, available on microfilm. Each form specifies the person's age, address, marital status and willingness to serve abroad. The series also includes a Qualification of Applicant form setting out her birthplace as well as current address, qualifications, work experience, present occupation, and names of two referees.

Finding aids

The catalogues to series WO 363 are arranged by initial letter A–Z, and by the first and last surname on each film. At the end of the catalogue is a similar alphabetical list of 'mis-sorts'; an index to the mis-sorts can be searched using our online catalogue.

What if you can't find your ancestors?

• Try the mis-sorts.
• The service papers don't appear to have survived. Try series WO 364, also on microfilm. These are pension papers relating to about three-quarters of a million men who were medically discharged during the Great War, or who retired as regular soldiers before 1921, so they also contain details about men serving before 1914 who re-enlisted. There is a 'maxi' and a 'mini' catalogue to this series, which is arranged in the same way as WO 363. The 'mini' catalogue is being fully indexed for inclusion in our online catalogue for WO 364.
• His service continued beyond 1920. You will need to write to the Army Personnel Centre in Glasgow.
• You don't know which regiment he served in and there are lots of soldiers of the same name. If he died or was reported missing the Debt of Honour Register of the Commonwealth War Graves Commission at **www.cwgc.org/ debt_of_honour.asp** should help sort out his regiment. This database contains entries relating to over 1.7 million men and women in the United Kingdom and Commonwealth units and regiments who were killed or reported missing during the two World Wars, with details of 23,000 cemeteries, memorials and other locations in the world where they are commemorated. Key in the person's surname and initials, the war, year of death if you know it, the force and person's nationality, and you can then inspect his or her regimental number, rank, the title of the last regiment, the date, age, circumstances and place of death and of burial or commemoration. Try also *Soldiers Died in the Great War*, available on CD-ROM in our Library and Resource Centre and in our Online Publications and Electronic Resources Archive, which is searchable by name, birthplace and place of abode. From this database you can learn the regimental number, rank, regiment, last address, date and place of birth, and when and where the soldier was killed or reported missing. The online database of indexed digital images of campaign medals at **www.nationalarchives.gov.uk/ documentsonline** will reveal the regiments, regimental numbers and ranks of the named recipients, and the names of their next of kin. Did you check similar family details in series WO 363, if the documentation survives, to eliminate at least a few of them? Have you a photograph of your soldier in uniform? The Imperial War Museum in London may be able to help you identify his regiment.

A selection of files about pensions awarded to soldiers discharged owing to sickness or wounds between 1920 and 1989 is in series PIN 26. Also included are pensions paid to dependants. However, this is only a 2 per cent representative sample, although it complements series WO 364. The records are arranged alphabetically in five different sections, according to the type of pensioner, the dates in the catalogue referring to the date of enlistment and cessation of payment of the pension. The content is similar to that in WO 364, and the series often contains copies of death certificates. You can search our online catalogue to PIN 26 by keying in the surname and initials of the soldier concerned.

Index cards recording the awards of First World War campaign medals to servicemen and women in the Army and Royal Flying Corps, in series WO 372, are available online at **www.nationalarchives.gov.uk/documents online**. On the cards is given each man's or woman's name, rank(s), abbreviated titles of his or her regiment(s), battalion, corps or unit, and regimental number(s) in coded form. You can find out from the index if he or she was awarded the Victory Medal for service between 1914 and 1919, the British War Medal from 1914 to 1920 (which with the Victory Medal became known as 'Mutt and Jeff'), the 1914 Star (otherwise known as the Mons Star) and the 1914–15 Star. Awards of either Star, plus the Victory and British War Medal were known as 'Pip, Squeak and Wilfred'. The index includes the Territorial Force War Medal (1914–19) and the Silver War Badge (awarded to men and women discharged because of sickness or wounds any time after 4 August 1914). If the solder was killed in action ('kia') the war theatre will be indicated too. In such cases the medals were sent to the next of kin. To work out what the abbreviations mean, consult *The Regimental List*, available in the Microfilm Reading Room.

To decode the medal references given in the WO 372 index and convert them to the original medal roll references in series WO 329, you will need to use the key to the Medal Roll Index in WO 329/1.

Honours, awards, decorations and Mentions in Dispatches were published in the *London Gazette*. You can search the indexed entries for 1914–20 online at **www.gazettes-online.co.uk/index** (see p. 29).

Awards of the General Service Medal and India General Service Medal between 1919 and 1938 are included in WO 100/411–93, available on microfilm.

To discover in which actions your ancestor's battalion or unit was involved, scour the diaries in series WO 95 (1914–22). Search our online catalogue for full document references for the battalion or unit number and regiment. You can read digital images of selected war diaries at **www.national archives.gov.uk/documentsonline**, which are searchable by battalion. Some confidential diaries are in series WO 154.

Personal details about soldiers who died in the Great War (1914–19) can be found on CD-ROM, as part of our Online Publications and Electronic Resources Archive and in many reference libraries and family history centres. Try also the Debt of Honour Register (see previous page).

You can search microfiche copies of the General Register Office indexes to deaths of army other ranks killed or dying in the First World War (1914–21), and of men in the Indian Services for the same period. Each of these identify the regiment or unit to which the deceased belonged. The indexes are accessible at **www.1837online.com/Trace2web/LogonServlet**. An incomplete set of death certificates of soldiers dying in France, Flanders and Belgium between 1914 and 1921 can be found in series RG 35, which is on microfilm both in the National Archives and in the Family Records Centre, as well as being available to search in family history centres. These complement the GRO indexes of Army War Deaths for the same period.

Don't forget to check our microfilmed back-issues of *The Times* (see p. 29). Announcements of war casualties were often delayed for many weeks, so the indexes are an invaluable finding aid. There should also be an account of the actions in which the troops were then engaged.

Later registrations Search the microfiche copies of the General Register Office indexes for births and marriages between 1796 and 1955, and to deaths from 1796 to 1950, recorded in the overseas chaplains' station (Army) Returns (see p. 42). Indexes to deaths of soldiers killed or dying between 3 September 1939 and 30 June 1948 are also available on microfiche. The indexes are searchable at **www.1837online.com/Trace2web/LogonServlet**.

To find out more, read our Research Guides:
British Army Soldiers' Papers: First World War 1914–1918
British Army: Courts Martial, First World War, 1914–1918
Women's Military Services, First World War
First World War: Disability and Dependants' Pensions
Medals: British Armed Services: Campaign Medals, and Other Service Medals
Medals: British Armed Services: Gallantry
Medals: British Armed Services: Gallantry, Further Information
British Army War: Campaign Records, 1914–1918, First World War Diaries
Military Maps of the First World War, 1914–1918
Prisoners of War (British), c 1760–1919
War Dead: First and Second World Wars
First World War: Conscientious Objectors and Exemptions from Service.

The Imperial War Museum holds a large collection of material relating to the First World War and later conflicts. Its website is **www.iwm.org.uk**.

Most regiments have their own museums, most of which host their own websites. Addresses and contact details of regimental museums can be located in *A Guide to Military Museums and Other Places of Military Interest,* by T. and S. Wise. Many regiments have published histories too.

Army officers in the First World War

We hold two groups of indexed service records of 217,000 commissioned officers who died or left the British Army before 1 April 1922. The first, in series WO 339, covering the period 1914 to 1939, relates to officers on Regular Army and emergency commissions, and the Special Reserve of Officers.

Because of the high number of officer casualties, men were frequently promoted from the ranks actually on the battlefield. Their records, too, are in series WO 339. Officers commissioned during the war were usually temporary. The second group, in series WO 374, for the years between 1898 and 1922, contains details about officers on temporary commissions and in the Territorial Army, officers coming out of retirement, and civilian specialists. No records are known to survive for women officers in the Women's Army Auxiliary Corps (WAAC).

What will you find?

In both series WO 339 and WO 374, there is a separately referenced personal file for each officer, which originally contained his attestation papers, a record of service, confidential reports and personal correspondence, accompanied by a note on the date of death where appropriate. The files were weeded, so not all of this information survives. You might find a dated and signed application for an appointment, stating the desired battalion or unit, which will disclose the candidate's date and place of birth, whether British born, a naturalized British subject or of European descent, his marital status, place of education, current address and occupation or profession. The application form made provision for any previous army service, the name and address of the next of kin, the relationship between them, and the candidate's level of physical fitness. Letters and memoranda are complemented by medical reports, and where relevant, details about any awards, decorations and Mentions in Dispatches, capture, pensionable wounds, discharge from service or death and the ultimate settlement of the officer's estate. For officers commissioned before 1901, try series WO 76, though the correspondence files no longer exist.

Finding aids

The personal-name indexes to series WO 339 and WO 374 are accessible via our online catalogue. The screen should display the surname, initials, rank and period of service, plus a document reference, so that you can order up and inspect the file itself.

What if you can't find your ancestor?

• The online catalogue hasn't recognized your request. You can always search the online indexes to the above long number papers in WO 339, in series WO 338, which relates to officers' services between 1870 and 1922, and consult the bound copy of the alphabetical index to series WO 374 for more information. If the long number in series WO 338 has a 'P' beside it, this means the officer's service continued beyond 31 March 1922, and you will need to write to the Army Personnel Centre in Glasgow. If it is a mixture of letters and numbers (usually the first letter and the first vowel of the surname), then the files will be in WO 374. However, some entries relate to personal files that were later destroyed.
• He was in the Foot Guards. These records are still in the care of the Guards Regimental Headquarters in London.
• The service records don't survive. You could try the battalion or unit diaries in series WO 95, which will tell you what was going on during his term of engagement. He might even have been mentioned.

- His service continued beyond 31 March 1922. Write to the Army Personnel Centre.
- He was in the Royal Army Medical Corps. Records about officers recruited for the war were destroyed, but their names are included in the printed *Army Lists*, and you can also find information about them in *Commissioned Officers in the Medical Services of the British Army, 1660–1960*, by A. Peterkin, W. Johnston and Sir W.R.M. Drew. Otherwise try series WO 339 and WO 374.

Other records about commissioned officers in the Army in the First World War in the National Archives

The indexed monthly *Army Lists* contain the names of all commissioned officers, even those on the Reserve list. You can use them to trace promotions and any changes of units over time. The quarterly and half-yearly *Lists* relate only to men on permanent commissions, but from these you can discover their dates of birth. Look in the 'War Services' section of the quarterly *List* published each January for details about campaigns and medals awarded to officers.

Medal rolls

Whilst campaign medals were automatically sent to non-commissioned officers, other ranks or their next of kin, officers or their legal representatives had to apply to the War Office, so not every officer claimed them. You can search indexed digital images of the card indexes to recipients of campaign medals, in series WO 372, at **www.nationalarchives.gov.uk/documentsonline**. For details on decoding the medal references, see p. 47. Only the rank and name of each officer is given on the British War Medal and Victory Medal rolls.

Gallantry medals, awards and Mentions in Dispatches were announced in the *London Gazette* (see p. 29).

War diaries

Arranged by battalion or unit, the war diaries, 1914–22, in series WO 95, come as a revelation to people with relatives who served in the Great War, because they provide a graphic eye-witness account of what it was like to be there. If your forebear was an officer, one of his duties might have been to compile the diary. Any commissioned officers who were casualties are always singled out by name, so you can find out how and where they died, were reported missing, were wounded or were taken prisoner. Digital images of selected war diaries are available at **www.nationalarchives.gov.uk/documentsonline**. These are searchable by battalion. Supplementary, confidential, war diaries are in series WO 154.

War dead

Consult *Army Officers Died in the Great War* in our Online Publications and Electronic Resources Archive. Key in your officer's name, and if you know it, the theatre of war where he was killed or last known. If his name can be found, the screen will show details of his rank, regiment, family home, his date and place of birth, and when and where he died. The Debt of Honour Register (see p. 46) will reveal his rank, regiment, age, date of death and exactly where he is buried or commemorated, as well as a brief summary of how he met his death or was reported missing.

You can search microfiche copies of the General Register Office indexes listing deaths of army officers killed or dying in the First World War (1914–21), and of commissioned officers in the Indian Services for the same period. The indexes can be culled at **www.1837online.com/Trace2web/LogonServlet**.

Have a look at *The Times* (see p. 29). Officers who were killed or reported missing, wounded or taken prisoner almost always merited mention in the death notices or obituaries in this broadsheet, though this frequently happened some time after the reported event.

To find out more, read our Research Guides:
British Army Lists
British Army: Officers' Records 1914–1918
British Army: Campaign Records, 1914–1918, First World War
Military Maps of the First World War, 1914–1918
Prisoners of War (British), c 1760–1919
First World War: Disability and Dependants' Pensions
War Dead: First and Second World Wars
British Army: Courts Martial: First World War, 1914–1918
Medals: British Armed Services: Campaign Medals, and Other Service Medals
Medals: British Armed Services: Gallantry
Medals: British Armed Services: Gallantry, Further Information.

Records about officers since 1 April 1922, and men and women in the Army since 1921

Contact the Army Personnel Centre in Glasgow for information about World War II officers and servicemen.

A small sample of disability pension records of officers discharged because of sickness or wounds between 1920 and 1989 is in series PIN 26. These are listed alphabetically by the name of each applicant, and you can search our online catalogue for document references by keying in the name of the officer concerned. There is also a selection of personal files of pensioners who died between 1923 and 1980, in series WO 324; they are listed alphabetically, enabling you to search our online catalogue by name for the original document reference. Some of the files are not yet open to the public.

You can read the original war diaries kept during the Second World War for a daily record of campaigns and actions in the following theatres of war:

WO 167	British Expeditionary Force	WO 178	Military Missions
WO 175	British North Africa Forces	WO 171	Northwest Europe
WO 170	Central Mediterranean Forces	WO 168	British North-West Expeditionary Force, Norway
WO 179	Dominion Forces	WO 257	Ships Signals Sections
WO 215	General Headquarters Liaison Regiment	WO 172	South-East Asia Command
WO 166	Home Forces	WO 218	Special Services
WO 174	Madagascar	WO 176	Various smaller theatres
WO 177	Medical Services	WO 165	War Office Directorates
WO 169	Middle East Forces	WO 173	West Africa Forces

Take care when using our online catalogue, though, because the titles of regiments are often abbreviated.

Details about medals awarded for long service (18 years) and good conduct between 1831 and 1953 can be found in series WO 123, whilst recommendations (citations) for gallantry awards or those for meritorious service up to 1967 are in series WO 373, available on microfilm. The surviving recommendations are arranged by operational theatre and usually by the date of the announcement in the *London Gazette*. For northwest Europe, in series WO 171, check our online catalogue for the names of individuals mentioned in the diaries. You can search for your relative's name from 1939 to 1948 in the *Gazette* at **www.gazettes-online.co.uk/index** (see p. 29).

Another source worth exploring is the *Army Roll of Honour* of servicemen and servicewomen killed or dying between 1 September 1939 and 31 December 1946, excluding 'dishonourable deaths'. This database, drawing on information in series WO 304, is available on CD-ROM, in our Library and Resource Centre, and as part of our Online Publications and Electronic Resources Archive. All you have to do is key in the person's name: this should give you the army service number, date and place of death, rank, first and last units served in, birthplace, place of residence, and any awards and decorations. Check the Debt of Honour Register (see p. 46).

Examine the microfiche copies of the General Register Office indexes listing deaths of army officers and of other ranks killed or dying during the Second World War, or dying of wounds between 3 September 1939 and 30 June 1948. Each of these identify the rank and regiment or unit to which the deceased belonged. You can also cull microfiche copies of the indexes of regimental registers of births and baptisms of children of officers and men between 1761 and 1924, and the Army Returns (see p. 42). Further microfiche copies, of General Register Office indexes to births and marriages in the Service Departments run from 1956 up to 1965, and for deaths from 1951 to 1965. Thereafter search the annual indexes to Births Abroad, Marriages Abroad and Deaths Abroad, available on microfiche up to 1992. You can also search these online up to recent registrations at **www.1837online.com/ Trace2web/LogonServlet**.

Have a look at our indexed digital copies of *The Times*. Death announcements and obituaries relating to officers killed during operations in the Far East, Korea and other actions are well worth tracking down in this newspaper, as well as publications of honours and awards.

To find out more, read our Research Guides:
British Army Lists
War Dead: First and Second World Wars
Prisoners of War, British, 1939–1953
Military Maps of the Second World War
Medals: British Armed Services: Gallantry
Medals: British Armed Services: Gallantry, Further Information.

THE MILITIA, YEOMANRY, VOLUNTEERS, RIFLE VOLUNTEERS, FENCIBLES AND HOME GUARD

From early times, local forces were raised in periods of emergency to protect the home front. Until 1871, the raising and training of local militias was the responsibility of the lord lieutenant of each county, who also appointed the officers. After 1285, adult males between the ages of 15 and 60 were expected to equip themselves with weapons and armour according to the value of their land and chattels, when summoned to appear for training or service. The resulting musters tell you parish by parish who was able-bodied, and who was not, and what weapons each man could provide. From the mid-17th century, special Trained Bands of mercenaries were used instead, at parish expense, so the lists of names of male parishioners are not so comprehensive. After 1757, as a result of a series of reforms, every county had its own militia regiment, and after 1881 each was attached to a Regular Army regiment as its third battalion. A kind of conscription was employed, and to 1831 a yearly list of men aged between 18 and 50 (lowered to 45 in 1762) was compiled by parish constables, from which an enrolment list was drawn up of those men selected by ballot to serve. In 1908, the Militia was renamed the Special Reserve, and the Supplementary Reserve in 1924. It was disbanded in 1953.

The Yeomanry was a cavalry corps and like the Volunteers was raised by private or municipal initiatives. The Volunteers were dissolved in 1813, but re-formed as Rifle Volunteers in 1859. The Yeomanry and Volunteers became the Territorial Force in 1908, and the Territorial Army in 1920.

The Fencible Infantry and Cavalry, which were regular regiments raised for home service, are often classed with the Militia.

In 1940, the Local Defence Volunteers (LDV) was set up, consisting of male civilians aged 17–62. This was later renamed the Home Guard.

Look at *Records of the Militia and Volunteer Forces, 1757–1945*, by W. Spencer, for more background information.

What will you find?

Surviving Tudor and Stuart militia musters are in a variety of E (Exchequer) and SP (State Papers) series. The earliest known surviving county militia musters date from 1522, in series E 101.

Militiamen's attestation papers, 1806–1915, in series WO 96, are arranged by the Regular Army unit to which they were linked after 1881, and then alphabetically by name within each regiment. From these you can discover each man's date and place of birth, and full military career details. You can identify the Regular Army unit to which the particular militia was attached from the 1882 and later printed *Army Lists*.

The militia muster rolls, dating between 1780 and 1878, are in series WO 13. These include not only forces raised in England, Scotland and Ireland, but the Colonial Militia, Fencible Infantry and Cavalry, Yeomanry, Irish Yeomanry and Volunteers. The first entry for each person gives his age and date of enlistment, and the last his date of discharge or death.

Some militia soldiers qualified for a pension after serving in the American Revolutionary (1775–83) and Napoleonic Wars (1793–1815), so their discharge papers will be found in series WO 97 (see p. 36).

The careers of militia officers can be tracked down in the annual *Army Lists* from 1865, and in the monthly *Army Lists* between 1798 and June 1940. There are incomplete service records of officers covering the period 1757 to

1925, in series WO 68, and a selection of their birth and baptism certificates, 1788–1886, in WO 32/8906–13.

Soldiers' documents, giving details about age, birthplace, usual trade, date of enlistment, and service of men in the Imperial Yeomanry, 1899–1902, are in series WO 128. They are arranged by regimental number, which can be located in the personal-name indexes in WO 129/1–7. This index has been uploaded at **http://hometown.aol.co.uk/KevinAsplin/home.html** and includes the Scottish Horse and Lovat Scouts. A copy of the printed index, compiled by K.J. Asplin, is available in our Library and Resource Centre. Similar service records and attestation papers of men serving in locally recruited volunteer forces during the South African (Boer) War are in series WO 126 and WO 127. The careers of members of the Territorial Army discharged or dying between 1914 and 1920, can be traced on microfilm in series WO 363, which is arranged alphabetically (see p. 44). Records of service of commissioned officers leaving the Army or dying between 1914 and 31 March 1922 are in series WO 374, which is indexed by personal-name (see p. 49). Otherwise most material is assumed to be held locally by regimental museums.

Service records of members of the Home Guard are held by TNT Archive Service, in Swadlincote. The names of officers in the Home Guard in October 1944 are listed in WO 199/3210–17.

Finding aids

You can discover document references to 16th- and 17th-century county musters in the National Archives in *Tudor and Stuart Muster Rolls* by J. Gibson and A. Dell. Many of the musters are held in county record offices. For a county-by-county listing of surviving later rosters, read *Militia Lists and Musters, 1757–1876* by J. Gibson and M. Medlycott. The musters may tell you the names, occupations and any noted infirmities of local men, and from 1802 onwards, the number of their children over and under the age of 14, and sometimes their precise ages. From 1806 expect to find the ages of the men too.

What if you can't find your ancestor?

• Try the records of the Regular Army.
• His service went beyond 1920. You will need to contact the Army Personnel Centre in Glasgow (see p. 194).

Other records about men in the militia, yeomanry, volunteers, rifle volunteers, fencibles and home guard

We hold microfiche copies in our Microfilm Reading Room of the General Register Office indexes to regimental registers of births and baptisms of children of Regular Army and militia personnel stationed at home and abroad between 1761 and 1924. Then there are similar copies of the indexes to deaths in the South African War, 1899–1902, to army officers and to other ranks killed or dying during the First World War, 1914–21, to army officers and to other ranks who were casualties during the Second World War, or who died of wounds between 3 September 1939 and 30 June 1948. You can search the indexes at **www.1837online.com/Trace2web/LogonServlet**.

To find out more, read our Research Guides:
Tudor and Stuart Militia Muster Rolls
Militia 1757–1914
British Army Muster Rolls and Pay Lists, c 1730–1898
Auxiliary Army Forces: Volunteers, Yeomanry, Territorials and Home Guard, 1769–1945
British Army Lists
Home Front: Second World War, 1939–1945.

Births, marriages and deaths of Britons at sea and abroad

BIRTHS, MARRIAGES AND DEATHS OF BRITONS AT SEA

When civil registration of births, marriages and deaths was introduced in England and Wales on 1 July 1837, similar returns of births and deaths of Britons at sea began to be made to the Registrar General in London. They were known as 'Marine Returns'. These registers are held in the General Register Office in Southport, although another useful series of records, known as the Registrar General's Miscellaneous Non-statutory Foreign Returns of births, baptisms, marriages and burials of Britons at sea between 1831 and 1958, is in the National Archives. The non-statutory returns contain extra entries not found in the Marine Returns, because by an accident of history the returns sent in the diplomatic or consular bags, and destined for the Bishop of London as the titular head of the Anglican Church overseas, often found their way to the Registrar General instead.

In 1851, it became obligatory for masters of merchant ships to send the wages and effects of dead crewmen to the Registrar of Shipping and Seamen so they could be distributed to the next of kin. From 1854 masters were required to keep official logs of births and deaths of passengers during each voyage. This information was conveyed by the Registrar of Shipping and Seamen to the Registrars General of England and Wales, Scotland or Ireland, depending on where the deceased had lived. Both series of records, filed with the Board of Trade, are now in the National Archives, and in many cases form a unique record of events at sea, such as when ships sank and there were no bodies whose deaths could be formally registered. Passengers of other nationalities are included in these returns as well.

You can search microfiche copies in our Microfilm Reading Room of the General Register Office indexes to the Marine Returns of births and deaths from 1837 to 1965, the annual indexes to Births Abroad and to Deaths Abroad from 1966 onwards up to 1992 (both of which embody maritime entries including those on board British-registered hovercraft from 1972 onwards, and deaths on offshore installations, lifeboats and other emergency survival craft belonging to them). Between 1914 and 1918, and 1939

**What will
you find?**

and 1945 the indexes also embrace war casualties on board merchant
vessels. Annual indexes to registrations from 1993 onwards can be inspected in the Family Records Centre.

Microfiche copies of the indexes to General Register Office returns of officers
and ratings in the Royal Navy, Royal Naval Air Service, Royal Marines
and Submariners dying at sea during the First World War, 1914–21, record
their rank or rating, ship or unit and year of death. These do not list men
reported missing. You can also search microfiche copies of the indexes to
war deaths of Royal Navy officers, Navy ratings and all ranks of the Royal
Air Force which occurred between 3 September 1939 and 30 June 1948, and
these include men and women reported missing and presumed dead.
Again, rank or rating, ship or unit and year are given. The indexes to First
World War deaths of army officers, and the indexes for other ranks, yield
the names of Royal Flying Corps and Royal Air Force personnel as well. For
the Second World War, there are similar indexes to the names of army
officers, and to other ranks. There are separate indexes to all ranks of the
Royal Air Force who were casualties. Like the previous indexes, these too
are searchable at **www.1837online.com/Trace2web/LogonServlet**.

The Registrar General's Miscellaneous Non-statutory Foreign Returns are
worth trawling because they may remove the need to purchase a certificate,
and you can examine microfilm copies of the original registrations yourself.

Births/baptisms at sea, 1831–1931	RG 32/1–16	Indexed in RG 43/2
Marriages on board naval ships, 1842–89	RG 33/156	Indexed in RG 43/7
Deaths at sea, 1831–1958	RG 32	Indexed in RG 43/4–7, 10–14, 20, 21
Deaths of Britons on board French ships, 1836–71 (written in French)	RG 35/16	Indexed in RG 43/4
Deaths of Britons on board Dutch ships, 1839–71 (written in Dutch)	RG 35/17	Indexed in RG 43/4

Microfilmed copies of registers of wages owed to and personal effects of
deceased merchant seamen covering the years 1852–81, and from June 1888
until September 1893, are in series BT 153. Each entry sets out the seaman's
name, register ticket number, date and place of engagement, date, place and
cause of death, name and port of the last ship, the master's name, date and
place of payment of wages, wages owed and when forwarded to the Board
of Trade. Monthly lists of their deaths can be located for the period 1886–90
in series BT 156, which is also on microfilm. In the lists are embedded
details of name, age, rating, nationality or birthplace, last known address
and cause and place of death.

Microfilmed copies of the registers of births of children to passengers at sea,
1854–87, and passengers' deaths from 1854 to 1890, extracted from the ships'
logs deposited with the Registrar General of Shipping and Seamen, are in
series BT 158. These contain integral indexes. Births at sea to British nationals and people of other nationalities between 1875 and 1891, and reported to
the Registrar General of Shipping and Seamen, are also in series BT 160.
The series is arranged in separate filmed volumes under England and
Wales (which includes non-Britons), Scotland or Ireland. Filmed registers

of their deaths from 1875 to 1888 can be studied in series BT 159, which is organized in the same way. For births at sea between 1891 and 1964 and deaths from 1891 to 1960, look in series BT 334. There is also an indexed register of marriages of passengers at sea between 1854 and 1972 in BT 334/117. You will need to search our online catalogue for references to the correct period and event, and then order each as an original document. The birth entries will tell you the name of the ship, her official number and port of registry, the child's date of birth, name, sex, father's name, his rank or occupation, mother's name and maiden surname, the nationality or birthplace and last place of abode of both parents. You will find that many of the babies were named after the vessels on which they were born. The death registers set out details of the ship, official number and port of registry, the date of death and place (or longitude and latitude), the name of the deceased person, sex, age, rating if a crewman, rank or occupation if a passenger, nationality or birthplace, last address, cause of death and any further comments. Many were drownings, but you can trace people who succumbed to epidemics during the voyage or who jumped overboard.

Such entries are not always in the General Register Office records; for instance, when a ship went down and no bodies were found, you will find a list of victims in BT 334, but not in the General Register Office indexes to Marine Returns. Marriages on board ship were probably not recognized by English and Welsh law, but the registers in BT 334/117 identify the date, ship, official number, and the names, ages, marital status, profession or occupation of both parties, plus their fathers' names and occupations.

You can discover details about deaths of merchant seamen between 1939 and 1950 in series BT 380, which were extracted from the log books and crew agreements of Allied and commandeered ships, and these mainly relate to World War II. Deaths on board ships engaged in the coastal trade, and similarly extracted between 1939 and 1945, are in series BT 381, which includes those which occurred off the Irish Free State as well as the UK coastline. A further series, BT 385, covers deaths during World War II, taken from the ships' log books and crew agreements which were received by the Registrar General of Shipping and Seamen. A final series, BT 387, includes details about the deaths between 1939 and 1946 of merchant seamen who served on Allied or foreign ships requisitioned by His Majesty's Government.

For information about Royal Naval personnel who died at sea, see p. 164.

Finding aids

You will already have seen that most of the above records are indexed, so are easy to access. The General Register Office indexes of Marine Returns are a good starting point for identifying many of the births and deaths recorded in the BT series. You can thus save yourself cost and delay in obtaining a certificate by reading the relevant Board of Trade registers. The indexed digital images of returns of births and deaths at sea from 1854 to 1890, in series BT 158, can be searched at **www.nationalarchivist.com**.

There are personal-name indexes to the pages in the registers of deceased seamen's wages and effects in series BT 154, which then enable you to establish the correct BT 153 microfilm reference. Series BT 155 is an alphabetical list of vessels mentioned in series BT 153.

Month June **Year** 1912 . **REGISTER OF DECEASED PASSENGERS.**

	PARTICULARS OF SHIP.													
	8. Name.	10. Official Number.	11. Port of Registry.	12. Date of Death.	13. Place of Death.	14. Name and Surname.	15. of Deceased.	16. Sex.	17. Age.	18. Rank, Profession, or Occupation.	19. Nationality, or Birthplace.	20. Last Place of Abode.	21. CAUSE OF DEATH.
	Titanic	131428	Liverpool	15.4.12	About Lat 41°16'N Long 50°14'W	Patrick	Fox	M			Irish	Queenstown	Supposed drowned
						Martin	Gallagher	M			Ireland	Queenstown	
						John	Sarfinch	M	22	shoe op	Eng		
						George	George	F	42	wife	Syra	Syria	
						Shahini					Syria	Syria	
						Josef	Sirio	M	21	farmhand	Syrian	Syria	
						Youssef	Serio	M	26	labourer	Syrian	Syria	
						Stanio	Theophff	M		Lab.	Bulgaria	Bulgaria	
						Leslie	Gilinsky	M	22	locksmith	Russia		
						Frank	Goldsmith	M	33	turner	Eng		
						Nathan	Goldsmith	M	41	bootmaker	Russia	Cape Town	do
						Augusta	Goodwin	F	43	Wife	Eng	Bath	do
						Charles E	Goodwin	M	14	child	do	do	do
						Frederick	Goodwin	M	40	Engr. Lab	do	do	do
						Harold V	Goodwin	M	9	child	do	do Melksham Wilts	do
						Josie A.M.	Goodwin	F	10	do	do	do	do
						Lillian A	Goodwin	F	16	do	do	do	do
						Sidney L	Goodwin	M	6	do	do	do	do
						William F	Goodwin	M	11	do	do	do	do
						Manuel Estanislau	Goncalves	M	38	Labourer	Portuguese	Brazil	do
						George	Green	M	40	farrier	English		
						Daniel D	Gronnestad	M	32	Labourer	Norwegian	Norway	
						Robert	Guest	M	23	do	English	London	
						Alfred	Gustafson	M	20	do	Swede	Sweden	
						Anders	Gustafson	M	37	do	Finn	Finland	
						Johan	Gustafson	M	28	do	do	do	

BT 334/52, p61: The entire emigrant Goodwin family were supposed drowned when RMS *Titanic* struck an iceberg in 1912, en route to the Port of New York. Only 711 of the known 2,201 on board were rescued.

- Have you tried each of the above options?
- The event happened before the records began. Try looking for a registered copy of the will or grant of letters of administration in the Prerogative Court of Canterbury (PCC), which had overall jurisdiction over property over a certain value left in this country by people dying at sea or abroad. You can search the indexed digital images of such registered wills between 1384 and 1858 at **www.nationalarchives.gov.uk/documentsonline**. For information on how to trace PCC administration grants, see p. 180. Warrants for grants of probate or of letters of administration issued by the PCC between 1657 and 1858, in series PROB 14, disclose the date of death of the testator or intestate, though this is more usual from the mid-18th century. This can be particularly helpful in the case of servicemen. Wills of people dying at sea leaving property within a single archdeaconry or diocese might be found in a local probate court. To discover their whereabouts, consult *Probate Jurisdictions: Where to Look for Wills*, by J. Gibson and E. Churchill.
- There is a gap in the records. For merchant seamen, investigate the ships' crew lists and agreements and official logs, in series BT 98, for the period 1852–60, and for 1861–1990 try series BT 99. These logs note deaths during a voyage, and the resulting auctions of personal possessions among the crew, though the latter series contains only a 10 per cent sample, the remaining 90 per cent being dispersed elsewhere. All the casualty and death lists between 1914 and 1918 are included in this series. For more information see pp. 136–7. Royal Naval ships' logs, in series ADM 50–55, and musters, in series ADM 36–ADM 39, ADM 41 and ADM 102, elicit details of personnel dying at sea. For more information about these, see pp. 160, 163.
- The baptisms of children born to passengers at sea might be located at the port of arrival or place of ultimate destination. Sadly, sometimes their burials will be recorded there too. The National Archives is unlikely to have copies of these registers. Otherwise, consult *The British Overseas: A Guide to Records of their Births, Baptisms, Marriages, Deaths and Burials available in the United Kingdom* for a survey of records in the Guildhall Library and elsewhere. The Guildhall Library holds two volumes featuring some baptisms and burials at sea between 1894 and 1952, and baptisms from 1955 to 1961. In the same library you can also inspect the 'International memoranda', which consist of returns made by overseas clergy to the Bishop of London of baptisms in 1810, 1822 and 1860–1921, and of burials at sea from 1860 to 1919. Don't forget to try the International Genealogical Index. For details of civil registration start-dates throughout the world, and where you can search copies of the indexes and registers, refer to *International Vital Records Handbook*, compiled by T.J. Kemp.

There is a register of births to emigrants and deaths at sea in CO 386/169, and two further books listing deaths on voyages between 1854 and 1869 are in CO 386/171–2.

To find out more, read our Research Guide:
Births, Marriages and Deaths at Sea.

Other records about births, marriages and deaths at sea in the National Archives

BIRTHS, MARRIAGES AND DEATHS OF BRITONS ABROAD

Up to 1980, the Bishop of London was responsible for Anglican dioceses abroad and overseas clergy's returns of baptisms, marriages and burials were made to his registry. Some of them were sent via the Foreign Office, Colonial Office or Registrar General, and these are now in the National Archives. The bishop's jurisdiction over American Episcopal churches ended in 1776, over Canada in 1787, the Caribbean in 1824, and southern Europe in 1842, when the diocese of Gibraltar was set up. Ecclesiastical returns of baptism, marriage and burial of Britons in India are now in the Asia, Pacific and Africa Collections of the British Library in London.

In July 1849 Consular Returns began to be made to the Registrar General in London of births, marriages and deaths of British subjects in foreign countries, and later on, from United Kingdom and British High Commissions in former colonies and Commonwealth countries from their date of independence.

What will you find? Search our online catalogue by keying in the name of the city, state, province or country of your choice, the type of event and date range. Alternatively, you can check the country-by-country listing of Foreign Office (FO), Colonial Office (CO) and other references in *Tracing your Ancestors in the Public Record Office*, by A. Bevan. For references to the Caribbean, look in *Tracing your West Indian Ancestors,* by G. Grannum.

The FO and CO records may take the form of local bound registers or loose bundles, many of which are written in the native language, especially those weddings performed '*lex loci*' (according to local law). There is a set of marriage returns from British embassies, consulates and legations covering the period 1846 to 1890, in FO 83/1136–47. This series includes correspondence relating to overseas weddings between 1814 and 1905. Other returns of marriages abroad, 1873–89, are in series FO 97.

Overseas newspapers contain birth, marriage and death announcements of British residents. Try the collections in the Newspaper Library, British Library. You could also consult *The Times* for births, marriages and deaths of expatriates and Britons working or stationed abroad (see p. 29).

The Registrar General's Miscellaneous Non-statutory Foreign Returns of births, baptisms, marriages, deaths and burials of Britons abroad between 1627 and 1965, in series RG 32–RG 36, are another fruitful source, though most before the late 18th century emanate mainly from The Hague, in the Netherlands.

The General Register Office indexes to Consular Returns of births, of marriages and of deaths from July 1849 to 1965, can be searched on microfiche in our Microfilm Reading Room, as can similar indexes to returns from United Kingdom and British High Commissions of births to 1966, and marriages and deaths to 1965 in Commonwealth countries since their date of independence. Some of these start in the 1940s. Later indexes to Births Abroad, Marriages Abroad and to Deaths Abroad up to 1992 can be examined on microfiche, but for later entries you will have to visit the Family Records Centre, where you can purchase a certified copy of the

(Page 96)

MARRIAGES *solemnized in the House of Her Britannic Majesty's Embassy at Paris, in the Year 1874*

Lord Randolph Henry Spencer Churchill, Bachelor of the Parish of Woodstock in the county of Oxford and Jennie Jerome, Spinster of the Parish of City of Brooklyn, State of New York, U.S.A. were married in this church with the consent of Her Majesty's Ambassador this fifteenth Day of April in the year one thousand eight hundred and seventy four By me, Edwd Forbes D.D. Offg Minister This marriage was solemnized between us, Randolph Henry Spencer Churchill Jennie Jerome In the presence of Leonard W. Jerome

RG 33/76, p96: Lord Randolph Churchill married Jennie Jerome at the British Embassy, in Paris, in 1874. Despite disapproving of the match, her father Leonard signed the register.

full registration. The indexes up to recent times are also accessible for a fee at www.1837online.com/Trace2web/LogonServlet.

Finding aids

There are no personal-name indexes or special finding aids to any of the FO or CO series, unless specified in the catalogue, except for FO 802/239, which is an index to the marriages recorded in series FO 83 and FO 97 described above. Foreign Office General Correspondence from 1808 to 1890 can be located via the registers in series FO 802, filmed copies of which are in series FO 605, to which you can help yourself. Other registers of General Correspondence, between 1817 and 1920, are in series FO 566, to which card indexes 1906–10 and 1910–19 in our Research Enquiries Room are linked. However, the document references on the cards need to be converted to archival ones, and some relate to papers which no longer survive. From 1920 to 1951 there are annual published index volumes, also in the Research Enquiries Room. Frustratingly, the records to which the printed indexes relate have been weeded, and you will similarly need to convert the cited record references to archival ones. For help in understanding the coded entries, read our three online Research Guides, *Foreign Office Records from 1782*, *Foreign Office: Card Index, 1906–1910* and *Foreign Office: Card Index, 1910–1919*. Our staff can help you too. For unindexed FO records you could first tackle the General Register Office indexes to Consular Returns of births, of marriages and of deaths from July 1849 to 1965, and then check to see if we hold copies of the registrations. If we do not, then try the indexes to the Registrar General's Miscellaneous Non-statutory Foreign Returns, in series RG 43, which span the period 1627–1960.

Miscellaneous registers of births, baptisms, marriages, deaths and burials, 1831–1964	Series RG 32	Indexed to 1960 in RG 43/2, 6, 10–14, 20, 21
Registers, notebooks and copies of registers kept by clergy, British embassies and legations, 1627–1958; the series includes some marriages performed by British consuls prior to 1859, and deaths from enemy action in the Far East, 1941–5	Series RG 33	Indexed in RG 43/1, 3, 7, 15–17, 19
Miscellaneous marriage returns, including those issued by foreign registrars, 1826–1921	Series RG 34	Indexed in RG 43/8, 9
Deaths abroad, 1830–1921; the series includes death certificates of British military personnel in hospitals in France and Belgium, 1914–21	Series RG 35	Indexed in RG 43/4–6 (excludes the military deaths, 1914–21)
Returns of births, marriages and deaths in British African and Asian Protectorates, 1895–1965	Series RG 36	Indexed, 1904–40, in RG 43/18

The indexes are not complete, so do search the copies of the actual registers to be really sure you have not missed that vital entry.

What if you can't find your ancestor?

• His or her birth, marriage or death was recorded locally. This is likely to be the case in the British Dominions and colonies. You will need to contact the relevant registrar. Consult *International Vital Records Handbook*, compiled by T.J. Kemp. A number of indexes and registers have been filmed and made available in family history centres. Try also the International Genealogical Index at **www.familysearch.org**, and the Vital Records Index for Scandinavia and for Mexico at the same website. You can search the Vital Records Index for Australia on CD-ROM, or as part of our Online Publications and Electronic Resources Archive. This index is composed of births, baptisms, marriages and deaths registered in New South Wales (1788–1888), Tasmania (1803–99), Victoria (1837–88), and Western Australia (1841–1905).

• There are online indexes to births registered in British Columbia, in Canada, at **www.vs.gov.bc.ca/genealogy/electronic_index.html** for the years between 1872 and 1884 (or 120 years after a birth was registered), marriages from 1872 to 1929 (or 75 years after the wedding), death registrations from 1872 until 1984 (or 20 years after demise), and deaths overseas of 3,423 British Columbians during World War II (1940–5). You can hire microfilm copies of the actual registrations to peruse in any family history centre.

• The birth, marriage or death might be mentioned in sources elsewhere. For instance, the Corporation of London Guildhall Library holds some bound volumes of 'International memoranda', consisting of returns of baptisms, marriages and burials made to the Bishop of London's registry between 1816 and 1924, the earliest recorded baptism being in 1788.

• Try Dr Williams's Registry of Births of dissenters registered in London between 1742 and 1837, in series RG 4 and RG 5, and the Wesleyan Methodist Metropolitan Registry of Births, 1818–40, in series RG 4, which both incorporate births overseas (see p. 142). Extracts from the birth registrations are available in the British Isles Vital Records Index.

- The Asia, Pacific and Africa Collections in the British Library hold the ecclesiastical returns of births, baptisms, marriages, deaths and burials in the three Presidencies of Madras from 1698, Bengal from 1709, and Bombay from 1713 up to 1948, and there are a few additional registrations as late as 1968. The returns exclude Roman Catholics before 1836. To access the returns, consult the indexes for each Presidency.
- Try the Debt of Honour Register (see p. 46).

See ARMY SERVICE RECORDS, MERCHANT NAVY, ROYAL AIR FORCE, ROYAL MARINES, ROYAL NAVY.

To find out more, read:
Guildhall Library Research Guide 2: *The British Overseas: A Guide to Records of Births, Baptisms, Marriages, Deaths and Burials Available in the United Kingdom*

Other records of births, marriages and deaths of Britons abroad in the National Archives

Cemetery records

Before 1850, most burials took place in churchyards or beneath the church floor; there might also be separate burying grounds for nonconformists and foreign congregations. The registers of burials kept by parish churches are now mostly in county record offices, and those relating to dissenters are in the National Archives, county record offices and elsewhere (see p. 139). *The Phillimore Atlas and Index of Parish Registers*, edited by C.R. Humphery-Smith, contains maps of English, Welsh and Scottish counties indicating Anglican parish boundaries and the start-dates of the first known registers, whilst the index tells you where the records are and for what period. The Society of Genealogists has an ongoing publication programme of compiling a *National Index of Parish Registers*, which includes details of known dissenters' chapel registers, their whereabouts and any copies. These county-by-county guides are available in the Family Records Centre and in many reference libraries. There is a special volume covering *Nonconformist Registers of Wales*, edited by D. Ifans.

After 1850 in London, and 1852 in the rest of the country, almost all urban and many rural churchyard burials were forbidden for reasons of hygiene and public health, so private cemetery companies started to be established as well as burial boards set up by local councils. Cremation began in 1902, the registers of which are kept in each crematorium. You can find a list of cemeteries and crematoria in England and Wales in the latest edition of *The Family and Local History Handbook* by R. Blatchford. For London, consult *Greater London Cemetries and Crematoria* by P.S. Wolfston, revised by C. Webb, and *London Cemeteries, An Illustrated Guide and Gazetteer* by H. Meller.

Check the National Burial Index (see p. 25) in our Online Publications and Electronic Resources Archive. Many family history societies and local record offices possess compiled burial indexes too.

RG 6/1332, p224: Jonathan Fardon was buried at Banbury, in Oxfordshire, four days after his death in 1763. The Fardons were a prominent Quaker family. The month is given as a number, in accordance with Quaker practice.

Very few burial entries are incorporated into the International Genealogical Index and British Isles Vital Records Index.

What will you find?

Records of many non-parochial burial sites are embedded in series RG 4, RG 8 and RG 6 (Religious Society of Friends), all on microfilm.

We hold the following London nonconformist cemetery registers:

• Bethnal Green Protestant Dissenters' Burying Ground (or Gibraltar Row Burying Ground), 1793–1837, in RG 8/305–14. A personal-name index is available in the Family Records Centre.

• Bunhill Fields Burial Ground, City Road, 1713–81, in RG 4/3974–4001, 4288–91, and 4633. There is an index in RG 4/4652–7. Another index, for the years 1827–54, is held by the Corporation of London Guildhall Library.

• Bunhill Fields Burial Ground (Golden Lane Cemetery), 1833–53, in RG 8/35–8.

• South London Burial Ground, East Street, Walworth, 1819–37, in RG 4/4362.

- Southwark New Burial Ground, 1821–54, in RG 8/73–4.
- Spa Fields, St James Clerkenwell, 1778–1849, in RG 4/4316–22, 4366–7.
- Victoria Park Cemetery, Hackney, 1852–76, in RG 8/42–51. The entries are arranged alphabetically.

For burials in the Anglican cemetery of the Royal Hospital in Greenwich between 1705 and 1864, look in RG 4/1669–76 and RG 8/16–8. Interments in the Royal Hospital, Chelsea, Burial Ground, 1692–1856, are in RG 4/4330–2, and 4387.

You can also discover lists of names of people buried in churchyards and cemeteries which have been cleared since the 1860s. Most stem from the 18th and 19th centuries, and note the places of re-interment. The lists, in series RG 37, are arranged by place. Correspondence and data relating to cemeteries closed within the last 30 years is held by the Office for National Statistics, in Southport.

Finding aids

See above for details of indexes to particular graveyards. Many of the Quaker registers, in series RG 6, contain integral personal-name indexes. You can also examine microfilm copies of the County Digests of deaths and burials of members of the Society of Friends in their library in London (see p. 141).

You can search Boyd's London Burials Index (see p. 25) of over 250,000 male London burials between 1538 and 1853, at **www.originsnetwork.com**.

What if you can't find your ancestor?

- You've looked in the wrong place. People were not always buried where they died. If your forebear left a will or the death was reported in a local newspaper, check these for clues about the resting place.
- Your ancestor might have been cremated. Contact the local district council for information on crematoria in the area where your relative died.
- The records are defective. If you know where your antecedent was buried, investigate the chance of a gravestone inscription. Some headstones refer to burial elsewhere, with a commemoration above the traditional family plot. Search *Monumental Inscriptions on the Web*, by S.A. Raymond, for addresses of online databases, and visit **www.ffhs.org.uk** for updated progress reports on memorial indexing projects currently being undertaken.
- Many dissenters did not have burying grounds of their own. Nonconformist ancestors might have been interred in the churchyard of the Established Church of England, so look in parish registers too.
- Not all nonconformist chapel registers were surrendered to the central authorities in 1840 or 1857 (see p. 139). You may have to hunt these down in a county record office, the chapel itself or the denominational archive repository. From the 1850s onwards nonconformists were likely to have been buried in special 'unconsecrated' parts of cemeteries run by local burial boards or in private cemeteries.
- Parish church burial registers shouldn't be confused with those of cemeteries, even if the funeral service took place in the church. The actual registers recording interments were compiled by the owners of the graveyards where the deceased were laid to rest, which might be the district council or a private company.

Burials of Britons at sea and abroad are included in the Registrar General's Miscellaneous Non-statutory Foreign Returns, and in those made to the Board of Trade (see p. 56).

See the Debt of Honour Register (p. 46).

To find out more, read:
J. Litten, *The English Way of Death: The Common Funeral since 1450.*

Census returns

1841–1901

The first complete population count (census) of the United Kingdom took place in 1801, and similar enumerations have been carried out at ten-yearly intervals ever since, apart from in 1941. Starting on Sunday 6 June 1841, the names of everyone have been listed, arranged under the households in which they slept on the appointed census night. From 1861 they embrace British naval and merchant vessels in port or at sea, though these are not complete.

You can study the returns of names of inhabitants and their personal details once the records are 100 years old. Microform copies of returns from 1841 to 1901 are widely available, but you can only scrutinize a complete set for the whole of England, Wales, the Channel Islands and Isle of Man in the Family Records Centre. They are not available in the National Archives. However, indexed digital images of the returns for Sundays 31 March 1901, 5 April 1891, 3 April 1881, 2 April 1871, 7 April 1861 and 30 March 1851 are searchable online. Indexed digital images of all of these census returns can be searched free of charge in the National Archives and in the Family Records Centre via the link at **www.nationalarchives.gov.uk/census,** which otherwise operates a pay-per-view scheme at **www.1901census.national archives.gov.uk** or **www.GenesReunited.co.uk** for the 1901 census, and a subscription service at **http://ancestry.co.uk** for the returns between 1851 and 1891; at the library of the Society of Genealogists, access is free to the last website as well. County-by-county indexed digital images of the 1841 census returns are gradually being uploaded into **www.originsnetwork. com** which also has a subscription service. The indexed transcriptions of the 1881 census returns of England and Wales are freely accessible at **www.familysearch.org** and are widely available elsewhere.

For more information read *Using Census Returns*, by D. Annal.

From 1851 onwards, the information gathered by local census enumerators was recorded in the same way, in special enumeration books. The returns are arranged by city or borough, ward and parish, or by town, village or hamlet. The house name or number, street, road or other address is given of all occupied buildings, divided into separate apartments where appropriate. A list of names of all the occupants of each numbered property is topped by that of the head of household, whose duty it was to complete the household schedule for collection by the local census enumerator after census night and then copied up into his enumerator's book. The relationship of each person to the householder was recorded, together with current marital status, age at last birthday, occupation, birthplace and any mental disability. Between 1851 and 1881, farm acreages were specified; details about a person's work status (employer, employee or neither) and size of living accommodation if less than five rooms began to be added in 1891.

In all cases, the digital images will be of a whole census page, and the transcriptions of a single household. You can opt to look at transcriptions of neighbouring households for the 1881 returns.

Finding aids

To access the digital image of a census page, or transcription of a particular household in 1901, first conduct an index search. You have seven options:

- Person search (for an individual name);
- Advanced person search (especially useful if there are lots of people of the same name: you can key in more specific information to narrow its scope);
- Address search (house or street name and property number);
- Place search (town, village, and so on);
- Institution search (buildings with over 100 inmates, such as a prison, army barracks, hospital, asylum, workhouse or school);
- Vessel search (including British ships at sea);
- Direct search (you will need a precise RG 13 piece number, folio and page reference for this).

You will need to key in the first two letters of both surname and forename.

If you prefer to search the microfiche copies of the 1901 census returns consult the place-name and street indexes on the open shelves in the Microfilm Reading Room and in the Family Records Centre.

You can interrogate the online 1881 census index at **www.familysearch.org** using a wildcard (*) for uncertain spellings. You are not obliged to key in the first two letters of the forename and surname. To see digital images of the 1891, 1871, 1861 and 1851 census returns at **http://ancestry.co.uk**, you can conduct an Exact Search for a named individual, or a Ranked Search for a person search, and select a county or civil parish. The Ranked Searches let you opt to view digital images of the returns of listed places within any county. The Exact Search lets you use a wildcard, but only after the first three letters of a surname, whereas the latter will automatically look for alternative spellings of surnames and forenames, and list the matches in descending order of relevance. In both cases, if you have already bought a copy of the returns for a particular year and county on CD-ROM, then the given National Archives document and page references will take you directly to the correct page entry. If you want to search the index to the digital images of the 1841 census returns at **www.originsnetwork.com**, you can do this by name, age, parish and county.

There are street indexes for towns with populations of 40,000 or more to help you find individual addresses in the 1841–91 census returns on microfilm in the Family Records Centre. There is a growing number of personal-name indexes to help you pinpoint census entries in particular places or counties, copies of many of which are in the Family Records Centre. Look in *Marriage and Census Indexes for Family Historians*, by J. Gibson and E. Hampson, for a county-by-county listing, though new ones are being compiled all the time.

What if you can't find your ancestor?

• The surname spelling is different to what you expected. This might be an indexing error, or a mistake made by the original census enumerator. Examine the returns for a specific address, try wildcard searches for missing letters, or look at the microfiche copy for 1901.

• Your search request has been too detailed. Try omitting parts.

• The given age and other personal details don't match what you have gleaned from other sources. The census information might have been supplied by a head of household who did not know much about him or her. Investigate the other indexed census years to see what was recorded about the person then. You may be lucky enough to find a personal-name index exists for the place or county in question.

• You don't know a woman's later married name. You can search for entries of people of the same forename, excluding the surname, which may help you sort out what became of female relatives.

• If you know the identities of other close relatives alive at the time of the census, try searching for them instead. You may find your ancestor in the same household, or at least not lose scent of the family altogether.

• There are some surviving lists of householders, with brief details about other occupants of the same property, for certain places and census years, principally those of 1821 and 1831. Consult *Local Census Listings, 1522–1930: Holdings in the British Isles,* by J. Gibson and M. Medlycott.

Other census returns in the National Archives

If you cannot decipher any part of the filmed returns of earlier census years in the Family Records Centre, ask a member of staff there to authorize a search by one of our staff of the original census enumerator's book for a particular address.

We hold microfilm copies of periodic censuses taken of convicts and of free settlers in Australia (see p. 80), and sporadic census returns for some other colonies too. Using our online catalogue, key in the name of the country or state, include 'census' and see what document references are given. However, most remain uncatalogued at present. For references to Caribbean census returns, look in *Tracing your West Indian Ancestors*, by G. Grannum.

To find out more visit:
www.familyrecords.gov.uk/ for details about other census years and how to access Scottish and Irish census returns.
Read our Research Guide:
Census Advice: Read This First; and
S. Lumas, *Making Use of the Census.*

Change of name

If your ancestor altered his name you may be able to trace this in the National Archives, but only if the name change was centrally registered. The majority were not.

There are several ways in which a name can be changed:
- By a deed poll, prepared by a solicitor. Copies of deeds poll which were centrally enrolled are held in the National Archives; otherwise the deed poll was a private transaction, as enrolment was not mandatory.
- By a private Act of Parliament. Such private Acts can be consulted by appointment in the House of Lords Record Office, in London.
- By Royal Licence. This method became common from the 18th century, particularly when a surname was in danger of becoming extinct in the male line. Copies of Royal Licences are held by the College of Arms, in London, and searches can be undertaken for you for a fee.
- By statutory declaration, sworn before a commissioner for oaths. There is no central record of them, because they are private documents.
- By announcement in the press. This can be done in any national or local newspaper. Few newspapers have been indexed, apart from *The Times* (see p. 29).
- By common repute. This is the most informal way of changing a name, and no documentation is needed. Sometimes this took the form of an alias, which eventually replaced the former name one or two generations later.

Look at *An Index to Changes of Name Under Authority of Act of Parliament or Royal Licence and including Irregular Changes from 1 George III to 64 Victoria, 1760–1901*, by W.P.W. Phillimore and E.A. Fry. The Royal Licences are those announced in the *London* and *Dublin Gazettes*, changes published in *The Times* and some other newspapers, Scottish name changes entered in the registers of the Lord Lyon King of Arms, and Irish surname changes recorded in the office of Ulster King of Arms. It does not include deeds poll, unless inserted in *The Times*.

What will you find?

To 1903, you can find central enrolments of deeds poll on the Close Rolls, in series C 54. From 1903 onwards the enrolments have been written into books, in series J 18. The enrolments give the original name, address, status or occupation of the person, and the new name by which he intended to be known, and the date when the deed was enrolled.

Petitions and warrants for Royal Licences between 1661 and 1782 are in series SP 44, from 1782 to February 1868 in series HO 38, and from then onwards (with gaps between 1922 and 1930, and 1957 and 1961) in series HO 142. Other petitions are in series HO 54 for the years 1783 to 1837, which includes reports from the College of Arms.

Finding aids

Search the yearly initial-alpha indexes to C 54 from 1851, and J 18 from 1903, on the open shelves in the Map and Large Document Room, and then order the original document. To 1903, the indexes list name changes by the former name; from 1904 there are cross-references to both names. There are usually integral indexes in series HO 38, HO 142, HO 54 and HO 45.

What if you can't find your ancestor?

• The name was changed within the last 8 years. If so, contact the Royal Courts of Justice, in London, as the records may not yet have been transferred to us.
• The deed poll wasn't centrally enrolled. If you cannot locate the document among your family papers, and you know the name of the firm of solicitors which dealt with the matter, it may still hold a copy, and any correspondence surrounding the application. You will probably have to pay for a search.
• The change of identity was informal. Ask your family when and why it happened for clues as to how it was done. If an alias was assumed, it might be for many reasons, so be open-minded and sensitive with your enquiries.

Other records about changes of name in the National Archives

Starting in 1914, enrolled deeds poll have been published in the *London Gazette, Edinburgh Gazette, Dublin Gazette* or *Belfast Gazette* as appropriate.

You can search bound copies of the twice-weekly editions of the *London Gazette* in series ZJ 1 (see p. 29). Try Phillimore and Fry's book for entries between 1760 and 1901. There is a copy of *London Gazette Index of Changes of Name 1938 to 1964*, containing former and new names, next to the catalogues for J 18, in the Map and Large Document Room. You can also read 20th-century digital images of issues of the *London, Edinburgh* and *Belfast Gazettes* up to 1979 online at **www.gazettes-online.co.uk/index**.

There are many examples in taxation lists of people using an alias, in army service records (see p. 39), navy personnel records, in wills and in legal records. Habitual criminals resorting to an alias between 1869 and 1876 are cited in PCOM 2/404.

To find out more, read our Research Guide:
Change of Name; and
H. Mead, *Change of Name*.

Civil War and Interregnum

The civil unrest between 1642 and 1649 led to a disruption of law and order and a breakdown of record-keeping, but also to the creation of new records. When the Church of England was abolished as the Established religion in 1653, its bishops ceased to have any authority, and church courts were suspended. Church congregations became largely autonomous and the parish registers of baptism and burial were thenceforward kept up-to-date by a lay officer rather than a priest, and were frequently removed from the church into their own homes, and subsequently lost. From 1653 to 1660, marriages were civil ceremonies performed by magistrates, and records of these are sparse. From 1653 to 1660 only one probate court functioned to approve wills, the Prerogative Court of Canterbury being converted into a civil court, sitting in Doctors' Commons, in London. During this period, many people did not make or have their wills proved because of the distance and cost of travel up to London (see **WILLS AND OTHER PROBATE RECORDS**). The ancient system of feudal tenure was effectively abolished in 1642, and formally in 1660. Some of the central law courts were swept away then too, depriving the king of yet another regular source of revenue.

For family historians, therefore, any material containing the smallest nugget of genealogical information in this era is invaluable, to compensate for the loss or lack of continuity of parish registers and wills, and to bridge the gap back to the first half of the 17th century.

Among the new records created in the 1640s and 1650s, and now in the National Archives, are the lists and returns of taxpayers regularly assessed to contribute towards the upkeep of the Parliamentary Army, the names of people who lent money or gave plate to be melted down, reports of the various county committees appointed by Parliament enquiring into the financial affairs of known or suspected Royalists, the resulting fines and seizures of property, county militia musters, and the memorials and transfers of estates to Adventurers for Lands in Ireland in exchange for money. All of these are written in English, which was the language of all legal documents between 1653 and 1660.

What will you find?

A series of weekly and monthly tax assessments was imposed from 1642 to 1660. These were based on a person's status or wealth. Surviving returns, in series SP 28, are arranged by county, then by administrative division. They name men and women considered liable and how much they were to pay, and identify individuals who were 'dead', 'gone away', 'in arrears' or 'in distraint' (when their goods had been seized by the local sheriff and sold to make up any tax shortfall). There are similar lists of contributors to the relief of the king's distressed subjects in Ireland, collected in 1642, in SP 28/191–5, and in series E 179.

The county committee returns to Parliament for the Advance of Money between 1642 and 1652, in series SP 19, set out the names of people who lent funds or sent plate to be melted down in aid of the cause, in return for an annual yield of 8 per cent of their capital value. Their names, places of residence and contributions are recorded. In 1650, this committee was amalgamated with the Committees for Compounding with Delinquents and for Sequestration of Delinquents' Estates.

The Parliamentary county committees for Compounding with Delinquents dealt with known and suspected supporters of the king, many of whom were Roman Catholics and recusants. The money raised was to pay the Army in Scotland. The records (also called Royalist Composition Papers), from 1643 to 1660, in series SP 23, are a genealogical goldmine, containing inventories, correspondence, disclosures, informations, and explanations about under-assessments, pleas for leniency and evidence offered by other family members, servants, tenants, neighbours and associates.

The papers of the county committees for Sequestration of Delinquents' Estates, covering the years 1643 to 1660, are in series SP 20. These relate to the seizure of land and personal property of the king's supporters. The documentation established the name of the landholder, with a detailed description of the estate and the nature of the tenure, its annual value, perhaps with the names of tenants, the date when it was taken into Parliamentary custody, and when and to whom it was later gifted, leased or sold at up to six or eight years' rent, and on what terms and conditions. Other books and papers concerning sequestered lands, 1643–53, are in series SP 20, and related accounts and papers between 1642 and 1660 can be found in SP 28/205–18. Details of bargains and sales of sequestered lands are enrolled on the Close Rolls, in series C 54. There is a series of certificates of seized land for 1649 and 1656, in C 203/2–3, yielding the name of each Royalist, their status, abode and date of sequestration, arranged alphabetically by county.

Extant lists of men between the ages of 15 and 60, mustered in militia districts set up by Parliament from 1642 to 1651, are in SP 28/120–5.

From 1642 until 1659, subscriptions of money in support of Parliament were invited in return for promises of land in Ireland. These returns of Adventurers for Lands in Ireland include receipts for contributions, papers of claims and later assignments. They are arranged by initial index of surname, in SP 63/288–302. This is an invaluable source of information about emigrants and off-shore investors during these years.

All the above records have to be ordered as original documents, apart from series SP 63, which is on microfilm in our Map and Large Document Room.

Finding aids

There is a typescript index to parishes covered by the surviving returns of contributions for the relief of the king's distressed subjects in Ireland, in 1642, which is attached to the bound catalogue for series SP 28. The identities and document references of parishes in series E 179 are searchable in a special database on our website at **www.nationalarchives.gov.uk/e179**.

Printed calendars or summaries are available of the proceedings of the Committees for Advance of Money in series SP 19, and for Compounding with Delinquents in SP 23. There is a place-name index relating to sales of sequestered land enrolled on the Close Rolls in series C 54, on the open shelves in the Map and Large Document Room.

What if you can't find your ancestor?

• You've relied on the printed calendars. Look at the actual records in case details have not been summarized. The indexes to the calendars chronicling the work of the various committees can be searched by place-name too.

• Try Chancery proceedings, which contain information about people and events long before the suit was first instigated (see p. 112). These records are in English, and are a cornucopia for historians of the 17th century.

• If you know your family was in a particular locality, discover which manor(s) served the relevant parishes (see p. 30). There may be surviving local family and estate papers you can glean for references to your ancestors as landowners, their relatives, tenants or employees. Key in the local landowner's personal or family name at **www.nationalarchives.gov.uk/nra** to discover the whereabouts of known documentation recorded by the

National Register of Archives. You could also try **www.nationalarchives. gov.uk/a2a** for catalogues to collections in many county record offices and other institutions, but do contact the county record office or local reference library as well, as the online catalogues are incomplete.

* If lands had been sequestered, pursue this in series SP 20, SP 23 and C 54, in case your antecedent was mentioned as a tenant. You might find details about them in Crown manorial records if the lands ultimately went to the Crown at the restoration of the monarchy in 1660 (see p. 122).

* Look at surviving records bounding either side of the Commonwealth period for evidence of continuity of your surname in a particular place or vicinity, if not of the individuals themselves. Examples are taxation lists, in series E 179 (see p. 171), wills (see pp. 175–85) and parish records (see pp. 23–5). Don't forget to look at wills made by other residents for mentions of your ancestors as relatives or friends.

Though the following sources seem formal and official, you will be surprised how many of them contain personal details about ordinary people who attracted the attention of or came into contact with central government during this period. State Papers, 1649–60, in series SP 18, are summarized in *Calendar of State Papers (Domestic Series), Commonwealth*. Privy Council Unbound Papers, 1481–1946, in series PC 1, and Privy Council Registers, 1540–1941, in series PC 2, record their discussions and decisions, as well as containing incoming correspondence and petitions. Sadly, many of the papers before 1698 in series PC 1 were destroyed by fire. There is a published and indexed set of *Acts of the Privy Council of England, Colonial Series, 1613–1783* for series PC 2. The contents of State Papers Colonial, America and West Indies, from 1574 to 1757, in series CO 1, and original colonial correspondence, 1606–1822, in series CO 5, have both been summarized and indexed in printed *Calendars of State Papers, Colonial, America and West Indies, 1574–1738*. There is a more detailed database to these in our Online Publications and Electronic Resources Archive.

Other records about the Civil War and Interregnum in the National Archives

To find out more, read our Research Guides:
Medieval and Early Modern Sources for Family History
Crown, Church and Royalist Lands: 1642–1660
State Papers Domestic: The Commonwealth [1642–60]
Privy Council Correspondence from c 1481
Privy Council Registers 1540 Onwards; and
G.E. Aylmer and J.S. Morrill, *The Civil War and Interregnum*.

Coastguard

The collection of duties on imported goods and policing against smuggling was long the responsibility of the Board of Customs. In times of war preventive officers were appointed by the Board to check on passengers entering and leaving our ports.

The Coastguard was set up in 1822. It merged the Revenue Cruisers, Riding Officers (both founded in 1698) and Preventive Water Guard (established in 1809), all tasked with preventing smuggling and avoidance of customs duty. Over the years its role included the defence of the coast, providing assistance to vessels in distress, and supervising the foreshore lifeboats and life-saving, lighthouses, signals, telegraphs, searches for mines and torpedoes lost at sea, and wrecks.

In 1925, the Coastguard was divided up into a Naval Signalling Force run by the Board of Admiralty, a Coast Prevention Force under the Board of Customs, and a Coast Watching Force (Coastguard) supervised by the Board of Trade. The Coastguard now concentrated on saving life, salvage of wreck and the foreshore. From 1923, it was administered by a succession of different government departments, resulting in the wide dispersal of records among different series in the National Archives.

What will you find?

Many coastguard officers were former naval men, so see **MERCHANT NAVY, ROYAL MARINES** and **ROYAL NAVY**.

You don't very often find information about births and families of Coastguard staff in our records, but they should give you clues to other sources to try, such as census returns (see pp. 66–8), parish registers (see pp. 23–5), and wills (see pp. 175–85). What you will uncover is evidence of men employed at a certain time and place, so you can build up a career profile.

Because the material is so scattered, what follows is unavoidably listy, but I have tried to choose those sources most likely to help you reconstruct your ancestor's working life.

The main series containing personnel records is ADM 175. All of these are available on microfilm in our Microfilm Reading Room. Succession books for the period 1816 to 1878, in ADM 175/1–73, list the names of nominated officers and ratings at the various coastguard stations, so you will need to know the locality or name of the vessel on which your forebear served. Registers of Admiralty nominations of officers and ratings to the Coastguard in England from 1819 to 1866 are in ADM 175/74–80, which are indexed between 1819 and 1862 in ADM 175/97–8. Other English nominations between 1831 and 1850 are in ADM 6/199, and for 1851–6, in ADM 175/101. Irish Coastguard nominations, 1820–49, are to be found in ADM 175/74 and 81 (indexed in ADM 175/99, 100), and for Scotland between 1820 and 1824, in ADM 175/74.

Admiralty appointments of lieutenants, masters and boatswains to Revenue Cruisers from 1816 to 1831 are in ADM 6/56, and for 1822 to 1832 in ADM 2/1127. There is an appointment book of boatmen from 1831 to 1850 in ADM 6/199, and for 1851–6 in ADM 175/101.

You can search the indexes to the registers of nominations for appointments of chief officers from 1886 to 1922, in ADM 175/103–7, and the indexes to their service records between 1919 and 1947 in ADM 175/109–10. There is an alphabetical series of service record cards for Royal Navy and Royal Marine ratings from 1900 to 1923 in ADM 175/82A–84B. Other service registers for Royal Naval ratings between 1919 and 1923 are in ADM 175/85–9, to which there is an index in ADM 175/108. For similar records about Royal Marines serving with the Coastguard between 1919 and 1923, consult ADM 175/90, and for members of the Naval Shore Service Signal Service from 1921 to 1929, try ADM 175/111.

Quarterly musters of Revenue Cutters 1824–57 are in ADM 119. Men serving on the Revenue Cruisers 1816–1879 can be traced in ADM 175/24–73, in the Ships' Establishment and Record Books.

Annual lists of enrolled volunteers for the Life-Saving Apparatus Companies, and the Watchers and Intelligence Section between 1920 and 1937, and for the Coast Life Saving Corps from 1932 are in BT 167/87–97. These may record dates of birth as well as of enrolment, places of residence and their distance from the nearest coastguard station.

Published Reports to Parliament can be searched on microfiche in the Microfilm Reading Room; they contain appointments and returns of active officers and men at certain dates, disclosing names, ages, birthplaces, and service details. There is an index covering 1801 to 1999 in our Online Publications and Electronic Resources Archive.

Indexed discharges from the Coastguard between 1858 and 1868 are in ADM 175/102, and indexed discharge registers for 1919, when the Coastguard was reduced, are in ADM 175/91–6 and ADM 175/107, the last of which includes an index to registers of nominations for appointments as chief officers in May the same year.

Civil Coastguard pension records of chief officers, 1855–1935, are in series PMG 23, and details about pensions paid by the Royal Hospital at Greenwich to chief officers from 1866 to 1928 are in series PMG 70. Coastguards' pensions paid by the Admiralty between 1866 and 1884 are recorded in ADM 23/17–21, whilst those paid to civil Coastguard staff from 1884 to 1926 are in ADM 23/71–75, and 194–199.

Many men in the Coastguard qualified for medals during the First World War. Their names can be located in series ADM 171, which is available on microfilm. A register of recipients of the Rocket Life Saving Apparatus Long Service Medal between 1911 and 1935 is in BT 167/84.

Finding aids

The names of officers serving in Revenue Cruisers are enshrined in the published annual *Navy Lists* from 1814 onwards.

The ten-yearly census returns between 1841 and 1901 may help you to establish where your ancestor was stationed, so that you can access the relevant Succession Books in series ADM 175. Indexed digital images of these returns are accessible online (see **CENSUS RETURNS**); and **Sources about Scots and Irish ancestors**.

What if you can't find your ancestor?

• You've selected the wrong coastguard station. Glean some of the other more general documents such as nominations for posts, discharges or pensions to see if you can pick out your forebear's name. Try the census indexes and digital images at **www.nationalarchives.gov.uk/census** to see if you can find him.

• The records are missing. You may still be able to locate your ancestor's discharge or pension payments.

• Our online catalogue hasn't been searched under 'coast guard' as an alternative to 'coastguard'.

HO 107/279/4, f6, p6: Census return of the Coastguard, at Worborrow, in Tyneham, Dorset, 6 June 1841. There were four of them, one of whom came from Scotland. They occupied two dwellings.

- Try local newspapers for write-ups of particular life-saving or wreck salvage operations. Local museums may contain exhibits about the work of the local coastguard service.
- If you live in the area, your local reference library or county record office should have copies of old newspapers. Otherwise you will need to visit the Newspaper Library, British Library (see p. 30). For full details of local newspapers search *Willing's Press Guide*, which is published every year.

Other records about the Coastguard in the National Archives

You may be able to discover register tickets issued to coastguards between 1845 and 1853, in series BT 113. These are available on microfilm. The numbered entries comprise age, birthplace and a physical description. Microfilmed indexes to the ticket numbers are in series BT 114.

There are occasional printed lists of coastguards to be found among the House of Commons Sessional Papers.

To build up a picture of what life was like as a coastguard, examine the plans of stations, officers' houses, cottages, gun batteries, watchrooms and other structures, 1844–1914, in series WORK 30, and then visit the site itself – many still exist.

To find out more, read our Research Guides:
Coastguard
Printed Parliamentary Papers; and
W. Webb, *Coastguard: An Official History of H.M. Coastguard.*

Crime, convicts and transportation

Records of criminal trials survive from the early Middle Ages. Unfortunately for us, they were written in Latin before 1733, except during the Commonwealth period, 1653–60, when they were in English. Often, too, legal phrases and words were abbreviated to save time and space.

Petty crime and misdemeanours were dealt with locally in the courts of the lords of the manor, and by unpaid magistrates sitting in petty, county or borough sessions. Their records are mostly now in county or borough record offices. Visit **www.nationalarchives.gov.uk/a2a** for catalogue entries to many of these. *Quarter Sessions Records for Family Historians: A Select List*, by J. Gibson, also provides guidance on local holdings.

Until 1971, when the following courts were abolished, more serious offences (except treason) were tried by justices of the peace sitting in county quarter sessions, or by professional judges of Assize on commissions of oyer et terminer (to hear and determine) or of gaol delivery, who from the late 13th century began to travel up to four times a year from Westminster in circuits around the country. Cases in London were heard either in the Middlesex Sessions or in the Old Bailey Sessions (renamed the Central Criminal Court in November 1834). You can search the Assize court records, Old Bailey and Central Criminal Court proceedings in the National Archives. There were special courts serving the Palatinates of Chester, Durham and Lancaster, and their records are in the National Archives as well. For Welsh Assize material before 1830, contact the Department of Manuscripts and Records, in the National Library of Wales, in Aberystwyth. Some early Assize material has been published. You can read indexed online transcriptions of the Old Bailey proceedings between 1674 and 1834 at **www.old baileyonline.org**. The period covered will eventually run up to 1913.

Read *Law and Society, an Introduction to Sources for Criminal and Legal History from 1800*, by M. Cale, for more background information.

People were usually arraigned in the Assize court of the county where they were apprehended. The preserved records are in various ASSI series according to the circuit to which a county belonged. The Palatinate of Chester records are in CHES series, those for the Palatinate of Durham in DURH series, and for the Palatinate of Lancaster in various PL series.

What will you find?

ASSI 44/168, pt1: Report on the Coroner's Inquisition on the body of Thomas Plenderleath, the late Registrar of Births and Deaths, in Longtown, Cumberland, 1851. The jury's verdict was that of murder by one of his census enumerators. At the Assizes, William Kirkpatrick was found guilty of manslaughter and sentenced to 6 months' gaol with hard labour.

If you know when and in which county an individual was tried, look for the catalogue reference to the bundle of indictments for that session. At the top of the indictment the defendant's plea was written in, plus the verdict and sentence if found guilty. Underneath are the defendant's name, place of residence, occupation, and details of the alleged offence, together with the date and place when taken into custody. If you turn over the indictment you can read the list of names of witnesses summoned to give evidence in court.

The evidence itself no longer survives unless a suspicious death was involved, but do trawl the local press for a write-up of the trial. Search *Local Newspapers 1750–1920, England and Wales, Channel Islands, Isle of Man, A Select Location List,* compiled by J. Gibson, B. Langston and B.W. Smith, for titles and whereabouts of local holdings. If there was a coroner's inquest, and the alleged assailant could be identified, his report served as the indictment, so the written and signed depositions of witnesses will be filed with it.

If you don't know when or where a person was indicted, try the Crown Minute Books for the entire circuit. These are arranged chronologically by session date for each county within the circuit. The volumes encapsulate sittings over a number of years. Each entry will lead you to the actual indictment for more information.

Gaol calendars are useful too because they list the names of people taken into custody to await trial, their addresses, ages and occupations, dates and places of apprehension, their alleged offences, and the names and addresses of the committing magistrates. Sometimes the occupation given in the calendar varies from the standard description of 'labourer' in the indictment. The gaol calendars may be listed in the catalogue to the ASSI series for each circuit, or are occasionally bound up with the indictments. Printed county calendars naming prisoners awaiting trial at quarter sessions and Assizes between 1868 and 1971, can be studied in series HO 140, and for London from 1855 to 1949 in series CRIM 9. The calendars reveal ages, occupations, standard of literacy, the name and address of each committing magistrate, the alleged offences, plus trial verdicts and sentences. Returns of prisoners committed for trial in the Old Bailey and Central Criminal Court between 1815 and 1849 are in series HO 16, and printed lists of defendants, together with details of the results of their trials in these courts from 1782 to 1853 are in series HO 77.

An incomplete set of printed proceedings of the monthly sessions in the Old Bailey and Central Criminal Court from 1801 to 1904 is in series PCOM 1. A more extensive set is held in the Guildhall Library. However, you should be able to discover all you need to know about trials between April 1674 and 1834 from the online transcriptions at **www.oldbaileyonline.org**, which you can search by personal-name, and by offence. After 1834, the indictments in the Central Criminal Court up to 1957 are in series CRIM 4, and the Crown Minute Books, 1834–1949, are in series CRIM 6. An incomplete set of printed proceedings, 1834–1912, is in series CRIM 10.

Finding aids

For trials on indictment in county quarter sessions and Assize Sessions in England and Wales between 1805 and 1892, search the Annual Criminal Registers in series HO 27. These are arranged alphabetically by county, and then chronologically by date, identifying the names of defendants, trial court, for what offence they were indicted, the verdict and sentence. From 1834 to 1848 the Registers include ages too. Between 1791 and 1849 there is a separate series of Annual Criminal Registers in series HO 26 for people tried in London and Middlesex, which furnish the ages of defendants, after which the entries until 1892 are also in series HO 27. From 1807 up to 1811, though, the Registers in series HO 26 relate only to cases heard in the Old Bailey, and for cases heard in other London and Middlesex courts you will have to search series HO 27. There is a personal-name index, arranged by county, to entries in the first part of the 19th century extracted from series HO 27, which you can search in our Online Publications and Electronic Resources Archive and on CD-ROM, floppy disk, or on microfiche.

For Central Criminal Court indictments in CRIM 4, you should first examine the catalogue to series CRIM 5, covering the period 1833–1971. This is arranged by session and then by initial letter of each defendant's surname.

People tried on indictment in the Palatinates of Chester, Durham and Lancaster are not always included in the Annual Criminal Registers, so you may have to track them down in the original documents.

CONVICTS

In the past, most offences carried the death penalty (often commuted to transportation) or convicted felons were punished by a fine and/or branding. Each county had its own gaol, and many also had houses of correction (or bridewells) where vagrants and convicted criminals were set to work. Extant records are usually now in county record offices.

Imprisonment was rarely used as a punishment until the 19th century. Court orders for imprisonment or transfer from one prison to another, with details of the convict's penal history, 1843–71, are in series PCOM 5, to which there are indexes in series PCOM 6. These comprise the name, age, marital status, trade or occupation, crime, date and place of committal and conviction, sentence, and previous convictions, a character assessment, the name and address of the next of kin, literacy level, religious denomination, and a physical description of each person. Most prison registers are kept locally, especially those of institutions set up after 1878. There are some government-administered prison registers in the National Archives. Interrogate our online catalogue by keying in the title of the gaol. Most of the registers are in series PCOM 2, which covers the years 1770 to 1951.

We also hold registers of names of convicts on prison hulks awaiting transportation. Microfilmed copies are in series HO 9, 1802–49, and in PCOM 2/131–37, which you will have to order as original documents. Both series are searchable by ship's name and by covering dates. The prison registers usually embody name, age, date and place of conviction, the sentence, a surgeon's report, and one on behaviour, a physical description and details about the occupation, marital status, any aliases, previous character, and discharge or transfer of each inmate. Quarterly returns of convicts in prisons and hulks from 1824 to 1876 can also be found in series HO 8.

TRANSPORTATION

After 1615, it became common for a pardon to be offered to convicts who were sentenced to death, on condition of transportation overseas. Transportation was formally ended in 1867, though effectively in 1857, after the introduction of penal servitude in 1853.

For information about convicted felons transported to America and the West Indies before 1776, consult *The Complete Book of Emigrants in Bondage 1614–1775*, by P.W. Coldham.

When transportation to America came to an end, there was a short hiatus period before convicts began to be shipped to New South Wales in 1787, to Van Diemen's Land (Tasmania) from 1803, and to Western Australia in 1850.

What will you find? There are two series of records about transported men, women and children, in the National Archives, both on microfilm. The first consists of transportation registers of convicts to New South Wales and Tasmania from 1787 to 1867, in series HO 11. These are arranged in date order, and then alphabetically by ship's name. There is a list of convict ships 1787–1870 in HO 11/20, recording their departure dates. The registers contain the name, age, date and place of trial, offence and length of sentence of everyone on board. The second series is made up of the periodic censuses and musters of convicts taken in New South Wales and Tasmania between 1788 and 1859, in series HO 10. These furnish their year of arrival and identify the ships on which the convicts sailed, enabling you then to find the appropriate convict registers in series HO 11.

Petitions of wives to accompany their husbands into transportation between 1819 and 1844 are in PC 1/67–92, and from 1849 to 1871 in series HO 12. For the latter, you will need to tackle the indexed registers in series HO 14, which give brief details of every letter and its subject-matter. Volumes containing details of applications by wives and families of convicts for passages to the colonies, 1848–73, are in CO 386/154, and these disclose the names and addresses of each family, their ages and marital status, the wife's maiden name, plus details about the relevant convict's date and ship of transportation.

Finding aids

There is an index to convicts and to names of ships arriving in New South Wales and Van Diemen's Land between 1788 and 1842, available on CD-ROM, and in our Online Publications and Electronic Resources Archive. An index to the convict transportation registers in series HO 11 has been compiled by Miss J.M. Chambers, 4 Quills, Letchworth, Hertfordshire SG6 2RJ; this includes additional personal and family details and petitions. Send her a stamped self-addressed envelope for information.

Details about convicts transported in the First Fleet of 1787 and Second Fleet of 1789 can be traced in *The First Fleeters*, edited by P.G. Fidlon and R.J. Ryan, and in *The Second Fleet Convicts*, by R.J. Ryan.

One of the censuses taken in New South Wales, in series HO 10, has been published in *Census of New South Wales: November 1828*, edited by M.R. Sainty and K.A. Johnson. It lists alphabetically the names of convicts, free settlers and those born in the colony, and gives age, religious denomination, abode, workplace, type of employment, any land or stock holdings, length of time in the colony, whether a person came free, as a convict or was locally born, period of transportation (7 or 14 years, or for life), date of arrival and on what ship. Other printed general musters and rosters of New South Wales, Norfolk Island and Van Diemen's Land in 1800–2, 1805–6, 1811, 1814, 1822, 1823, 1824 and 1825, have been edited by C.J. Baxter, and a general return of convicts in New South Wales in 1837 has been edited by N.G. Butlin, C.W. Cromwell and K.L. Suthern.

What if you can't find your ancestor?

• The Annual Criminal Registers in series HO 26 and HO 27 divulge who was sentenced to transportation. However, many such convicted felons spent a long time in hulks before transfer to a convict ship.

• Try the Vital Records Index for Australia (enfolding New South Wales from 1788 to 1888, Tasmania between 1803 and 1899, Victoria from 1837 to 1888, and Western Australia between 1841 and 1905) for marriage and death entries of convicts, former convicts and their families. This is available as part of our Online Publications and Electronic Resources Archive. Some registrations reveal details about length of stay in the colony, any pardon granted to a former convict, any change of name, and the names of the deceased's parents.

• The person wasn't transported. Try the petitions for pardons between 1787 and 1829 in series HO 47 (see below).

Other records about convicts in the National Archives

Judges' reports on applications for mercy by convicts and their representatives between 1784 and 1829, are in series HO 47. A database is currently being compiled of appellants' names, summarizing the trial evidence, the grounds for appeal, and the trial judges' opinions. This is gradually being uploaded into our online catalogue, which you can search by personal-name for specific document references.

You can learn about applicants for pardons and reprieves between 1782 and 1849 in series HO 13 in our Online Publications and Electronic Resources Archive and on CD-ROM or microfiche. For the years between 1850 and 1871 such applications are in series HO 15, and from 1887 to 1960, in series HO 188. Each volume contains a rough index.

In 1853, licences (or tickets of leave) began to be issued to prisoners for good behaviour, so they could be released early. Records of these from 1853 to 1887 are in series PCOM 3 for male convicts, to which there are indexes up to 1881 in series PCOM 6. For females there are similar records for the same period, in series PCOM 4, which is indexed to 1885 in series PCOM 6. You can find information about convicts' pardons and tickets of leave issued in New South Wales and Tasmania from 1839 to 1859 in series HO 10, and conditional pardons granted to convicts in Western Australia between 1863 and 1873 in series HO 45. When searching our online catalogue, key in the name of the colony and the words 'AND pardons'.

An alphabetical national register of habitual criminals was compiled between December 1869 and March 1876, and you can consult this in PCOM 2/404. There are further registers for 1881–2, and 1889–1940, in MEPO 6/1–52, though these are not open to the public for 75 years. Other surviving copies of the national register may still be held by prisons or police constabularies. The register volumes indicate each person's name, any known aliases, age, a physical description (including any distinguishing marks), trade, prison from which released, date of discharge, offence, sentence and term of supervision, any previous convictions, and intended place of residence.

To find out more, read our Research Guides:
Assizes: Criminal Trials
Assizes (English), Key for Criminal Trials, 1559–1971
Assizes (Welsh), 1831–1971: Key to Classes for Criminal and Civil Trials
Old Bailey and the Central Criminal Court: Criminal Trials
Convicts and Prisoners, 1100–1986, Sources in The National Archives
Criminal, Tracing a 19th Century
Transportation to America and the West Indies, 1615–1776
Transportation to Australia 1787–1868; and
D.T. Hawkings, _Criminal Ancestors, a Guide to Historical Criminal Records in England and Wales_
R. Hughes, _The Fatal Shore: A History of Transportation of Convicts to Australia, 1787–1868_
C. Bateson, _The Convict Ships 1788–1868_
L.L. Robson, _The Convict Settlers of Australia._

Customs and Excise officers

Customs officers were responsible for the collection of duty on imports and the prevention of smuggling, whereas Excise men collected taxes on home products. Indexed directories of their names are included in *Ham's Customs Year Book*, from 1875 to 1930. *Ham's Inland Revenue Year Book* began to list Excise officers from 1849, when the Board of Excise and Board of Stamps and Taxes were amalgamated to form the Board of Inland Revenue. Copies from 1875 to 1930 are also available in our Library and Resource Centre.

Read *Something to Declare: 1000 years of Customs and Excise*, by G. Smith.

What will you find?

You can harvest a lot of information about the daily activities, concerns, hirings, disciplinary proceedings, firings and deaths of officers from the correspondence books of the various customs out-ports and for the Port of London, in the relevant CUST series (CUST 50–CUST 105). These also include registers of appointments, giving ages, capacities and character assessments of local officers.

Pension records of customs officers between 1803 and 1922 can be tracked down on microfilm in series CUST 39, and for Ireland from 1785 to 1851. Applications for pensions made by staff and their dependants, 1777–1920, in series T 1, are indexed in series T 2, to which there are subject indexes in T 108. Superannuations of staff in the United Kingdom 1803–1912 are in CUST 39/145–51, also indexed. They record widows' pensions, and the names and dates of birth of children of customs officers. Similar indexed information relating to customs officers in Ireland, between 1785 and 1898, is contained in CUST 39/161–2.

Finding aids

An index to the superannuation allowances made to customs officers between 1831 and 1881, listing name, age, office held, last port of service, superannuation date, and date of death, is being assembled. For a paid search of this index, contact Mrs J. Underwood, 174A Wendover Road, Weston Turville, Buckinghamshire HP22 5TG, enclosing a stamped self-addressed envelope.

EXCISE OFFICERS

Many of the sources are similar to those about customs officers.

Excise Entry Papers, 1820–70, in series CUST 116, usually elicit two letters folded together for each officer: a letter of recommendation, giving the name of the applicant, his age, birthplace and marital status, plus a character reference, and a report from the officer in charge of his training on his proficiency in writing, spelling and arithmetic. There is an alphabetical index. Records referring to the appointment of Irish Excise officers, 1824–33, and Irish Revenue Police, 1830–57, are in series CUST 110 and CUST 111 respectively.

Pensions awarded during the period 1856 to 1922 can be found in CUST

39/157–9, and include those to officers' widows, which set out the names and dates of birth of their children.

• Check the published *Year Books* to see if you've searched the wrong service.

Starting in 1845, the Excise (from 1849, Inland Revenue) Life Assurance and Benevolent Fund Society granted annuities and allowances to widows and orphans of its members. You can find information about the dates of birth, careers, movements and deaths of members up to 1972 in IR 92/15, which also consists of membership registers 1843–1966, and details about payments of annuities 1897–1972.

To find out more, read our Research Guide:
Customs and Excise Officials and Tax Collectors.

Death Duty registers

In 1796, a Stamp Duty was introduced on certain legacies and annuities. Until 1849, it was supervised by the Board of Stamps, and thereafter by the Board of Inland Revenue. Succession Duty was added in 1853, to be followed by Estate Duty in 1894. From this date the three were jointly called Death Duties. Legacy and Succession Duty were abolished in 1949, and in 1975 Estate Duty was replaced by Capital Transfer Tax (currently known as Inheritance Tax).

The Death Duty registers, in series IR 26 run from 1796 to 1903. They are available on microfilm up to 1857. From 1858 you will need to study the original registers. No records are known to survive after 1903. Only those estates or parts of estates attracting duty feature in the registers, so many of lower value escaped attention, especially in the early years. Always look at the original will for the complete picture.

To 1811, there are discrete registers of wills and administration grant entries for each English and Welsh probate court. From 1812 up to 9 January 1858, the will extracts were filed together regardless of court. However, details extracted from grants of administration were filed independently after 1812 to 1858, a system that continued up to 1881. The later entries of wills and administrations were merged. Administration grants made by the Prerogative Court of Canterbury from 1796 to 1858 were also written up in separate registers.

From 1853 until 1894, separate sets of registers contain details of payments of Legacy and Succession Duty. There is one set of registers for Estate Duty (IR 26/6283–8690), in which the numbered entries indicate liability for Legacy (L) and/or Succession Duty (S). The collection of Legacy and Succession Duty from 1894 onwards is recorded in IR 26/8691–8743.

Each entry records the full name, last abode and occupation or status of the deceased, usually disclosing the date of death, the date when the will was made, the names and addresses and occupations of the executors (or administrators if no will had been made, when the person was said to have died intestate), the date and court where the will was proved (or where letters of administration were granted), and the gross value of the estate before deduction of debts. Before 1853 this excluded realty (freehold property). Extracts from the will relating only to those legacies, annuities and residuary estate on which duty fell due were written into the register by the names and exact relationship to the deceased of each beneficiary.

The registers are immensely important because they tell you how a person's estate was finally distributed. Their contents disclose names and kinships of people which might be unstated or unclear in the will itself. Many wills made provision for what was to happen to the estate should the widow remarry or die, and for children as yet unborn. The division of the estate might also be affected by deaths of beneficiaries predeceasing the testator, sometimes increasing the share taken by survivors having a joint share, and liability to tax.

The registers were kept up to date by regular enquiries made by the clerks in London. When annuities were set up, the ages of the beneficiaries were given at their dates of entitlement. The dates of death were recorded of future beneficiaries, their marriages, and any absences abroad during their wait for the death or remarriage of the testator's widow, or pending their succession to a part of the estate under the terms of a trust set up in the will. The whereabouts over time and date of demise of the testator's widow were noted, together with the final distribution of the estate and payment of duty on the directed sale of her share in the property. Names of successive heirs to property, their relationship to the deceased, and their dates of succession to the estate, may be included, some of whom might not have been born at the time of the testator's death, and may stretch over several generations, perhaps spanning more than a century. Death Duty register entries for the beneficiaries themselves might be cited too.

If you don't know in which local court a particular will was proved, the Death Duty registers will tell you, so long as the person's estate was liable.

Finding aids

To access the Death Duty registers in series IR 26, you will need to glean the annual indexes in series IR 27. These are on microfilm from 1796 to 1903. You can also search the indexes relating to wills attracting Death Duty free of charge online at **www.nationalarchivist.com,** but will have to pay to view the actual digital images of the full index entries.

There are no separate indexes to Succession Duty registers prior to 1894, though there are cross-references to them in the Legacy Duty registers in series IR 26, and some Succession Duty entries are indexed in the Legacy Duty indexes from 1889 to 1894 in IR 27/486–533.

If you know when a person's will was proved or a grant of letters of administration was made, search the index in series IR 27 for that year and part of the alphabet to see if there is an entry in the registers in series IR 26. You can also do this even if you only know when the person died, but you may have to cull the indexes for several years. From 1889, the indexes contain dates of death as well as dates of probate or administration grants.

The series IR 27 indexes are arranged as follows:

IR 27/1–16	Prerogative Court of Canterbury wills, 1796–1811
IR 27/17–66	Prerogative Court of Canterbury administration grants, 1796–1857
IR 27/67–93	Wills and administration grants in all other English and Welsh probate courts, 1796–1811 (listed alphabetically by the name of the court)
IR 27/94–139	Administration grants in all English and Welsh probate courts excluding the Prerogative Court of Canterbury, 1812–57
IR 27/140–419	Prerogative Court and all other English and Welsh probate court wills, 1812 to 9 January 1858, and all civil probate court wills, 11 January 1858–81
IR 27/420–29	Administration grants in all English and Welsh civil probate courts, 1858–63 (there are no indexes 1864–81)
IR 27/430–533	Wills and administration grants in all English and Welsh civil probate courts, 1882–94
IR 27/534–605	Wills and administration grants in all English and Welsh civil probate courts, on estates assessed for Legacy Duty, Succession Duty and Estate Duty, 1894–1903

Indexed digital images of the Death Duty register extracts from 'country wills', (those proved in courts other than the Prerogative Court of Canterbury) before 1812, are at **www.nationalarchives.gov.uk/documentsonline**.

What if you can't find your ancestor?

• Many people didn't make a will. Any land was automatically transferred to the next legal heir in the absence of a will, and personal property might have been negligible. To be really sure, peruse the indexes or lists of wills and administration grants registered in all the courts serving the area where they kept their personal possessions and cash. Look in *The Phillimore Atlas and Index of Parish Registers*, edited by C.R. Humphery-Smith, for the probate court boundaries within each county, and then establish the where-abouts of indexes in *Probate Jurisdictions: Where to Look for Wills*, by J. Gibson and E. Churchill.

• The legacies and residuary estate were not worth enough to attract duty. Only those over a certain value were liable. When 'NE' is written against an entry in the index in series IR 27, this indicates there is no entry in the register, usually because the estate valuation was too low. Have a look in the above two guides for help in finding wills and administration grants escaping tax. See **WILLS AND OTHER PROBATE RECORDS**.

• If you know your ancestor was a beneficiary but you can't find his or her name in the relevant register entry, this may be because the relationship to the deceased granted exemption from duty. To 1805, gifts to spouses, direct ancestors and descendants did not attract tax; from 1805 to 1815, gifts to spouses and direct ancestors remained exempt; after 1815, only gifts to spouses were excluded.

Other Death Duty records in the National Archives

Only a sample survives in the National Archives of the residuary accounts produced by executors and administrators, detailing the payment of bills, debts, legacies, and receipts of debts to estates in order to quantify what was left in the pot to distribute to the residuary legatees. The accounts, in series IR 19, cover 1796 to 1903, and are arranged by year. A number of residuary accounts relating to the estates of some famous and public figures, spanning 1805 to 1981, can be examined in series IR 59.

Reversionary registers relating to outstanding claims for payment of Legacy Duty, 1812–1852, are in IR 26/4856–67, and correspondence over contested cases from 1812 to 1836 is in series IR 6. Reports made to the Treasury by the Board of Stamps on Legacy Duty cases between 1800 and 1825 are in series IR 49, and from 1825 to 1833 in series IR 50. Later reports, covering the period 1853 to 1866, are in series IR 67. Succession Duty registers of arrears of payment of duty accruing between 1853 and 1878 can be searched in IR 26/6263–82. Alas, there are no indexes to any of these volumes.

To find out more, read our Research Guides:
Death Duty Records from 1796
Wills and Death Duty Records, after 1858
Death Duty Registers, Interpretation; and
K. Grannum and N. Taylor, *Wills and Other Probate Records, a Practical Guide to Researching Your Ancestors' Last Documents.*

Divorce petitions

Before 11 January 1858, marriages could only be ended legally by the death of one of the partners, on a declaration of nullity *a vinculo matrimonii*, issued by a church court, or, from about 1670, by a private Act of Parliament on the grounds of the wife's adultery, or the husband's adultery plus proof of his life-threatening cruelty or unnatural practices. These were the sole means of releasing a person to remarry.

The written proceedings of the church courts are now usually in county record offices. By the 18th century the Consistory Court of London presided over matrimonial disputes brought to it by people travelling from all over the country, attracted by its relative speed and efficiency. The resulting records are in the London Metropolitan Archives. The divorce petitions and private Acts of Parliament are held in the House of Lords Record Office, in London.

On 11 January 1858, a new civil Court for Divorce and Matrimonial Causes was set up in London, and in 1923 a wife became able to sue her husband for divorce based solely on his adultery, giving her equal rights of complaint, whereas before she had been additionally required to prove his life-threatening cruelty towards her. Various statutes since then have broadened the grounds on which a person can petition a court for divorce. The court issues a decree nisi, which becomes a full decree of divorce on the application of the petitioner after a further six weeks (originally six months).

Until 1922, cases were heard in London, but subsequently certain Assize towns were given authority over undefended suits, and such petitions were filed locally in district registries from 1927. After a statute passed in 1967, county courts were empowered to hear divorce cases too.

What will you find? You can search the filed numbered petitions for decrees of divorce, judicial separations (equivalent to an annulment or a divorce *a mensa et thoro* before 1858), protection of earnings and property of married women (which before a series of Acts of Parliament starting in 1882 legally belonged to the husband), declarations of legitimation of children, and for restitution of conjugal rights (the restoration of cohabitation under the same roof). These are in series J 77, and extend from 1858 to 1954. They have to be ordered as original documents.

It is thought that all the petitions survive up to 1927. After 1927, only those petitions filed in London are included. Don't forget that petitions were often filed several years before a case was heard, and some never progressed to court, although unsuccessful petitions are included in this series. The petitions filed in London from 1938 onwards have been severely weeded and merely a tiny sample now exists, listed by name and year of the petition; you can search for these document references using our online catalogue. In the files you will find a copy of the petition, a defence or counter-claim if any, sworn affidavits, birth, marriage and death certificates, and from 1870 onwards, copies of the decrees might be attached too.

Assize court records are described at p. 77.

County court records generated more than 30 years ago are generally transferred to county record offices, although there may be research restrictions. More recent material is likely to be retained by the court itself. You can find county court addresses at **www.hmcourts-service.gov.uk/HMCSCourt Finder** or from a phone book.

Finding aids There are surname indexes to series J 77 in series J 78, which is available on microfilm in the National Archives and the Family Records Centre, and free to search online for the years 1858 to 1903 at **www.nationalarchivist.com**, though you will have to pay to view the digitized index entries. The indexes run from 1858 to 1958, though from November 1946 to 1949 inclusive they constitute divorce receipt books rather than indexes to petitions. Look for the year you want, and then drill down the list of surnames, which are arranged in initial letter order. The surname of any co-respondent will be cited as well, with an abbreviated reference to the type of petition. Match up the petition number with the relevant year range in series J 77, so that you can order up the documentation.

Although the indexes run to 1958, files relating to London cases heard after 1954 are not yet open to the public.

What if you can't find your ancestor? • You've searched the wrong year. The petitions in series J 77 are numbered according to the date they were filed in the registry, while the decrees held by the Principal Registry of the Family Division, in London, are listed by the date they were granted. Pre-paid searches of the Principal Registry indexes can be conducted for you in blocks of ten years at a time, but any Principal Registry search will only yield a copy of the decree nisi or decree absolute. For any more information surrounding the case, look at the petitions and supporting evidence in series J 77, and read the local press.

• You can't find any documentation. Sadly, the numbering sequences in series J 77 seem to overlap, so you may have to try several indexes to obtain the correct file reference. If this doesn't work, approach the Principal Registry of the Family Division, pay for a search and copy of the decree, and then scour the local press for an account of the court hearing. You can examine copies of these in the Newspaper Library, the British Library (see p. 30). Alternatively, consult *Willing's Press Guide* for details about local newspapers or look in *Local Newspapers 1750–1920, England and Wales, Channel Islands, Isle of Man: A Select Location List*, by J. Gibson, B. Langston and B.W. Smith. You can also try *The Times* for a write-up. For petitions after 1937, this is probably your only option to make up for the loss of the records.

• The petition was filed in a district registry after 1927. You will have to approach the Principal Registry of the Family Division for an index search and copy of a decree. The Registry does not hold unsuccessful or abandoned petitions, nor any other paperwork than the decrees.

• The divorce was granted after 1954. Contact the Principal Registry of the Family Division for a copy of the decree, and then study the local or national press for an account of the hearing. If the case was heard within the last five years, and you know which county court was used, contact this direct as the search will be cheaper. Only the decrees themselves have been preserved.

Other divorce records in the National Archives

Before 1858, a cuckolded husband could sue his wife's lover in the Court of King's Bench (Crown Side) on a writ of *crim. con.* (criminal conversation), alleging trespass on his goods (his wife), and seeking damages against him. This was often used as a preliminary to a petition for divorce by a private Act of Parliament, and these civil proceedings were instituted at the same time as a request for a divorce *a mensa et thoro* in a church court. Like the records of the church courts, they were written in Latin until 1733, and are not easy to access. The original Plea Rolls, in series KB 27, run from 1536 to 1701, and the Crown Rolls, in series KB 28, cover the period 1702 to 1857. There is a card index to entries between 1844 and 1859 in series KB 28, in the Map and Large Document Room.

Appeals about matrimonial disputes heard in church courts were presented to the Court of Arches of the Archbishop of Canterbury, sitting in London. Consult *Index of Cases in the Records of the Court of Arches in Lambeth Palace Library, 1660–1913*, by J. Houston for brief references.

Final appeals relating to church court applications went from the Court of Arches to the High Court of Delegates. Its proceedings, from 1609 to 1834, are in series DEL 1. You can search the online catalogue to this series by the names of the parties, type of case and date. The cause papers (consisting of the allegations, answers, depositions, exhibits and so on), arranged alphabetically by name, from about 1600 to 1834, are in series DEL 2. Case Books, containing the printed appeal cases running chronologically from 1796 to 1834, are in series DEL 7. Some of the books are integrally indexed. Later appeals were heard before the Judicial Committee of the Privy Council, and copies of their proceedings between 1834 and 1880, and brief summaries of the originating proceedings in a lower court are in series

PCAP 1. Printed Appeals Case Books, 1834–70, are in series PCAP 3. These are in date order too.

To find out more, read our Research Guides:
Divorce Records before 1858
Divorce Records after 1858; and
L. Stone, *Road to Divorce: England, 1530–1987.*

Dockyard employees

Until 1832, dockyards and naval establishments came under the overall control of the Navy Board, and thereafter the Board of Admiralty was responsible. As well as Chatham, Deptford, Plymouth, Portsmouth and Sheerness, there were naval dockyards servicing British shipping throughout the world.

The Royal Dockyards were run by yard officers, who were civilian employees of the Board, serving as naval but not sea officers, although staff often moved between the dockyard and seagoing branches of the Royal Navy. The commissioners, in charge of the yards, and the masters attendant (harbour masters and pilots), in charge of yardcraft and ships afloat and in reserve, were usually retired sea captains and masters appointed by the Admiralty. Other master craftsmen and boatswains were recruited from service afloat. Each yard had its own surgeon and chaplain, who had usually transferred from the Navy.

What will you find?

Yard officers' names are embedded in the annual printed *Navy List* from 1814, which is indexed from 1847. The entries are given in order of seniority. Starting in 1870, you can find the names of boatswains and carpenters too.

Personal details about dockyard and other naval apprentices may be found in series ADM 106. The description books of artificers, labourers and shipwrights in listed dockyards at various dates between 1748 and 1830, in ADM 106/2975–3005, and ADM 106/3625, furnish their physical descriptions. Some of the volumes are alphabetical.

Passing certificates of qualified carpenters, 1856–87, and of boatswains, 1851–8, are in series ADM 13. Earlier passing certificates of boatswains, 1810–13, are in ADM 6/122. These often include birth or baptism certificates, and almost certainly their ages, dates and places of birth, ships on which they served, and the periods spent on board.

Certificates of service of boatswains, carpenters and shipwrights, at various dates in the 19th century, can be examined in series ADM 29. These were issued in support of claims for pensions or gratuities. They disclose the ship's pay book number and number of years, weeks and days on each vessel, which can then be linked to the ships' musters in series ADM 36 and ADM 37, described below.

Yard Pay Books from 1660 to 1857, in series ADM 42, relate to the larger dockyards, whilst the ships' pay books and musters in series ADM 36 (1688–1808) and ADM 37 (1792–1842) include minor yards. Victualling Yard records are in series ADM 113, and cover the years 1703 to 1857; there are also similar records for Portsmouth and Gosport between 1712 and 1903 in series ADM 224.

Salaried officers' civil pensions, and those paid to their widows and orphans between 1836 and 1918, can be found in series PMG 24, and in Additional Pension Books, covering 1834 to 1926, in series ADM 23. Try also series ADM 18 (1661–1781) and series ADM 22 (1781–1821) for superannuation and retirement pensions and payments made to yard officers and their widows. Neither series is indexed. ADM 22 embraces out-pensions paid by Greenwich Hospital from 1814 to 1846. Details of retirement pensions and superannuation paid to artificers and labourers on the Naval Establishment between 1836 and 1928, are in series PMG 25, and records of retirement pension payments from 1830 to 1926 in series ADM 23. Registers of pensions paid out of the Chatham Chest to wounded men and widows of dockyard employees killed in action or in service from 1675 to 1799, are in series ADM 82. There are annual alphabetical lists of names of recipients, which were compiled each 25 March.

Some service records of dockyard personnel between 1892 and 1939 are kept by TNT Archive Service (Navy Search), at Swadlincote. You will need to write for information, and there will be a fee.

Finding aids

The certificates of service in series ADM 29 are partially indexed, in ADM 29/97–104, but you can search a complete personal-name index to the series by using our online catalogue. From this, you can discover the name, date and place of birth, age on joining the Navy, rank or rating at the end of each man's career, his start- and end-dates of service, date and type of financial application, and an ADM 29 document reference, including the page number of the service record, and cross-references to other service returns of ratings in series ADM 139 and ADM 188, together with service numbers. Indexed digital images of the returns in series ADM 188, covering careers extending over the years between 1853 and 1923, can be viewed at **www. nationalarchives.gov.uk/documentsonline**.

The material in series ADM 36, ADM 37 (ships' musters), ADM 42 (yard pay books), ADM 106 (description books) and ADM 113 (victualling yard records) is signified by dockyard. Volunteers are currently listing the 17th- and 18th-century correspondence from dockyard personnel, in series ADM 106.

What if you can't find your ancestor?

• Try the wide range of other sources in the National Archives about men in the Royal Navy (see **ROYAL NAVY**). Look in *Naval Records for Genealogists*, by N.A.M. Rodger, for a detailed list of series and document ranges. The online catalogue should also help too.

• You could also contact the Naval Dockyards Society, in Southsea, for any information it might hold about your forebear.

Other records about dockyard employees in the National Archives

Registers of baptisms, marriages and burials performed in the dockyard church at Sheerness between 1688 and 1960 are in ADM 6/429–33, and 438. Similar registers, 1826–1946, relating to the naval dockyards in Bermuda, are in ADM 6/434, 436 and 439. Recorded deaths of dockyard and victualling yard employees between 1893 and 1956 can be found in series ADM 104, though some of the volumes are closed to the public for 75 years. There are separate indexes in ADM 104/102–08.

To find out more, read our Research Guide:
Royal Naval Dockyards (this includes an alphabetical list of dockyards worldwide with details of personnel records held by the National Archives); and
B. Pappalardo, *Tracing Your Naval Ancestors.*

Emigrants

Britons have ventured abroad since early times, to engage in trade, colonize, settle, fight, police, explore, to find work or a better life, escape from persecution or war, or to pay the price for their crimes. Details about them are therefore scattered throughout many records in this country and in their places of destination.

From time to time various government schemes were set up to boost the British population of its colonies by sending out ex-servicemen and their families, or by providing free or assisted passages for particular types of worker to help with building construction, land clearance and development, and by dispatching young people and orphans to begin a new life as servants and employees in agriculture.

Private charities also funded the emigration of children to be educated and settle in the colonies. Child emigrants were usually sent as servants, apprentices, and to boost the labour force under various parish, Poor Law Union and charitable schemes from 1618 until 1967. After the outbreak of war in 1939, about 30,000 children were dispatched to the British colonies and to the USA to ensure their safety.

If you are descended from an emigrant it is a good idea to learn as much as you can about them in their adopted state, province or country, before attempting to trace them in British sources. By first tackling sources in the country of settlement you should be able to find enough clues to bridge the gap back to the approximate date of departure and place of provenance.

For more information read *Emigrants and Expats, a Guide to Sources on UK Emigration and Residents Overseas,* by R. Kershaw.

What will you find?

If your forebear set sail between 1890 and 1960, you may be able to trace his or her name in a United Kingdom ship's passenger list, in series BT 27. There are no lists after 1960, and none at all for air passengers. The manifests are arranged chronologically by date of sailing, under the port of departure, but no rosters survive for ships calling only at European or Mediterranean ports. It helps to know the name of the vessel, an approximate date and port of embarkation, which can sometimes be gleaned from the lists of arrivals at the end of the voyage. Try **www.cyndislist.com/ships.htm** and **http://home.att.net/~wee-monster/onlinelists.html**, both portals for links to or information on country-by-country lists and indexes of passenger arrivals and departures. For instance, **www.ellisislandrecords.org** contains details about people arriving in the Port of New York between 1892 and 1924. Try also **www.vitalrec.com/links2.html** where you can search for the names of passengers arriving at all America's major Atlantic ports (you will need to subscribe). Such databases, lists and indexes should help you identify the ships, ports and dates of departure in series BT 27 described below. Every emigrant was an immigrant somewhere, and in countries such as Australia, New Zealand and Canada, indexers have been very active in creating nominal lists of arrivals, which will supplement or even predate our own collections.

For busy ports like London, Liverpool and Southampton there may be several boxes of ships' passenger lists in series BT 27 for a single month, making your task a long one if you don't have much to go on. The top sheet of each manifest reveals the ship's name, official registration number, shipping line, the name of the master, the port and date of departure, all ports of call and final destination. Information about each passenger is recorded according to class of ticket, starting with first class bookings. Alien passengers on board were listed separately on special forms, so you will find names of trans-migrants from all over Europe who changed ship in the UK for larger ocean-going liners and steamers.

The lists give each passenger's ticket number, port of boarding, name, age, occupation, nationality if an alien, and port of destination. From 1922, they provide the last address, and from 1956, the date and place of birth. At the end of each manifest any births and deaths during the voyage were noted. You can also search for births at sea between 1890 and 1960 and deaths from 1891 and 1964 in series BT 334. There is also a special register of marriages at sea between 1854 and 1972 in BT 334/117. If you know a relative was born, married or died at sea, but not the name of the vessel, try these records first, or the microfiche copies of the General Register Office indexes to Marine Returns of births and deaths, which commenced on 1 July 1837. The last set of indexes are searchable at **www.1837online.com/Trace2web/Logon Servlet** though you will have to pay to use them. See **BIRTHS, MARRIAGES AND DEATHS OF BRITONS AT SEA AND ABROAD.**

There is no continuous run of ships' passenger lists before 1890, but if your ancestor went abroad between 1773 and 1776, you can inspect the weekly returns of passengers leaving English and Welsh ports in series T 47. Also in the same series are weekly returns of emigrants leaving Scottish ports for America in 1774 and 1775. The returns relate to vessels of all types, and disclose the date and place of embarkation, the destination, name, address, age, occupation and purpose of the voyage of everyone on board, and to where they were ultimately travelling. The series is catalogued by year, and the original lists are arranged chronologically by date.

An earlier collection of licences to pass beyond the seas, 1573–1677, and

No.	Surname	Forename	Port		Sex		Date of Birth		Address	Profession	Relation		Nationality
84647	WHITMAN	Joseph			M	M	29.12.11		3 Seno St., Glasgow, S.E. 29	Van Salesman			U.K.
84648	WHITMAN	Lily			F	M	17. 8.38		-- do --	Wife			U.K.
84649	EVANS	Ralph	SYDNEY		M	M	23. 4.25		58 Skelwith Rd, Sheffield, Yorks	Railway Wkr		11	U.K.
84650	EVANS	Margaret			F	M	13. 1.23		-- do --	Wife			U.K.
84651	GIBB	Harold			M	M	15. 1.16		71 Northern Grove, West Didsbury - Mr. Manchester	Collector Salesman			U.K.
84651	GIBB	Barbara			F	M	17.11.20		-- do --	Wife		13	U.K.
84651	GIBB	Leslie			F	S	12. 1.45		-- do --	Daughter			U.K.
84651	GIBB	Barry			M	S	1. 9.46		-- do --	Son		14	U.K.
84651	GIBB	Maurice			M	S	22.12.49		-- do --	Son			U.K.
84651	GIBB	Robin			M	S	22.12.49		-- do --	Son		15	U.K.
84651	GIBB	Andrew			M	S	5. 3.58		-- do --	Son			U.K.
84652	TOMAS	William			M	S	4.10.28		13 Palmer Ave., Cheadle, Cheam	Salesman			U.K.
84652	TOLLITT	William			M	S	11.12.30		-- do --	Clerk		16	U.K.
84653	SHEPPARD	John			M	M	18. 5.30		17, Clifton Place-Off Staple-ton Road, Bristol	Upholsterer			U.K.
84654	SHEPPARD	Edith			F	M	20. 7.31		-- do --	Wife		17	U.K.
84654	SHEPPARD	Lynn			F	S	17. 8.53		-- do --	Daughter			U.K.
84655	TOJATT	Leslie			M	M	4.10.14		c/ Bowden, 28 Mount Bennett Rd Plymouth, Per, Cornwall	Clerical Wkr		18	U.K.
84656	TOJATT	Ethel			F	M	31. 8.14		-- do --	Wife			U.K.
84656	TOJATT	Lesley			F	S	23. 1.42		-- do --	Daughter		19	U.K.
84656	TOJATT	Judith			F	S	6.11.44		-- do --	Daughter			U.K.
84656	TOJATT	Penelope			F	S	29. 4.46		-- do --	Daughter		20	U.K.
84657		Leonard	MELBOUR		M	S	13.10.28		c/83 The Broadway, Biloor, Berks	Naval Rating			U.K.
84658	RUSSHAW	Ernest	STNEY		M	M	22. 8.19		457, Bilston Rd, Wolverhampton Staffs	Draughtsman		21	U.K.
84659	RUSSHAW-Joyce				F	M	20.10.27		-- do --	Wife			U.K.
84659	RUBSHAW	Donald			M	S	16. 4.56		-- do --	Son			U.K.
84660	KILNON	Robert	MELBOUR		M	M	25. 4.20		32, College Ave, Mannamead Plymouth --Devon	Motor Body Build		22	U.K.
84661	KILNON	Evelyn			F	M	9. 3.26		-- do --	Wife			U.K.
84660	KILNON	Robert			M	S	29. 8.47		-- do --	Son		23	U.K.
84661	KILNON	Susan			F	S	10.11.48		-- do --	Daughter			U.K.

BT 27/1851: The emigrant Gibbs family sailed from Southampton to Fremantle, in Western Australia, on board MV *Fairsea*, in 1958. The four young Gibbs brothers later became the Bee Gees.

registers naming passengers aged 18 and over swearing the Oath of Allegiance to the English Crown under an Act of Parliament of 1610, is in series E 157. These take in people including merchants and soldiers going to the Continent as well as to the New World. Published details about passengers bound for the American colonies and the West Indies have been extracted and included in *Passenger and Immigration Lists Index, 1538–1900*, edited by P.W. Filby and M.K. Meyer, which has annual *Supplements*.

For lists of convicts transported to America up to 1776 and to Australia, 1787–1868, see **CRIME, CONVICTS AND TRANSPORTATION**.

The wills and death certificates of emigrants can be key sources of information about their origins. Conversely, the wills of members of the family left behind often refer to relatives overseas. Consult indexed abstracts in *American Wills and Administrations in the Prerogative Court of Canterbury, 1610–1857*, and *American Wills proved in London, 1611–1775*, both by P.W. Coldham. See **BIRTHS, MARRIAGES AND DEATHS OF BRITONS AT SEA AND ABROAD, WILLS AND OTHER PROBATE RECORDS**, and **DEATH DUTY REGISTERS**.

The indexed digital images of the census returns may provide invaluable clues as to where particular emigrants came from. See **CENSUS RETURNS**.

Finding aids

You can inspect the yearly registers of ships' passenger lists between 1906 and 1951, in series BT 32. To October 1908, only Bristol, Southampton and Weymouth are covered, but thenceforward the monthly (from 1921 daily) departures from the United Kingdom record the names of ships (specifying the shipping line) leaving every port, enabling you to go to the catalogue for series BT 27 to select your document reference. However, series BT 32 does not specify destinations. *The Morton Allan Directory of European Passenger Steamship Arrivals*, in our Research Enquiries Room, identifies ships docking in the Port of New York between 1890 and 1930, and in Philadelphia, Boston and Baltimore from 1904 to 1930, indicating both the port of departure and arrival. The directory is arranged by year, with an index listing each steamship line.

There is a card index to names of passengers sailing to North America extracted from series T 47, giving the name, age, occupation, ship's name and ultimate destination of each person, plus the document reference. These entries have also been culled and published in *Emigrants from England to the American Colonies 1773–1776*, by P.W. Coldham, and in *A Dictionary of Scottish Emigrants to the USA*, by D. Whyte.

What if you can't find your ancestor?

• There are no passenger lists for the year you want. Try the lists of ships' arrivals, immigration lists and naturalization certificates of the destination state or country. You can do this by visiting the websites of the relevant state or national archives offices, accessed via **www.nationalarchives.gov.uk/archon**. You will need to know at least an approximate year or short period in which to start looking. Some of the overseas lists of ships' passenger arrivals begin much earlier than our collection in 1890. Utilize a website portal such as **www.cyndislist.com**.

• You are not sure when your ancestor emigrated. Consult W. Filby's *Passenger and Immigration Lists Index, 1538–1900*, and its *Supplements* for any printed references. Try Immigrants to the New World 1600s–1800s, the Mormon Immigration Index, 1840–90, and Irish immigrants to North America 1803–71 in our Online Publications and Electronic Resources Archive. Have a look at the cited books to which the entries refer for contextual information about each immigrant, which may add extra clues to their places of provenance. The Mormon Immigration Index consists of ships' manifests, and you can search the database by personal-name and then look at the list of other passengers sharing the same voyage.

• The online indexes to digitized images of wills proved in the Prerogative Court of Canterbury, at **www.nationalarchives.gov.uk/documentsonline** are well worth checking for details of testators of the same surname in the same generation, the previous one and the next in case they left anything to your migrant antecedent or his children. You may even locate the will of that person himself! Search the International Genealogical Index and the British Isles Vital Records Index for entries of the surname, to discover its geographic spread in the same, the previous, and next generation, and trawl the will indexes of the various local probate courts serving those areas for references. Look at the county maps in *The Phillimore Atlas and Index of Parish Registers*, edited by C.R. Humphery-Smith, for the boundaries of each court, and then in *Probate Jurisdictions: Where to Look for Wills*, by J. Gibson and E. Churchill, for a county-by-county listing of availability of indexes.

• Visit **www.nationalarchives.gov.uk/a2a** for any online catalogue references to local material in England relating to specific emigrants or migrant groups. Often a party of local people joined together to emigrate, so if you can find the place of origin of one of the group, this may be a pointer to your ancestor's home too. Sometimes an individual emigrated ahead of his family and once settled, sent for the rest to follow him; you may be able to locate the ones who remained behind, once you know where he came from.

• Try the indexes to the overseas returns of births, marriages and deaths to the General Register Office and the Registrar General's Miscellaneous Non-statutory Foreign Returns (in series RG 43), described on p. 56. The vital records of the state, province or country of settlement may provide clues on origins, particularly the death registrations. Consult *International Vital Records Handbook*, compiled by T.J. Kemp, for start-dates and whereabouts of any copies of indexes and registers. Some indexes are also available online. The Vital Records Index for Australia in our Online Publications and Electronic Resources Archive, covers births, marriages and deaths registered in New South Wales between 1788 and 1888, Tasmania from 1803 until 1899, Victoria between 1837 and 1888, and Western Australia from 1841 until 1905. The actual registration may reveal the length of time in the colony, current age, parentage, birthplace and any name changes.

• Don't forget that descendants of emigrants may be looking for you! The annual *Genealogical Research Directory, National and International*, edited by K.A. Johnson and M.R. Sainty since 1981, is made up of brief accounts of surnames, places and periods under investigation, and the contact details of the contributors.

A calendar summarizing original correspondence and papers in State Papers, Colonial: America and West Indies, 1574–1739, in series CO 1 and CO 5, can be accessed in our Online Publications and Electronic Resources Archive. This can be searched by personal-name, place and subject, and will give you full document references. The correspondence includes various petitions from settlers, colonists and merchants, applications for land grants, offices and privileges, reports and complaints about other settlers, and is well worth a look. For information on other sources about emigrants to the West Indies, read *Tracing your West Indian Ancestors*, by G. Grannum.

State Papers Foreign, and after 1782, correspondence from various overseas British embassies and consulates can often throw up useful genealogical information about Britons abroad. These are all arranged chronologically by date. Look in *Never Complain, Never Explain: Records of the Foreign Office and State Paper Office, 1500–1960*, by L. Atherton for guidance on series numbers.

Between 1740 and 1772, foreign Protestants in America could be naturalized as British subjects by taking the Oath of Allegiance to the Crown. The records, in series CO 5, have been extracted and published in *Naturalization of Foreign Protestants in the American and West Indian colonies, 1740–1772*, by M.S. Giuseppi. Under the Naturalization Act 1870, Britons born abroad but not registered at a British consulate, and excluding the colonies, could petition for a certificate of British nationality. The petitions, birth certificates of the petitioners and of their fathers, plus their parents' marriage certificates were sent by British consuls to the Home Office in London for consideration. These were supposed to be returned in due course. Surviving information may be found in series HO 45, and in the relevant consular correspondence files in FO series.

As a result of the Revolutionary War in America, many of the colonists loyal to the British Crown were forced to flee and abandon their estates and possessions. Many eventually made their way to Canada (particularly Nova Scotia) or sailed to England. Crown Loyalists were able to apply to the Treasury for compensation for their losses under the Treaty of Peace, signed in 1783. The actual memorials (petitions for compensation), from 1780 to 1835, are in series AO 13, and lists of claims, evidence, examinations and decisions of the Commissioners in London between 1776 and 1812, are in series AO 12. There is a personal-name index to each claimant at the front of the bound catalogues. Read *The Lives, Times and Families of Colonial Americans who Remained Loyal to the British Crown*, by P.W. Coldham, for summaries of entries in AO 13. Reports of investigations, payments of temporary allowances and pension lists of Loyalists compiled by the Treasury from 1780 to 1835, are in series T 50 and American Loyalist Claims Commission papers concerning claims prosecuted between 1777 and 1841 are in series T 79.

British subjects interned during World War I and World War II in enemy countries may be mentioned in series FO 371. Look in the indexes (on cards to 1919, and thereafter in yearly volumes). Some of the listed files no longer exist due to heavy weeding. For internees overseas, look too in series FO 916, which contains reports on internment camps. Details about civilian internees in enemy and enemy-occupied colonies may be found in series CO 980.

The Emigration Commission was founded in 1833 to encourage workers and skilled craftsmen to populate the new colonies of Australia, New Zealand, South Africa and Canada. All they had to do was apply to local government agents, submitting their name, age, address, occupation, marital status, and the number and ages of any children. If the occupation appeared on the approved list and the person was aged between 14 and 35, and preferably married and childless, the chances of success were high. Successful candidates were expected to supply their own clothing, bedding, food and cooking utensils for the journey, an inventory of which was published by the Commission. You may be lucky and come across something relevant to your family amongst the numerous applications and letters between 1817 and 1896 in series CO 384. This series includes lists of settlers in Australia, North America and the West Indies in 1819, and between 1820 and 1825, and CO 384/51 contains a list of North American settlers in 1837/8. For British North America, try CO 327/12, which is a register of correspondence logged between 1850 and 1863, and series CO 328, which relates to the period 1864 to 1868.

Emigration Commission Papers from 1833 to 1894, in series CO 386, contain embarkation registers of land purchasers and labourers between 1835 and 1841, a partially indexed register of emigrant labourers' applications for free passages to South Australia from 1836 until 1841, and registers of applications from convicts' families for assisted passages between 1848 and 1873. In the Emigration Entry Books, 1814–71, in series CO 385, are enfolded letters about bounties and loans to Australian emigrants in 1831 and 1832. Each series is arranged chronologically by date, and you will need to order items as original documents. Original Correspondence relating to the relevant colony is also worth searching for letters and petitions from settlers and for reports and complaints. These are to be found in CO, DO and FCO series, each of which is catalogued by colony. There are registers to these, logging the daily receipts and outgoing correspondence, and petitions. For Dominions Office correspondence on post-war assisted emigration look in DO 35/3366–3443. For a full list of series numbers, consult *The Records of the Colonial and Dominions Office*, by R.B. Pugh, and *Records of the Colonial Office, Dominions Office, Commonwealth Relations Office and Commonwealth Office*, by A. Thurston.

For details concerning early settlers in Australia you can try *Census of New South Wales: November 1828*, edited by M.R. Sainty and K.A. Johnson (see p. 81 for more information about this and other censuses in series HO 10). Look also in *Musters and Lists New South Wales and Norfolk Island, 1800–1802, Musters New South Wales, Norfolk Island and Van Diemen's Land, 1811*, and *General Muster and Land and Stock Muster of New South Wales, 1822, General Muster of New South Wales 1823, 1824, 1825*, all by C.J. Baxter, for names of inhabitants. The records of the New Zealand Company, 1839–50, in series CO 208, elicit indexed personal details about applicants for free passages as emigrant labourers, some ships' passenger lists, and applications for investment in land.

Look in the Immigration Database at **www.collectionscanada.ca** for details of ships' passenger arrivals from abroad between 1925 and 1935. The Library and Archives Canada, in Ottawa, holds ships' passenger lists and immigration records of border entries from the United States of America from 1865 up to 1935.

It is also worth trying government *Gazettes* and colonial newspapers for announcements which might refer to British links. We hold a small selection of these publications, which are listed by colony, but the Newspaper Library, British Library, in London, has a much larger collection (see p. 30).

Particulars about the ages, marital status, occupations and destinations overseas of emigrating individuals or family groups awarded financial assistance by their parish between 1834 and 1909, may be found in dated lists among the Poor Law Union papers in series MH 12, to which there are subject indexes in series MH 15. The papers are arranged by Union title, and then chronologically by date. If you are uncertain as to which Union your ancestor's parish belonged to, consult *Poor Law Union Records: Part 4: Gazetteer of England and Wales*, by J. Gibson and F.A. Youngs, Jr. A growing index of names extracted from series MH 12 for the period 1834–60, is held by Miss J.M. Chambers, 4 Quills, Letchworth, Hertfordshire SG6 2RJ. Send her a stamped self-addressed envelope for information. The names of people benefiting from free or assisted passages after 1890 and before 1960 can be found in the ships' passenger lists in series BT 27, described earlier.

Soldiers encouraged to retire to the colonies where they were last stationed, especially between 1846 and 1851, can be traced through their quarterly receipts for pensions, in series WO 22, which covers the period 1842–83, and in series WO 23 (1817–1903). Both of these are arranged by pay district and then according to the date the pension board first granted the pension. The soldier's name, last rank and regiment are invariably given, and the entries frequently contain details of his birthplace, later career and death, as well as bearing the pensioner's signature, and record any move to another pay district. Similar lists of ex-army emigrants in Australia and New Zealand between 1830 and 1848, are in WO 43/542–3. For army pensioners settling in Canada and South Africa mentioned in series WO 120, study *British Army Pensioners Abroad, 1772–1899*, by N.K. Crowder. Soldiers and their families emigrating under special schemes on demobilization after 1920 can be traced in the ships' passenger lists in series BT 27.

Occasionally you will come across lists of emigrant children or correspondence relating to poor or orphaned youngsters considered for emigration between 1834 and 1909 by the local Boards of Poor Law Guardians, in series MH 12. Trawl the correspondence between local Poor Law authorities and the Emigration Commissioners from 1836 until 1876 in MH 19/22 for references to individual cases. The Union workhouse records, held in county record offices like most parochial material, may yield details of their dates and circumstances of admission and discharge, and the local parish registers set out their family baptisms, marriages and burials. You can find catalogue references to many Poor Law Union sources at

www.nationalarchives.gov.uk/a2a, and refer to *Poor Law Union Records*, by J. Gibson and C. Rogers for a listing of their dates and known whereabouts.

Reports on pauper child emigrants who were sent to Canada can be located in MH 19/11 for 1887–92. These are highly informative as they disclose the children's own view of their new homes (not always flattering), as well as giving their names, ages, host's name and address, and comments by the agents of the Secretary Department of Agriculture as to their condition, health, character, attendance at school and frequency of church attendance. Details about children who were sent from 1910 up to 1967 to America, Canada, the Caribbean, Rhodesia, South Africa, New Zealand and Australia, under the sponsorship of various government or charitable initiatives, may be traced in series MH 102. Series HO 144 contains material relating to child emigration, though some of these files are subject to closure. Search our online catalogue by using the keywords 'children AND emigration'. Other sources about child emigrants between 1947 and 1952 are in series DO 35, including appointments of escorts under the Big Brother Scheme between 1947 and 1952 in DO 35/3383. The Home Children database, at **www.collectionscanada.ca**, ranging from 1869 until the 1930s, is composed of details about more than one million children sent to Canada during this period, extracted from records in North America and Canada. The Child Migrant Central Information Index serves as a conduit to the sending agencies, and is open to former child emigrants, their parents and siblings, or nominated representatives. Contact The National Council of Voluntary Child Care Organisations, in London, for more information. The ships' passenger lists in series BT 27 will include such children up to 1960, and of course, the recorded lists of arrivals at their destination ports.

You can examine a selection of case files relating to children evacuated to Canada, South Africa, New Zealand and Australia under the auspices of the Children's Overseas Reception Board in 1940, in DO 131/94–105. There is a child applicants' register in DO 131/106–13, and the names of their escorts can be identified in DO 131/71–87.

For information about people going to India, the Asia, Pacific and Africa Collections, in the British Library, in London, are probably your best starting point. You can find out more about genealogical sources, particularly the archives of the East India Company from 1600 to 1858, of the India Office from 1858 until 1947, the Burma Office between 1937 and 1948, and of a number of related British agencies overseas at **www.bl.uk/collections/orientaloffice/html**. The National Archives holds a limited amount of material, such as printed directories of residents, and service records of officers and men in the British Army stationed in India. Don't forget the ships' passenger lists in series BT 27. Army pensioners in India between 1799 and 1899 are included in Crowder's book, cited above. We have copies of the *East India Register* and its successors, published annually between 1791 and 1947, and *Indian Army Lists*.

Look in the annual editions of the *Imperial Calendar, Colonial Office List* (up to 1925, and from 1941 to 1966), *Dominions Office and Colonial Office List* (1926–40), *Commonwealth Yearbook* (from 1967), and *Foreign Office List* for information on postings of British officials throughout the world. Copies of many issues of these are available in our Research Enquiries Room.

For details about how to trace transported convicts, see pp. 80–2.

To find out more, read our Research Guides:

Passenger Lists
Titanic
Emigrants
America and West Indies: Calendar of State Papers, Colonial
State Papers, Foreign
Foreign Office Records from 1782
Foreign Office Records: Card Index, 1906–1910
Foreign Office Records: Card Index, 1910–1919
American and West Indian Colonies before 1782
Government Gazettes of the British Empire and Commonwealth
American Revolution Emigrants to North America after 1776
Transportation to Australia, 1787–1868.

Immigrants

We are all likely to have at least one immigrant ancestor in our family tree, as this country is a rich mix of people of different cultural origins. There are lots of references to foreigners (aliens) in England in our archives from early times to the present day. Their origins can be traced back not only to the near Continent, but to much further afield.

Many immigrants wanted to become established as British citizens, and thus be treated as native-born subjects, so probably the best way to begin eliciting an immigrant ancestor's place of origin is to trawl through the alphabetical indexes of names of men and women who were granted naturalization or denization. After 1844, the wives of native-born or naturalized British subjects were deemed to be naturalized too. Under an Act of 1731, children whose fathers were already or were to become naturalized British citizens were also taken to be naturalized British subjects. Previously, both parents had to have been naturalized for this to happen. In 1773 this measure was extended to include grandchildren.

From 1870, applications were only considered after five years' residence in the United Kingdom. Naturalization was originally by private Act of Parliament, but since 1844 it has been by a certificate issued by the Home Secretary. Naturalized British subjects are entitled to the same rights as natives, following the legislation of the day. Denization was in the gift of the Crown, under letters patent. This did not bestow full rights of citizenship: for example, after 1571, denizens were liable to pay double tax, and although able to purchase land they could not inherit it or pass it on, so were treated as if they were still aliens. Denizens frequently applied for full citizenship later. No denizations were granted after 1873. However, not every immigrant went down this route and instead clung onto their original national status.

The Commonwealth Immigrants Act 1962 required Commonwealth citizens wishing to work in Britain to qualify for an employment voucher, which thereby limited right of entry, and a further statute in 1968 obliged such immigrants to provide proof of their or their parents' or grandparents' birth in the United Kingdom. Current legislation on Commonwealth immigrants has been in force since 1973, and like citizens of other countries (except for nationals of countries within the European Union) they now have to have prospective employers before admission to the United Kingdom.

The British Nationality Act 1981 created five categories of citizenship: British Citizenship, British Dependent Territories Citizenship, British Overseas Citizenship, British Protected Person, and British Subject.

Read *Immigrants and Aliens, a Guide to Sources on UK Immigration and Citizenship*, by R. Kershaw and M. Pearsall, and visit **www.movinghere. org.uk**.

What will you find?

The original private Acts of Parliament granting naturalization are in the House of Lords Record Office and survive from 1497. You can study enrolments of abstracts of the bills in the *House of Lords Journal* and *House of Commons Journal*, copies of which are in our Library and Resource Centre.

The naturalization and denization papers and certificates run from 1509 to 1987; you will need to order them. You can search copies of enrolments of naturalizations from the reign of Henry VIII to 1800, in series C 89, and from 1801 to 1840 in series HO 1. Some 17th-century enrolments are in series SP 44, and those relating to the simultaneous naturalization of whole groups of foreign Protestants between 1708 and 1711, having sworn the Oaths of Allegiance and Supremacy in an open court of law, are in E 169/86 and series KB 24.

When naturalization certificates began to be issued by the Home Office in 1844, each certificate was allotted its own unique number. Copies of certificates issued between 1844 and 1873 are enrolled on the Close Rolls, in series C 54, and duplicate copies from 1870 to 1987 are in series HO 334. Embedded in our dated certificate copies are the person's name, current marital status, place of residence, occupation, date and place of birth, and the names and nationalities of his or her parents.

For later naturalizations you will need to contact the Departmental Records Officer of the Home Office, in London. There is also a gap between June 1969 and 1987, so if you want proof of naturalization during this time the Immigration and Nationality Directorate, in Liverpool can furnish a letter of confirmation, but this will add nothing to our index references.

Enrolments of denizations up to 1801 can be located on the Patent Rolls, in series C 66, and then to 1844 in series C 67. Other copies, enrolled between 1681 and 1688, and relating to Protestant refugees, are in SP 44/67, and still more, from 1752 to 1792, are in series C 97, from 1804 to 1843, in series HO 4, from 1844 until 1873, in series C 54, and from 1872 to 1878, in series HO 45. They should all contain the person's name, current address, occupation and native abode, as well as the date when they became denizens.

Between 1740 and 1772, foreign Protestants settling in the English American colonies could be naturalized as English subjects, and lists of their names are in series CO 5. You can find details about these in *Naturalizations of Foreign Protestants in the American and West Indian Colonies, 1740–1772,* edited by M.S. Giuseppi.

Duplicate copies of Imperial Certificates of Naturalization granted by governments of British possessions overseas from 1915 to 1949 are in series HO 334. The certificate numbers are prefixed by the letter 'O'. Some of the volumes contain nominal indexes, and the entries will tell you the name of the applicant, plus his or her address, trade or occupation, the country of origin, as well as the spouse's name and those of any children. Since the British Nationality Act 1948 citizens of the United Kingdom, Republic of Ireland, the Channel Islands, Isle of Man, British colonies, Protectorates or Trust Territories have been able to register themselves as British subjects. The numbered certificates of citizenship, also in series HO 334, are prefixed by the letter 'R'. For such certificates issued after 1987, contact the Departmental Records Officer, at the Home Office. Series HO 334 does not include duplicate certificates of the self-governing Dominions of Australia, Canada, Newfoundland, New Zealand or South Africa. For these you will have to approach the national archives of each country.

Conversely, under the Naturalization Act 1870, people born in the United Kingdom of foreign parentage could renounce their British nationality, and the resulting 'declarations of alienage' from 1871 to 1944 are in series HO 45, those between 1868 and 1959 are in series HO 144, and a few others are to be found in series HO 1 and HO 213. Duplicate copies of the certificates between 1871 and 1914 are in series HO 334.

You can search the petitions, applications and correspondence relating to naturalizations between 1688 and 1784 in series SP 44, those between 1798 and 1829 in series HO 5, 1801 and 1871 in HO 1/1–176, 1872 and 1878 in series HO 45, 1879 and 1934 in HO 144, and from 1934 until 1948 in series HO 405. Although the records in the last series are closed for 100 years, the Home Office will review this on request to the National Archives for surnames beginning with the initial letters between A and N, and once opened, the files will remain open. Files for surnames starting between O and Z should be transferred to the National Archives by 2008. Until then, enquiries for information should be made to the Departmental Records Officer, in the Home Office, in London. The applications include a memorial from the immigrant, setting out his or her name, address, occupation and country of origin, to which was added any further background information, and government departmental decisions and action surrounding the application. There are no memorials before 1800. After 1844, they give the length of time the applicant had lived in the UK, his or her age, present address and occupation, plus a statement of intent to reside and settle in Great Britain. From 1847 the memorials were supported by signed affidavits from at least four independent householders, called resident referees. Starting in 1870, the memorials also mention the name of any spouse, the duration of the marriage, the names of any children under 21 living with the applicant, and all the addresses at which he or she had lived within the last five years. The papers were endorsed with the Home Office decision. If the application was rejected, the reason is recorded, though this was not communicated to the applicant, and no appeal was possible.

Most of the application papers in series HO 405 relate to people of European origin, and the files for married couples are attached together. Police reports, applications for visas, employment permits, changes of name, business name, and internment papers for World War II may be found in these files too. The files in this series start when the person first applied to enter the United Kingdom, and end when naturalization was granted or the immigrant died.

Applicants for denization presented petitions to the Crown, but these only survive from 1801. However, we do hold the stamped or sealed Signet Bills in series SP 39 for the years between 1567 and 1645, and in series SO 7 for the years between 1661 and 1853. The related docquet books of the Signet Office running from 1585 to 1851 in series SO 3, provide short summaries of the bills. Applications and correspondence about denizations from 1801 until 1840 are in series HO 1, from 1801 to 1832 in series HO 44, and from 1841 to 1873 in series HO 45.

If you know your relative arrived in this country after 1890 and before 1960, try searching the ships' passenger lists of incoming vessels in series BT 26. There are also a few manifests for the years between 1878 and 1888 in the same series. They are arranged chronologically by date of arrival at each port, and usually only include ships commencing their voyage from ports other than those in Europe or the Mediterranean Sea, so embrace people coming from the Caribbean and elsewhere in the Commonwealth, from North America, the East and South Asia. Each list will tell you the name of the ship, its official registration number, shipping line, master's name, the date and port of embarkation, and the dates and ports of call as well as the final destination. Every passenger's name, profession or occupation, age, nationality and country of last permanent abode and the intended place of residence are given. On the back of the list provision was made for any births and deaths on board, which were duly reported to the Registry of Shipping and Seamen, and are now included in series BT 334 (1891–1972), which includes indexes. (See **BIRTHS, MARRIAGES AND DEATHS OF BRITONS AT SEA AND ABROAD.**)

Finding aids

Indexed abstracts of naturalizations and denizations from 1509 to 1800 have been published in *Denization and Naturalization of Aliens in England, 1509–1603,* by W. Page, and *Letters of Denizen and Acts of Naturalization for Aliens in England, 1603–1800,* edited by W.A. Shaw. There are typescript indexes for the period 1801 to 1935, in series HO 1. These cover denizations from 1801 to 1873, Acts of naturalization between 1801 and 1900, and naturalization certificates issued by the Secretary of State for Home Affairs from 1844 to 1935. They give the date and number of the certificate, and original Home Office references to the applications and other papers. Document references to background papers relating to naturalizations and denizations between 1844 and 1871 in series HO 1, between 1872 and 1878 in series HO 45, and between 1879 and 1934 in series HO 144, are now searchable by personal-name, using our online catalogue. You can also search our online catalogue by personal-name for the background papers to naturalizations or denizations by Act of Parliament from 1801 to 1840, in HO 1/6–16. All the indexes disclose the applicant's name, any alias, the country of origin, date of naturalization or denization, and from 1878, the current place of residence. Bound copies of the indexes are available on the open shelves in the Research Enquiries Room. The indexes only concern successful applications. A nominal index of people granted British nationality between 1801 and 1900 is in HO 409/1, and later indexes up to 1980, are in HO 409/2–32, the volumes being listed in date order. The indexes furnish the original nationality, certificate number and number of the related Home Office file for each person. Once you have identified the correct certificate number you can then track down the duplicate certificate reference in series C 54 or series HO 334. Later indexes are held by the Home Office. There are no personal-name indexes to the 'O' or 'R' or 'M' (relating to the registration of a minor, under the 1948 British Nationality Act) certificates in series HO 334, so if you do not have the certificate number, you will need to write to the Immigration and Nationality Directorate, in Liverpool, for details. The document references to declarations of alienage in all but series HO 334 are searchable by personal-name online.

Name indexes to the docquet books in series SO 3 are in series SO 4 (1584–1851). The indexes between 1584 and 1624 have been published by the British Record Society, Index Library, vol. IV. Copies of this are available in our Map and Large Document Room and in our Library and Resource Centre.

Interrogate our online catalogue to series HO 45 and HO 144, for the names of people renouncing British citizenship between 1874 and 1944 and 1868 and 1959 respectively.

Yearly registers of ships' passenger lists arriving in UK ports from 1906 to 1951 are in series BT 32, though these are incomplete. Until October 1908 merely the ports of Bristol, Southampton and Weymouth are covered. Up to 1920, the handwritten registers are arranged by month, and thereafter by day. If you already know the name of the ship, but not the date and port of arrival, then this series may prove invaluable. Armed with the date and port, you can then search the catalogue for series BT 26 to identify the relevant box of ships' passenger lists for that month. A project called 'Travel to the UK' is underway to list the names of vessels, their shipping companies, and details of their voyages, extracted from series BT 26, and working backwards from 1960. The information will be uploaded into our online catalogue.

What if you can't find your ancestor?

• Not all the naturalization records survive, nor did every immigrant seek to become a British citizen. You may have to consult other sources such as the ten-yearly census returns (see **CENSUS RETURNS**). If your forebear was a 19th-century immigrant, you are probably better off starting by looking in the census returns, particularly those in and around ports. However, their given birthplaces are frequently limited to their native countries, states, towns or cities.

• Many Irishmen were recruited into the British Army and Royal Navy, and their personnel records should be trawled for details of age on joining, birthplace and careers (see **ARMY SERVICE RECORDS** and **ROYAL NAVY**). Recruits from other nationalities served as army mercenaries, for instance the King's German Legion, other German Corps and Hessian Troops during the American Revolutionary War of 1775–83. You can find details about their ages and birthplaces as well as their careers in series WO 97 if they went to pension, and you can search this catalogue online by personal-name between 1754 and 1854. Service records of officers in the King's German Legion are in series WO 25, which is listed by regiment. There are nominal indexes to the returns in our Research Enquiries Room. Birth, baptism, marriage and death certificates, other personal papers and statements of service of German officers in the above units are in WO 42/52–8, which is arranged alphabetically. Similar information about the Loyal American and Canadian Corps is in WO 42/59–63, and of French, Greek and Italian Corps in WO 42/64–5, though the latter are arranged in numerical order. Three days' notice is required to examine all but the German officers' records. You can unearth numerous references to foreign merchant seamen on board British ships in the crew lists and agreements, registers of seamen and seamen's pouches, particularly after 1913. See **MERCHANT NAVY**. For those who died at sea look at **BIRTHS, MARRIAGES AND DEATHS OF BRITONS AT SEA AND ABROAD**, which includes references to foreign nationals too.

• The relevant naturalization papers have been misfiled, and are not yet embedded in our indexes. Try an online catalogue search, keying in the name of your ancestor, in case they have turned up elsewhere, for instance in series HO 144. The Departmental Records Officer of the Home Office might be able to assist in locating post-1948 files, which haven't yet been transferred to the National Archives.

• Have you tested variant spellings of your family name, including Anglicization? If the surname was changed you may have to tackle our indexes under both the original and adopted names. Until 1916, aliens could alter their names in the same way as any British subject (see **CHANGE OF NAME**), but thereafter citizens of enemy states were proscribed from doing so. This regulation was extended to embrace all aliens up to 1971 by an Act of Parliament in 1919. Exemption was only granted to people changing their names by Royal Licence, or with the consent of the Home Secretary, or when a woman took her husband's surname on marriage. Changes effected within the first two categories were announced in the *London Gazette* (see p. 29).

• No names of unsuccessful applicants for naturalization are included in our indexes, but you can explore some of their preserved memorials from 1872 to 1878 in series HO 45, and some later ones up to 1934 in series HO 144, which might reveal the Home Office's reason for their rejection. You can search our online catalogue by personal-name for both series. Details about unsuccessful applications between 1934 and 1948 may be discovered in series HO 405, especially in cases where a later application succeeded. Series HO 5 contains correspondence about unsuccessful applicants between 1794 and 1921, and series HO 136 holds similar material for 1871 to 1873.

• He or she didn't apply for naturalization. Many immigrants were wrongly described as naturalized before the outbreak of war in 1914, and you can find numerous examples in the census returns.

• You don't know when he or she arrived, or on what ship. If you know where your ancestor came from, local passenger lists of ships leaving ports abroad and bound for the United Kingdom may help, as some of these pre-date our collection. Use a portal such as **www.cyndislist.com/ships.htm** or **http://home.att.net/~wee-monster/onlinelists.html**, and visit the websites of the national archives of the relevant country or individual state archives for other information on emigrants and ships' manifests. The websites often include readers' guides similar to ours, so are well worth visiting. You could also try the ten-yearly census (see **CENSUS RETURNS**). The census will give at least a decadal cut-off date for arrival in this country, but generally only the foreign country or state where each immigrant was born will be given.

• Your ancestors arrived before 1890, and they weren't naturalized. If they were here between 1826 and 1869, and you have located them in the 1851, 1861 and/or 1871 census returns, it is worth delving into the signed individual certificates of arrival of aliens between 1826 and 1869 in series HO 2 (1836–52), to which there are indexes up to 1849 in HO 5/25–32. The indexes actually go back to 1826, but no certificates are known to survive before 1836. The certificates list the name, nationality, profession or occupation of each passenger, with the port of embarkation, date and port of landing, and last country visited. Returns of the names, occupations and country of origin of immigrant passengers made to customs officers by ships' masters on arrival in this country between 1836 and 1869, are in series HO 3. These are arranged chronologically by date, but there is a gap between 1861 and 1866. In both cases, the lists are largely confined to the Port of London. There is an alphabetical index of German, Polish and Prussian passengers during the years between 1847 and 1852 in our Research Enquiries Room, and members of the Anglo-German Family History Society have created a further index of the names of 36,000 passengers between 1853 and 1869 extracted from this series. Consult its website (**www.art-science.com/agfhs**) for more information.

• Don't neglect the records of the known country of origin. It is often worth seeking out copies of any census returns, published directories and lists of names of people in the estimated period of emigration if you have a rough idea of where your antecedents came from. These will localize the family name at least. An excellent website portal is **www.cyndislist.com**. A published history of your ancestral area will arm you with much useful background information too

• Family historical research is one of the most popular global pursuits. You could consult the bulletin boards hosted by various major websites for people posting their interests and seeking contact with people sharing their ancestry or knowing something they don't. Another good resource is *Genealogical Research Directory, National and International,* edited by K.A. Johnson and M.R. Sainty (see p. 96). Family historians with a shared ancestral nationality often collaborate to form an Anglo/relevant country society, and host a website publicizing its activities, offering advice and information. Some of these are affiliated to the Federation of Family History Societies, whose website, **www.ffhs.org.uk**, can be used as a link to theirs. However, anyone can load anything onto the internet or submit anything for publication without it necessarily being accurate or authentic, so use such information with caution, and evaluate the evidence to see if it is reliable and the interpretation of it correct.

**Other records
about immigrants
in the National
Archives**

For foreign Protestant congregations in England, especially those of Dutch Walloons, Huguenot refugees in the late 16th and 17th centuries, and German Lutherans, their births, baptisms, marriages and burials recorded in the deposited registers of their own churches are available on microfilm in series RG 4 and RG 8. Usually these will have been written in the vernacular. All the registers in series RG 4 have been transcribed and published by the Huguenot Society of London, and copies are widely available. The dated baptism entries in the registers generally include the names of the sponsors (godparents) as well as of the child and his or her parents. The traced places of origin of the sponsors often provide clues to where your forebears came from too, if you are otherwise at a loss to know where to look next. Extracts from the birth, baptism and marriage registers in series RG 4 are enshrined in the International Genealogical Index.

The National Archives hold myriad records relating to refugees. Some of these deal with appeals for and grants of financial support, so the best way to discover document references is to use our online catalogue and key in the nationality 'AND refugees' plus the dates in which you are interested. We possess a good collection of material about French émigrés fleeing the Revolution of 1789, including paylists in series T 50 for the period 1793 up to 1831, and in series T 93 for the years between 1792 and 1828 tracking the work of the French Refugees' Relief Committee.

We hold family history cards relating to about 260,000 Belgian men, women and children who fled here between 1914 and 1918, in MH 8/39–93. Each card indicates the ages, married and former names, and family relationships of the named people, plus the allowances awarded them and the address for payment. We have a set of specimen personal files of Czech refugee families between 1938 and 1975, in HO 294/235–486. You can search our online catalogue to those up to HO 294/385 by surname and the date range covered by each file is indicated too. Post-war refugees coming here from 1948 onwards (in HO 294/386–486) are listed by personal-name. Numerical case papers relating to other Czech refugee families from 1938 and during World War II are in HO 294/487–585, and from 1948 onwards up to 1979 in HO 294/586–611, to which there are indexes in HO 294/612 and 613. However, the files and case papers are subject to a 50- or 75-year closure period. The information contained in the dated and signed files includes the name and settlement plans of the head of the family, and whether any family member was already settled abroad and if so where, the person's occupation in this country, nationality status, current address, and the names, ages and relationship to him or her of the rest of the family in this country.

In 1793, an attempt was made by an Aliens Act to regulate the arrival and movements of foreign subjects in and around this country. As well as having to furnish declarations of name, occupation and address on arrival, foreigners already resident in this country or householders with whom they were lodging were obliged to supply details of their names, ranks or occupations, and addresses to a local magistrate or parish overseer respectively, for transmission to the county quarter sessions. A special Aliens Office was established in the same year, which was absorbed into the Home Office in 1836 after a new regulatory enactment. The local returns of declarations are now in county record offices; check the online catalogue at **www.national archives.gov.uk/a2a**, though this is far from complete as yet. From 1793 aliens were restricted to certain entry ports and areas of residence inland. Passes were issued allowing them to leave London or specific English ports for the Continent within a prescribed period. You can find out-letters between 1794 and 1921 relating to foreigners and their movements, particularly French people in the early years, in series HO 5, and from 1871 to 1873 in series HO 136. The letters are arranged chronologically by date. The Aliens Registration Act 1914 made compulsory the registration with the local police force of all aliens aged 16 or more. They had to notify details of their age, race, place of domicile, employment and employer, and marital status. Unfortunately, there is no central register, so any surviving records will now be in county record offices or among county police archives. However, more than 1,000 sample cards have been preserved in series MEPO 35, relating to registrations made to the Metropolitan Police Force, which cover the period 1876 to 1991. The listing is by personal-name, date of birth and the dates between which they were of alien status in the UK and obliged to register after 1 January 1961 under the Aliens Order 1960. A number of these individuals later became naturalized as British subjects, so look in these sources too.

During both World Wars, enemy aliens were interned in special camps in the United Kingdom. Many of the records relating to internment camps are kept locally, so try **www.nationalarchives.gov.uk/a2a** for references to some of these. A classified list of enemy aliens who were internees from 1914 until 1918 is in HO 144/11720, and nominal rolls of male enemy aliens aged 45 or more held in internment camps is included in a census of UK aliens undertaken from 1915 to 1924 and recorded in HO 45/11522. References to individual internees may be extracted from Foreign Office General Correspondence, to which there is a card index from 1906 to 1919 in our Research Enquiries Room. The cards also concern material which no longer survives, and the references need to be converted to archival ones.

Internment of enemy aliens began on the outbreak of war in September 1939. You can search a microfilmed copy of an index of internees and people considered for internment between 1939 and 1947, in series HO 396, in our Microfilm Reading Room. This mostly relates to Germans, Austrians and Italians and their wives. The index is usually arranged by nationality, and then alphabetically by name, and the details recorded are date and place of birth, address, occupation and employer's details, and the date and nature of the Tribunal decision. The personal case histories, on the back, are not open to public inspection, but you may obtain a copy by writing to the National Archives. Indexed digital images of the index relating to aliens in HO 396/1–106, who were exempted from internment between 1939 and 1942, are at **www.movinghere.org.uk**. These mainly refer to German Jews. The series also embraces details about German and Austrian internees sent to Canada between 1939 and 1942, and those who returned to the United Kingdom after release between 1939 and 1945, and about non-resident seamen who were interned here from 1939 until 1940. Other particulars about camp transfers of internees within the UK or shipped abroad to Australia and Canada in 1940 and 1941 are in series HO 215. As many ships were lost at sea, the Home Office dealt with claims from the survivors for the loss of or damage to their property, and these can be found in the same series.

Nominal listings of detainees interned between 1941 and 1943 are in HO 215/2, and are arranged by camp. They contain the names, dates of birth and of release of internees. Delayed release returns from all camps from 1942 until 1945 are in HO 215/9–11. The last internees were let go in late 1945, and many remained in this country. There is a small sample of personal case files of internees between 1940 and 1949 in series HO 214. These are listed in our online catalogue by personal-name, occupation, the conditions under which kept, and the dates of internment. Finally, the files of applications for naturalization between 1934 and 1948, in series HO 405, include internment papers where appropriate, and the names of unsuccessful candidates too.

Many of the records relating to prisoners of war held in this country are to be found in local archives, and very few survive for the Second World War. The International Council of the Red Cross, in Geneva, keeps lists of all known prisoners of war and internees of all nationalities for both world wars. You can make a written request for a search, and an hourly fee is charged. We have two specimen lists of German subjects interned as prisoners of war in 1915 and 1916 in WO 900/45 and 46 respectively, which are arranged by Army, Navy and civilians, and recording the regiment, ship or home address of each person.

The Aliens Act 1905 created the power to deport aliens. You can obtain the names of deportees in the outward ships' passenger lists in series BT 27, which run up to 1960. Use the registers of ships' passenger lists from 1906 to 1951 in series BT 32, to ascertain the ships' names, ports and dates of departure. There is a register of deportees between 1906 and 1963 in series HO 372. This is listed according to the prevailing statutes and in date order.

Look in series BT 334 for the births and deaths of aliens at sea from 1891 until 1960 and 1964 respectively. This series has separate registers of deaths of seamen reported to the Registrar General from 1896 onwards, a number of whom were of foreign nationalities.

The names of aliens who were taxed double from 1335 feature in the lay subsidy returns in series E 179, which run up to 1689. They were also subject to a separate poll tax between 1439 and 1487, householders paying a higher rate. Consult the online database at **www.nationalarchives.gov. uk/e179** for details of dates, places and document references. You can study indexed published tax lists and other sources in *Returns of Aliens in London 1523–1625,* edited by R.E.G. Kirk and E.F. Kirk.

To find out more, read our Research Guides:

Immigrants
Naturalization and Citizenship: Grants of British Nationality
Passenger Lists
Anglo-Jewish History, 18th–20th Centuries: Sources in The National Archives
Refugees and Minorities
French Revolution, Great Britain and the
Internees: First and Second World Wars Prisoners of War in British Hands: 1698–1949
(Ex-POWS and Displaced Persons, 1945 onwards); and
R. Winder, *Bloody Foreigners, The Story of Immigration to Britain*
A. Joseph, *My Ancestors were Jewish: How Can I Find Out More About Them?*

Legal proceedings: civil actions

The National Archives holds surviving records of the central law courts of England from early medieval to recent times. See **CRIME, CONVICTS AND TRANSPORTATION**. The civil actions relate to disputes between the monarch's subjects over matters such as land, business and personal debts, inheritance, trusts, fraud, marriage settlements and wills.

There were two types of court, those practising common law and those following the rules of equity. Actions at common law were instigated on the issue of a writ on behalf of the plaintiff, but the legal arguments of the lawyers, expressed orally in the court itself, were not written down. To 1875, the central law courts all sat in Westminster Great Hall, part of the Palace of Westminster. The Assize judges went out from Westminster on circuit three or four times a year (see p. 77). There were special courts serving the Palatinates of Chester, Durham and Lancaster, the Duchy of Lancaster, and the Principality of Wales. The records of all except those for Wales are in the National Archives. The Welsh court records prior to 1830 are in the National Library of Wales, Aberystwyth, whilst later material is in the National Archives.

In 1875 the central courts were brought together to form the Supreme Court of Judicature. The records of the five Divisions of the new High Court of Justice (King's Bench, Common Pleas, Exchequer, Chancery, and of Probate, Divorce and Admiralty) are in various 'J' series, but they have been heavily weeded.

The extant common law court records are not generally very informative for the family historian, because only the content of the initiating writs and enrolments of judgements were preserved. Conversely, equity suits were determined by consideration of the written petitions or bills of complaint presented on behalf of the plaintiffs, the answers of the defendants, any further responses, counter-allegations and other supporting material. Such flurries of documentation can help you to build up a detailed picture stretching back a sizeable length of time. They were almost always written in English.

The church courts followed a separate legal system, based on ecclesiastical (canon) law, and dealt with matrimonial causes, wrangles over wills, non-payment of tithes, and matters referred to them by parish officers. The records of causes in the Prerogative Court of the Archbishop of Canterbury (PCC) are in the National Archives whilst those of other church courts are held locally, either in diocesan or county record offices. The Court of Arches was the appeal court for the PCC and a complete index to cases between 1660 and 1913 held in Lambeth Palace Library, London, has been published. The ultimate court of appeal was the High Court of Delegates (DEL), set up in 1532 and superseded by the Judicial Committee of the Privy Council (PCAP) in 1834 (see **WILLS AND OTHER PROBATE RECORDS**). You can search the foregoing material in the National Archives.

Manorial and many local courts relied on the application of customary law. Crown manorial court records from about 1200 until about 1900 are in series SC 2, with some duplicate court rolls and other manorial documents running from 1286 to 1837 in series LR 3, though these range mostly from the 16th century up to 1800. The Duchy of Lancaster manorial court rolls between about 1272 and 1954 are in series DL 30. Both series are indexed.

For more information, read M. Cale, *Law and Society, An Introduction to Sources for Criminal and Legal History from 1800*; H. Horwitz, *Chancery and Equity Proceedings 1600–1800*.

What will you find?

The busiest court for litigation, and the one where you are most likely to find information about a warring family, was the Court of Chancery, set up in the late 14th century. Until the early 17th century the bundles cannot be dated more precisely than the period of office of the Lord Chancellor to whom they were addressed. It has been reckoned that more than 90 per cent of cases never actually came to court, so it is best to start by looking for the pleadings themselves rather than for any resulting court orders or decrees.

The early pleadings, from about 1386 until 1690, are in series C 1 to series C 3. All those covering a particular action should be fastened together. Series C 4 consists of miscellaneous pleadings which may be related to those in series C 1, C 2 and C 3. Series C 5 to series C 10 cover the period 1613–1714, and because of the filing system employed during this period papers relating to a single case may be scattered over several of these series. In 1842, a new and simpler filing system was introduced.

From 1715 onwards to 1875, all the papers relevant to any one suit were tied together in series C 11 (*c* 1700–58), C 12 (*c* 1758–1800), C 13 (1797–1842), C 14 (1842–52), C 15 (1853–60), and C 16 (1861–75), with some miscellaneous pleadings in series C 18 (1664–1868, though most date between 1850 and 1860). Series C 17 is concerned with cases involving the administration of estates of deceased persons. Surviving pleadings in the Chancery Division of the High Court of Justice from 1876 onwards are in series J 54.

The bill set out the plaintiff's side of the story. From it you can discover the names, places of residence, status or occupation of each party. A crib of the bill, summarizing the allegations, was addressed to the defendants. Their answer(s) might be made individually or jointly, sometimes the answers made counterclaims, and so on. Proceedings could therefore be protracted and slow, so you may need to search for them over a wide period.

It is worth persevering with Chancery proceedings, because they may recall people and events over a hundred years before, perhaps even in the Middle Ages. They deal with disputes about land inheritance, mortgages, loans of money, legal entitlement to land deeds, family trusts, marriage settlements and wills, material evidence of which otherwise no longer survives anywhere else. You can find out about apprenticeships, descent of property, changes of land occupancy, the circumstances, terms and conditions of borrowings, business enterprises, travel overseas, family marriages, ages at mortality, the intentions and contents of wills and trust deeds, and the causes and duration of family fractures.

The sworn and signed written depositions of witnesses are especially useful. They were made by people who knew the suitors and were thus often their relatives, friends, servants, employees, tenants and neighbours. The answers tell you who and how old they were, where they lived and for how long, what were their occupations, and their length of acquaintanceship with the suitor for whom they were lending support. The depositions were filed with the pleadings from the 15th century until about 1558 in series C 1, then became separated and were hived off into a series of Town (London) depositions in series C 24 (1534–1853), and Country (elsewhere) depositions in series C 21 (1558–1649), and C 22 (1649–1714). Later Country depositions, 1715–1880, are filed with the pleadings in series C 11–C 14, whilst from 1854 up to 1880 Town depositions are filed with the pleadings in series C 15, C 16 and J 54, and thereafter both are merged to April 1925 in series J 17.

Finding aids

You can interrogate our online catalogue by personal-name for series C 1 (about 1386 to about 1558), C 2 (1558–1603), C 3 (1484–1690), C 4 (about 1272 to about 1790, for the first part of the catalogue only), C 5 (1613–1714), C 6 (from about 1625 to 1714 – for more information about this read on), C 9 (from about 1643 until 1714), C 10 (from about 1640 to 1714, for surnames so far only up to those beginning with the letter 'P'). The catalogues to these include the names of the first plaintiff and first defendant only. You can likewise search our online catalogue to series C 11 (running from about 1700 until 1758), though merely the surnames of the first plaintiff and first defendant are given, and the date of the document. For series C 12 (from about 1681 until 1800), the online catalogue will disclose surnames and dates as for series C 11, but also the nature of the documents. Our online catalogues can be trawled by surname for the first plaintiff and first defendant for series C 13 (1797–1842), C 14 (1842–52), and C 15 (for the first few years between 1853 and 1860). Only the deceased's name, rather than that of the parties to each suit, is searchable online for series C 17 (1852–5). The online catalogue to series C 18 (1664–1868) lists the personal-names of suitors.

The complete catalogues to series C 2 and C 4 are not yet searchable online, but there is a printed list to the former series, arranged sequentially by bundle number, and then initial-alphabetically under the name of the first plaintiff. The bound catalogue to series C 4 is arranged in alphabetical order by first plaintiff's name, but most of the causes are not listed in any detail. The bound catalogues to series C 5 and to C 7–C 10 contain a brief account of each case. An online Equity Pleadings database has been created at **www.nationalarchives.gov.uk/equity** for part of series C 6, which incorporates the names of every plaintiff and defendant, plus brief case summaries; a similar database is in progress for series C 4. The database is searchable by personal- and place-name, and by subject. You will otherwise have to cull the bound catalogue to series C 6, which spans the period from approximately 1625 until 1714.

The bound manuscript catalogues to series C 11–C 15 are arranged according to the six divisions of the Six Clerks Office, and then in rough alphabetical order under the name of the principal plaintiff. There are manuscript indexes to the records in series C 16, which are arranged by year and then initial-alphabetically by the surname of the first plaintiff. Each entry gives the cause number.

There is an index to series J 54 (1876–90) in IND 1/2218–2226.

It is also worth pursuing the index to *The Times* (see p. 29). Investigate the Bernau Index too, available on microfilm in the library of the Society of Genealogists, and for hire in family history centres. This index contains the names of all the suitors in series C 1 up to 1529, all the parties and deponents in the pleadings in series C 11 and C 12, all the Town deponents from 1534 to 1800 in series C 24, the Country deponents to the end of the reign of Charles I in 1649 in series C 21, and 8 per cent of the remainder (the first 75 bundles prior to 1714 in series C 22). The index entries give the name, abode, occupation, age and year the documentation was filed. For more information about the index, read *How to Use the Bernau Index*, by H. Sharp.

For cases involving disputed wills and intestate estates located in series C 6 to C 8, and in series C 10, read *Indexes to Disputed Estates in Chancery*, by P.W. Coldham. The entries are listed by the name of the deceased rather than by those of the suitors. You can also examine this (under the title of 'Inheritance Disputes Index 1574–1714'), at **www.originsnetwork.com**, which offers a subscription service.

What if you can't find your ancestor?

• Your forebear might have been 'and another' or one of the unnamed 'others' cited in the series lists or catalogues. If you know the case revolved around a particular place or piece of property, key this in instead when searching our online catalogues, or cast your eye down the final right-hand column headed 'county or subject' in the bound catalogue.

• Your ancestor used another court. Sometimes plaintiffs instigated legal proceedings by issue of a writ in a common law court and if there was no remedy at common law for the alleged act or omission the case would be thrown out, so they might have recourse to the equity courts.

• The Court of Requests was in existence for less than 200 years, from 1483 to 1642, when it was abolished. Proceedings in this court were similar to those in the Courts of Chancery and of the equity Court of Exchequer. The proceedings, including depositions, are to found in series REQ 2, to which the personal-name index of suitors is available in our online catalogue, and the Bernau Index includes both the names of suitors and deponents throughout the period.

• The equity Court of Exchequer received bills of complaint from aggrieved subjects where royal revenue or Crown debts were ultimately involved. As such these embraced disputes about tithes, the administration of estates, mortgages and copyholds. The Court was abolished in 1841 and merged with the equity Court of Chancery, which itself became the Chancery Division of the High Court of Justice in 1875. To find cases brought in the Court of Exchequer, use series E 111, covering the years between about 1485 and about 1558, and series E 112, extending from approximately 1558 until 1841. These consist of bills and answers. You can search our online catalogue for the names of the suitors mentioned in series E 111, but you will need to consult the contemporary Bill Books in IND 1/16820–53 for series E 112 references. These are arranged in county sections and new book(s) were opened for each reign. The full names of all the parties and the subject matter of each case are listed. The Town depositions made by witnesses from 1558 until 1841 are to be found in series E 133, and Country depositions, from about 1558 until 1841, are in series E 134. Both series are listed by the names of plaintiffs and defendants rather than those of the various deponents. You can scour these catalogues online. However, there is a published chronological calendar of Country deponents between 1558 and 1760, a copy of which is on the open shelves in our Map and Large Document Room. The names of the plaintiffs and defendants are encased in the Bernau Index, together with those of Country deponents from 1559 to 1800 (in series E 134).

• The Court of Star Chamber was set up in 1485 to enforce public law and order, but included disputes over property rights as well. This court was dismantled in 1641. The court records, in series STAC 1 to STAC 9, consist of the case papers but not the eventual outcomes. You can trawl our online catalogue for the names of petitioners and defendants. The names of suitors and deponents between 1485 and 1509, in series STAC 1, are enshrined in the Bernau Index.

• You didn't search a long enough period. Try each of the catalogues to the pleadings, because many of the equity court actions relate to situations that first arose perhaps more than a hundred years before the actual complaint.

• You searched under the wrong name. Explore the Bernau Index as an alternative.

Chancery Masters' Exhibits, in series C 103 to C 116 (which extend from the 12th century until 1859), C 171 (1350 to about 1850) and J 90 (from 1700 until 1918), are well worth delving into. The Exhibits are listed by case title, so you can search our online catalogue for document references.

The entry books of Chancery decrees and orders made between 1544 and 1875, in series C 33, and from 1876 until 1954, in series J 15, plus the formal enrolments of final decrees and judgements from 1534 to 1903 in series C 78 and the supplementary decree rolls, 1534–1903, in series C 79, help you track the progress of a case to its conclusion, though from 1875 the enrolments have no genealogical value. Series C 33 and J 15 include interlocutory

Other civil litigation records in the National Archives

[10]

The GREEN-HOUSE, *Numb.* LI.

Twenty bay Trees in Tubs, 30 Orange Trees in Tubs, 10 Orange Trees in Pots, 8 *Mecnemplanny's* or Winter cherries, 29 Myrtles in Pots, 23 Orange Trees in Pots, 3 *Adam's* Needles, 4 Ragworths in Pots, 2 Honey Trees, 1 Currant Tree, 1 Hollander in a Tub, 1 Strawbery Tree, 6 Watering Pots, 25 blue and white Earthen Pots, 17 brown Earthen Pots, a Brass Pump, Water-Tub, 2 Casting Nets, Drag Net, 8 Forest Chairs, 2 Sieves, 8 Forms, Spanish Table, Earthen Pots, 34 Iron Hoops, 4 Tubs iron-hoop'd, Iron Dogg, 4 Scythes, 2 Pair of Sheers, Turfing Iron or Reel, 4 Hoes, Iron Bar, a Gun, 3 Wheel-barrows, Hand-barrow, 2 Rakes, 20 Lead Pots, 10 large Earthen Pots, 4 Stone Rolls and Frames, large Iron-cast Roll, Wood Roll, 2 Stone Jarrs, 3 blue and white Earthen Pots, Hair-brush, 2 large Settles.

NUMB. LII.

Matted Bedstead, Feather-bed, Bolster and Pillow, brown Rug, 3 Blankets, 2 Chairs, Close-stool, Chest, Pewter Pot, Skillet, 2 Prongs, Chariot box.

NUMB. LIII.

Corded Bedstead, Flock-bed and Bolster, 3 Blankets, Table and Lanthorn.

NUMB. LIV.

Seven Collars, Corn Bins, 2 Buckets, a Sconce, Wheelbarrow, Shovel and 3 Prongs, a Berline Chariot lin'd with blue Cloth, Tar-barrel, and Tub-cloth to cover the Chariot, 2 Water-brushes.

NUMB. LV.

Bedstead, Serge Furniture, Feather-bed, 2 Bolsters, 3 Blankets, Coverlid, Elbow Chair, Cane Chair, Wood Chair, Stool, Table, Pair of Doggs, Cupboard, 2 gilt Sconces, 13 Pair of Bowls, and 3 Jacks.

In the WARDROBE, *Numb.* LVI.

A large Quantity of Table-Linnen, Bed-Linnen, and all other Sorts of Linnen, with several large Boxes to keep Linnen in.

C 110/136: All good things come to an end. After a disastrous series of court cases and an overburdened estate, the Walter family's possessions at Sarsden, in Oxfordshire, were auctioned off in 1732. Chancery Masters exhibits include this sale catalogue, listing the contents of the greenhouse.

(interim) orders by the court for the delivery of certain specified documents by a set date, dates of receipt of sworn depositions and affidavits and injunctions, plus details of the final decree deciding the case. They are arranged by case title, and before 1733 they may be in Latin. You may unearth any number of such orders issued after the original bill of complaint was received, but each entry refers back to the previous order, making the trail of documentation easier. The means of access to the entry books in series C 33 and J 15 is via the 'A' and 'B' books, on the open shelves in the Map and Large Document Room. The 'A' books start in 1544 and the 'B' books in 1547 and both end in 1955. They are organised by legal year, which, up to 1859, commenced with Michaelmas Term (the end of September), and ended with Trinity Term (in June the following year), with Hilary and Easter Terms in between. From 1860, the books run by calendar year. The entries are listed chronologically and initial-alphabetically by first plaintiff's surname and by order number. To Trinity Term 1629, the 'A' and 'B' books overlap; thereafter plaintiffs' surnames between A and K appear in the 'A' books and from L to Z in the 'B' books. The two series were amalgamated in 1932.

The final decrees, enrolled in series C 78 (1534–1903) and in a supplementary series for the same period, C 79, are much more instructive. The rolls set out a summary of the case put by each side, and provide an explanation of how the written decision was reached. Only a very small percentage of cases ever achieved this stage, as proceedings could drag on for years and be a constant drain on family finances, so an out-of-court settlement might be reached instead. The catalogues to series C 78 and C 79 are not yet searchable online, but there are some printed calendars and contemporary indexes available on the open shelves in our Map and Large Document Room.

Other Masters' papers, and pedigrees lodged with the court between 1852 and 1974, are in series J 46, J 63, J 64, J 66 and J 67. The indexes to these, in series J 68, are listed by the name of the earliest known progenitor, the earliest date on the family tree, and by case title.

117

The Records A to Z

To find out more, read our Research Guides:
Assizes: English, 1656–1971: Key to Series for Civil Trials
Assizes: Welsh, 1831–1971: Key to Classes for Criminal and Civil Trials
Chancery Proceedings: Equity Suits before 1558
Chancery Proceedings: Equity Suits from 1558
Chancery Masters' and Other Exhibits: Sources for Social and Economic History
Chancery Masters' Reports and Certificates
Money Funds in Court
Equity Proceedings in the Court of Exchequer
Supreme Court, Chancery Division: Cases after 1875
Court of Requests, 1485–1642: A Court for the 'Poor'
Court of Star Chamber, 1485–1642
Bankrupts and Insolvent Debtors: 1710–1869
Bankruptcy Records after 1869
Lawyers: Records of Attorneys and Solicitors; and
H. Horwitz, *Exchequer Equity Records and Proceedings 1649–1841.*

Maps, Tithe and Valuation Office records

You can learn a lot about how and where your ancestors lived just by looking at a map of the area – large-scale Ordnance Survey maps are especially good. There are two other important series of maps, both of which tie in very nicely with the census returns and other records of the same period. These are the Tithe maps and apportionments drafted between 1836 and 1852, and the Valuation Office record sheets and field books compiled from 1911 to 1915.

Read *Maps for Family and Local History, the Records of the Tithe, Valuation Office and National Farm Surveys of England and Wales, 1836–1943*, by G. Beech and R. Mitchell.

We have a full set of Ordnance Survey maps on a scale of one inch to the mile. These were drawn up between 1805 and 1879, when a second, revised, edition began to appear. You can also find larger scale maps, up to a scale of 25 inches to the mile, which were produced after 1840, though our holdings of these are incomplete.

If your forebears were country folk (in the first half of the 19th century the majority of the population was rural), it is well worth poring over the Tithe maps. These maps were compiled between 1836 and 1852 when a survey was undertaken by special Tithe Commissioners of the boundaries, size, shape

What will you find?

and usage of private property owned in all those parishes in England and Wales (over 4,000 of them) which hadn't yet converted to a money payment (rent-charge) the occupiers' contribution to the incumbent or other entitled person of a tenth (the Tithe) of the annual produce in crops or animals on each piece of land. Three copies were made: the two local copies are now usually in county record offices, and the Commissioners' signed and sealed copies, in series IR 30, are available in our Map and Large Document Room.

The maps indicate parish boundaries, rivers, ponds, forests, woods, parkland and scrub, as well as road routes, and the names of adjoining parishes and townships. Each plot of land is denoted by number, so the maps are no use on their own. You will need to inspect the accompanying series of Tithe apportionments, in series IR 29, available only on microform in our Map and Large Document Room. These schedules of apportionment set out the date of the agreement or award, landowners' names, the names(s) of the occupiers of each numbered plot, plus any name and a description of the property, its state of cultivation, its size, the Tithe owner, the annual rent-charge, and any additional remarks. You can link these records to the householders' schedules in the census returns of 1841 and 1851.

The Finance Act 1909/10 introduced an Increment Value Duty in the United Kingdom, entailing a complete land survey and valuation between 1911 and 1915 to estimate each property's value as of 30 April 1909. The numbered record sheets, in series IR 121 (London Region) and IR 124–IR 135, have to be ordered as original documents in our Map and Large Document Room. On each record sheet are marked in colour the numbered hereditament (assessment) boundaries. To discover who owned and tenanted any one of these you will need to locate the relevant field book for the civil parish in series IR 58. In 1914, every landowner completed a special form answering a series of questions about their property, the details of which were then copied into a special book. The resulting field books are arranged sequentially by hereditament number, some of which are united with other connected hereditament numbers, enabling you to tot up the total property value. There is usually a cross-reference to the numbered record sheet on which the plot can then be identified. The full name, title or address of the property is given, with the name of the owner, the tenant, the nature of the tenancy (for instance a lease or a periodic rent), the purchase price of the property if it had been bought within the last 20 years, a detailed room-by-room description of their individual function, the fabric of construction of the building and roof, plus any outbuildings, and the approximate age and present condition of the property. The gross value of the land and buildings on the open market were recorded, the full site value after deducting the estimated worth of the buildings, timber or fruit trees, followed by the calculated total gross value minus any fixed charges or encumbrances, which were all used to reach an assessable site value. Duty was to be paid on the difference between this and its later transfer value. The Great War intervened and the idea was dropped. Similar Valuation Books (also known as 'Domesday Books'), in county record offices, list the properties alphabetically by the names of their owners, rather than by consecutive hereditament number, and contain the addresses of non-occupying owners, but exclude the property descriptions. The Valuation Books for the City of London and for Paddington (Westminster), compiled in 1910, are in the National Archives, in series IR 91.

For the Ordnance Survey maps, there is a key map of England and Wales, available in our Map and Large Document Room, which cites the individual map numbers, so that you can go straight from this to the relevant map sheet in the bound books on the open shelves.

The Tithe: Maps of England and Wales, Cartographic Analysis and County by County Catalogue, by R.J.P. Kain and R.R. Oliver, lists parish by parish the known whereabouts of the dated maps and gives full National Archives references to series IR 30 and IR 29 where appropriate.

There is a bound index of civil parishes which names the numbered local Valuation Office district offices to which they each belonged, so you can identify which record sheet to look for in series IR 124–IR 135. A separate street index for London specifies the relevant parishes or districts in series IR 121. If you can't find your parish, look at the *Board of Inland Revenue, Alphabetical List of Parishes and Places in England and Wales*, or the large map of England and Wales for the numbered Divisions and district boundaries covering your area. Also look in G. Beech and R. Mitchell's *Maps for Family and Local History* for an index of Divisions, districts and record sheet references. Copies of all of these are in our Map and Large Document Room. Use the catalogue covering the relevant regional Division, in series IR 121, or IR 124 through series IR 135 to find the correct record sheet reference for the numbered Valuation Office district.

• He was a landowner who lived somewhere else at the time of the Tithe commutation. Try contemporary printed poll books and registers of voters in parliamentary elections, since land ownership was the means by which a person was qualified. See *Poll Books and Lists c.1696–1872: A Directory of Holdings in Great Britain*, by J. Gibson and C. Rogers, and *Electoral Registers since 1832; and Burgess Rolls*, by the same authors for details about locally held copies. The books and registers should reveal not only the location and nature of the qualifying land, but also the owner's place of abode.

• Your ancestor was described only as 'and another' or 'and others' in the list of given occupiers in the Tithe apportionment. He and his family might have been sub-tenants of the listed individual, and too low down the chain to be of interest to the Commissioners. The chief tenant was liable, and ultimately the landowner, for the annual rent-charge.

• There is no Tithe map and apportionment because conversion to a monetary payment had already come about at the time of enclosure of the common land, pasture and manorial waste in the parish. For details about individual Enclosures, consult *A Domesday of Enclosure Acts and Awards*, by W.E. Tate.

• Your ancestor was a sub-tenant or lodger of the main tenant or occupier cited in the Valuation Office field book. By the time of the survey between

1911 and 1915, nearly every adult male aged over 21 was entitled to vote. Look in surviving electoral registers for the area.

• Your family might not yet have moved to this address, or had moved on. Rate books, now in county record offices, list for every property the name of the householder and the half-yearly payments, and note any changes of occupancy or householders' deaths.

Other maps in the National Archives

We have sets of printed registration district maps in series RG 18. The maps were produced by the Ordnance Survey, with boundary lines demarcating the registration and sub-registration districts at the time of the census picked out in colour. There is a fully comprehensive run for England and Wales for 1871 but excluding London, a set for London only in 1861, and an incomplete set for England and Wales for 1891 and for 1921. These maps are helpful if you are uncertain in which district a particular hamlet or township lay when searching for a birth, marriage or death registration, or for census returns on microfilm.

To find out more, read our Research Guides:
Maps in The National Archives
Ordnance Survey Records
Tithe Records
Valuation Office Records: The Finance (1909–1910) Act
Enclosure Awards
Enclosure Records (an Example).

Marriages – 'Fleet' and other clandestine weddings in London

It has been estimated that from about 1667 until 24 March 1754, between 250,000 and 400,000 weddings were held in London taverns, in 'marriage shops', in and around the Rules of the Fleet Prison (bounded by Ludgate Hill, the Old Bailey, Farringdon Street and Fleet Lane), in the King's Bench Prison (south of the River Thames, in Southwark), the Mint (in the East End), the Minories (between Aldgate and Whitechapel, in the East End), and in certain churches and chapels in London and throughout the country. Such ceremonies were secret (clandestine), and were generally performed by ousted or debt-ridden clergy without a living, in return for cash, dispensing with the formalities of the public reading of banns in church. Because the weddings were covert and speedy, they were preferred by heirs marrying for love in defiance of their parents' wishes, by under-age couples whose parents' consent would be unlikely, by women trying to escape their creditors and foist responsibility for their debts onto their hapless new husbands, by opportunists preying on or kidnapping an innocent heir or heiress for financial gain, pregnant single women, and by soldiers and sailors on short-term leave. Sometimes one or both of the parties was so inebriated during the ceremony that they didn't know they had been married until it was too late.

Because the records of such unions were so badly kept and were notoriously inaccurate, they were regularly thrown out by courts of law as inadmissible evidence of a valid and legal marriage. The Earl of Hardwicke's Act 1753 put an end to such 'clandestine' ceremonies as from 25 March 1754, and henceforward, until 30 June 1837, a couple could lawfully marry only in an Anglican church or according to the rites of the Society of Friends (Quakers) or Jews.

A number of the London registers of clandestine marriages are on microfilm in series RG 7.

Each clergyman kept his own notebook or register. The books are often identified by their names. The information about the parties is often fairly sparse, but surprisingly it is sometimes better than that in parish registers. The date, the couple's names, maybe their places of residence, groom's occupation or status, and their current marital status were noted, plus the name or initials of the priest. Any or all of this might be false. The registers reveal people travelled from all over the country up to London to wed in this way. The registers occasionally include baptisms too.

Some of the deposited registers have been transcribed and indexed in *Clandestine Marriages in the Chapel and Rules of the Fleet Prison, 1680–1754*, by M. Herber. You could also utilize the typescript index of entries of people emanating from Kent, Surrey and Sussex, whose names were extracted from the registers by S. Hales. This is available in the Family Records Centre, and in the library of the Society of Genealogists. About 2,000 clandestine marriages between 1709 and 1754 in the Fleet are also included in Boyd's Marriage Index (see p. 25).

It is worth hunting for your ancestor's name in the indexed Old Bailey Proceedings between 1674 and 1834, at **www.oldbaileyonline.org** in case he or she was tried for bigamy and cited a clandestine wedding ceremony. Proof of this had to be supplied in the form of the register book itself, or the name of the officiating clergyman given. If the latter, then examine our online catalogue for series RG 7 and look for his name and the relevant date to see if the register has been deposited.

• The registers haven't survived, or haven't been deposited in the National Archives. Some held elsewhere, like those of the MayFair Chapel, have been transcribed and printed (for instance, *The Register of Baptisms and Marriages at St George's Chapel, MayFair*, edited by G.T. Armytage). Since the registers were the private property of the clergymen concerned they were frequently lost or destroyed.

• The wedding was performed in a London church well known for clandestine or irregular services. Examples were Holy Trinity Minories and St James's Duke's Place. Neither of these has deposited its marriage registers in the National Archives. Look in *The Phillimore Atlas and Index of Parish Registers*, edited by C.R. Humphery-Smith, for details of their present whereabouts and any copies or indexes.

• Your forebear may have been secretly married in a country church, where

What will you find?

Finding aids

What if you can't find your ancestor?

the priest had obtained the right to sell marriage licences. You can detect the incidence of clandestine and irregular marriages in certain parishes when the number of marriage entries far outstrips those of baptisms and burials. Most older, full parish registers are now in county record offices; check *The Phillimore Atlas and Index of Parish Registers*. Explore the International Genealogical Index and the British Isles Vital Records Index: either might show that your ancestor married in a place you hadn't previously thought of.

Other marriage records in the National Archives

Hundreds of thousands of people came to London in search of work or to pass through the Metropolis on their way to somewhere else. It is worth searching Pallot's Marriage Index 1780–1837, in our Online Publications and Electronic Resources Archive.

Details about marriages can also be found in divorce petitions, British Army records, and those of the Royal Navy. See the relevant sections.

To find out more read:
J.S. Burn, *History of the Fleet Marriages*
R.B. Outhwaite, *Clandestine Marriage in England 1500–1850*.

Medieval ancestors – before parish registers

Tracing your ancestors before the introduction in 1538 of parish church registers of baptisms, marriages and burials can prove tricky, unless they left or were mentioned in wills (see **WILLS AND OTHER PROBATE RECORDS**), or were recorded in the pedigrees prepared by heralds during their periodic Visitations to check the authenticity of coats of arms used by county gentry and the merchant classes, or compiled for other purposes, such as court cases.

The official Visitation pedigrees of the heralds between 1530 and 1689 are in the College of Arms, in London, where searches of them and other registered family trees can be conducted for you for a fee. Many other unofficial pedigrees, based on or adding to the Visitation material, have been published by the Harleian Society and elsewhere, but these should be used with caution as they may be unreliable. Examples of manuscript genealogies abound in the British Library in London; check **www.bl.uk/catalogues/manuscripts.**

A selection of pedigrees from the common law courts has been published in *Pedigrees from the Plea Rolls 1200–1500*, compiled by G. Wrottesley. Family lineages are frequently outlined in legal suits, especially those brought before the equity Courts of Chancery, Exchequer, and Requests where disputes over inheritance, trusts and settlements were involved (see p. 112).

Manorial records, some dating as far back as at least the 13th century, note the annual appointments of manorial officers, changes of land tenancy, and fines and punishments meted out to tenants for misdemeanours. Documents concerning Crown manors are in the National Archives.

In feudal times (before 1660, but in practice until about 1642) when a landowner died holding an estate directly from the Crown as a tenant-in-chief, an inquiry (Inquisition post mortem) was held by the sheriff in each county where his or her land lay, to establish its value and extract a fine for the monarch before the next heir was allowed to take possession (seisin). Enrolments (Chancery office copies) of Crown grants, sales or leases of land, offices or privileges are worth gleaning too.

Landless labourers are unlikely to feature in official sources unless they were in trouble with the law.

Most of our early documents were written in Latin or Norman French. The words were often heavily abbreviated. The terminology can be difficult to understand too. The text may be dated according to the number of days before or after a particular religious feast or saint's day, and by the number of years that the monarch had been on the throne, making them awkward to identify by our modern calendar. Don't allow these problems to put you off. Rely on a good Alphabet, such as the one provided in *Examples of English Handwriting 1150–1750*, by H.E.P. Grieve, or hone your skills using our online Palaeography tutorial at **www.nationalarchives. gov.uk/palaeography**. *Palaeography for Family and Local Historians,* by H. Marshall, contains a mixture of copies of English and Latin documents for you to transcribe. You can look up the meanings of words in *The Record Interpreter, a Collection of Abbreviations, Latin Words and Names used in English Historical Manuscripts and Records*, compiled by C.T. Martin, and *Latin for Local and Family Historians*, by D. Stuart, and read line-by-line copies and translations of Latin documents in *Medieval Local Records, A Reading Aid*, by K.C. Newton. Since many of the documents were formulaic and repetitive you will learn where to predict the points at which personal-names, place-names, and dates should appear. For converting dates, use *A Handbook of Dates for Students of English History*, by C.R. Cheney, and revised by M. Jones. If you really can't face the task, hire an independent professional researcher specializing in records of this era.

Finally, don't forget that surnames were not hereditary like they are today. They only began to develop in the 13th and 14th centuries as personal-name tabs, which might take the form of a nickname, or refer to a person's occupation or trade, place of origin or residence, or parentage. By the 14th century these personal tags began to be passed on to the next generation and become hereditary. For the family historian, therefore, there are practical difficulties in being certain whether a person described by one name in an early document is the same as someone of another name at another date, even if other evidence points towards it. Because the pool of first names was small you can't always rely on this as a clue. If details of land occupancy, parentage or other family relationships are consistent in all available sources, then the evidence will be strongly circumstantial that you have one and the same individual.

Probably the most productive series of records is going to be wills (see p. 175). You can peruse digital images of registered copies of wills at **www. nationalarchives.gov.uk/documentsonline** of people that were proved

What will you find?

from 1384 until January 1858 in the Prerogative Court of Canterbury (PCC). This served as the chief church court for dioceses in the counties roughly south of the River Trent. The index is freely searchable by personal-name and by place-name, though the digital images are freely accessible only in the National Archives, or in the Family Records Centre. Even if you don't find your own direct ancestor or family name, work your way through the wills of maternal kindred and other people in the neighbourhood as you might strike lucky and locate your antecedents as beneficiaries or relatives by marriage. Grants of letters of administration, when a person died intestate without leaving a will, only survive in the PCC from 1559. There are printed indexes to these microfilmed records, which are in series PROB 6.

Chancery proceedings, dating from the late 14th century, are another possibility. The bundles of bills of complaint, answers and depositions filed in this court and in the equity Court of Exchequer from the late 15th century onwards, and in the Court of Requests between 1483 and about 1642, refer retrospectively to thousands of people and to events perhaps several generations before, for whom no other written evidence of their existence might survive. Because they were written in English, this makes them easier to explore, though the way in which they were filed can present problems. For more about these, see **LEGAL PROCEEDINGS: CIVIL ACTIONS**. Pedigrees lodged by lawyers in the Court of Chancery between 1852 and 1974 are in series J 46, J 63, J 64, J 66 and J 67 in the National Archives, and are listed by the name and date of the earliest ancestor, and by case title, in series J 68.

In the Middle Ages the country was to a large extent governed through the agency of local magnates acting on behalf of the Crown. As lords of manors they or their stewards called a court meeting once or twice a year to transmit to writing annual appointments of manorial officers, the fines and punishments dished out to tenants for non-appearance at the court, for offences such as non-repair of ditches or hedges or straying livestock and to formally enrol changes of tenancy on death, by exchange, purchase or by surrender on leaving the manor. Each manor had its own customs of tenancy, so when a tenant died his or her property passed automatically to the next heir predetermined by that particular manor. This might be the eldest son (primogeniture, or impartible inheritance), the youngest son (Borough English), youngest daughter, all the male issue equally (partible inheritance, or gavelkind), or all the daughters might share the estate equally if there were no sons. Some customary tenants held their land for a single life or lives (perhaps his own, that of his wife and one child), on the expiry of which the land reverted back to the lord of the manor to grant to whoever he wished. The formal surrender of the previous tenant's land back to the lord of the manor recorded, in Latin, a description of it, its size, the annual rental and the date the court admitted him or her. An entry fine was payable by the incoming tenant (generally amounting to one or two year's rent) and a heriot (usually the best beast) would also be exacted on the death of the last occupier. The new tenant was given a copy of the enrolment of his or her admission, giving rise to the term 'copyholder'. It was his or her proof of title to the plot. The manorial court rolls, rentals, surveys,

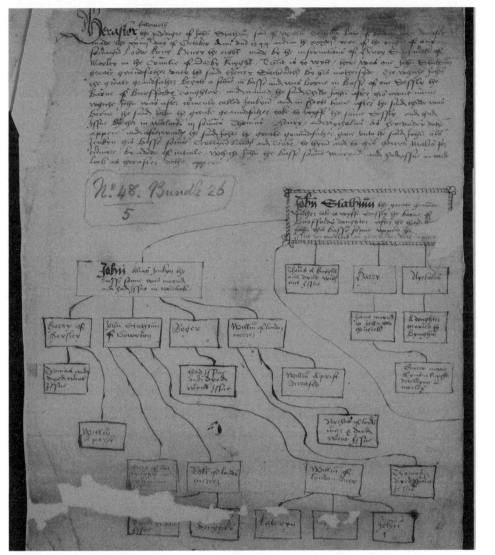

REQ 2/26/48, no 5: This pedigree, compiled in 1544 for Sir Henry Sacheverell, shows his descent in the female line from his great-grandfather, John Statham. The plaintiff in the Court of Requests in 1556 was John Statham, who claimed his right to John's estates via the male line from his own great-grandfather, John alias Jenkyn, the progenitor's illegitimate son. John was eventually awarded a judgement in default.

and custumals, in series SC 2, relate only to those manors which at some stage were held by the Crown. You can ascertain the whereabouts of other known surviving manorial records from the Manorial Documents Register (see pp. 30–1).

The king's secretariat, or writing office, of the royal Chancery, sent out writs containing instructions to local sheriffs and officers of the Crown. The county sheriff's inquisitions post mortem (IPMs) were taken on the estates and manors of dead tenants-in-chiefs to calculate and ensure payment of a feudal entry fine to the Crown by the next legal heir prior to taking formal possession of them. The documents were written in Latin. There are two sets of Inquisitions, those filed in Chancery between 1230 and about 1649, in series C 132–C 142, and duplicates filed in the Exchequer between about 1216 and about 1603, in series E 149 (from about 1216 to about 1485), and E 150 (from about 1485 until about 1603). Further enrolments from about 1216 until about 1547 are in series E 152. A third copy, in the Court of Wards and Liveries, established in 1541, and whose records run to about 1641, is in series WARD 7. This court dealt with the estates of heirs under the age of 21, and of lunatics, whose lands and person passed into the care of the Crown or its nominees for the time being. IPMs regarding land in the Duchy of Lancaster are in series DL 7, the Duchy of Cornwall in series E 306, for the Palatinates of Chester in series CHES 3, Lancaster in series PL 4, and Durham in series DURH 3. Each dated Inquisition gave the name, status and date of death of the landowner, with a full description of the estate, its current value, how he or she came by it, and ended with the name, age and relationship of the next heir to the deceased. The payments of feudal fines were recorded on the Fine Rolls, in series C 60.

If the estates were spread over several counties an Inquisition was held in each. The IPMs may incorporate extracts from long-vanished title deeds and wills, in which tenants occasionally receive a mention.

Copies of petitions for and grants of offices, privileges and liberties, confirmations of earlier grants of land, appointments of wardships of under-age heirs and of lunatics, proofs of age or lucidity of such heirs seeking to take possession of their estates, were enrolled in Chancery too. Look for these on the Patent Rolls from 1201 onwards in series C 66, Charter Rolls between 1199 and 1517, in series C 53, Close Rolls from 1204 onwards, in series C 54, and Fine Rolls from the late 13th century until 1641, in series C 60. They were written in Latin. Letters and Papers of the reign of King Henry VIII, 1509–47, in series SP 1, include correspondence and petitions received from his subjects. Although most of the foregoing relate to the nobility, landowners and prominent merchants, they contain frequent references to servants, retainers and tenants.

The Crown relied on feudal aids and taxes collected from its subjects for most of its income in the Middle Ages. From 1290, regular subsidies of a fixed percentage of the value were imposed on a person's movables (goods and chattels) over a certain value. Lists of assessed inhabitants or payers only up to 1332, arranged by town, village or hamlet, are in series E 179. Thereafter, until 1523, merely totals were recorded. The lists were compiled in Latin. See **TAX LISTS**.

Finding aids   See **LEGAL PROCEEDINGS: CIVIL ACTIONS** for details of finding aids to the Court of Chancery, equity Court of Exchequer and the Court of Requests.

Manorial boundaries were not conterminus with those of parishes, so different parts of a parish might be carved up among several manors, or conversely a single manor might extend its boundaries over more than one parish. To discover to which manor or manors your family's parish belonged, look at any 19th-century county directory (see p. 30) and read the preface. Alternatively, you can search the parish index of the Manorial Documents Register in our Research Enquiries Room. This will identify the relevant manors. The companion manorial index will then disclose details about the last known lord of the manor, his steward, any surviving records, their type, period of coverage, and whereabouts. The index is not fully comprehensive, as the information was supplied voluntarily, so if no material is listed, contact the steward to see if any exist, and if you may be allowed to study them yourself. You can also search the Manorial Documents Register at **www.nationalarchives.gov.uk/mdr**, but as yet only catalogues for Hampshire, Isle of Wight, Middlesex, Norfolk, Surrey, Yorkshire and Welsh manors are uploaded. For references to manorial material concerning Crown manors you can interrogate our online catalogue by keying in the name of the one you are interested in, and then order the documents as originals.

So far, indexed calendars (summaries) of the Inquisitions post mortem have been published up to 1432, and for the reign of King Henry VII (1485–1509). The summaries are in English. There are separate lists for the C and E series for the intervening years and a joint catalogue from 1509 onwards, which includes series WARD 7. You can trawl our online catalogue for the name of the dead landowner, the county and regnal year of the IPM document reference in series C 139 (from about 1422 until 1461), C 140 (from about 1461 until 1483), C 141 (from approximately 1483 to 1485) and C 142 (1558–1603 so far) and then order the original parchments. The catalogue to series E 150 (*c.* 1485–*c.* 1603) is also searchable by personal-name online.

The printed and indexed calendars of the Patent Rolls, Charter Rolls, Close Rolls and Fine Rolls up to the 16th century, and Letters and Papers of King Henry VIII can be extremely helpful in unravelling family relationships and activities, because they translate and summarize the contents of each roll, as well as cross-referencing them to the original material.

Feudal Aids 1284–1431 is a fully indexed set of lists of names of nobles, knights, landed gentry and others plus the dates, circumstances and amounts mulcted by the Crown. For lay subsidy assessments and particulars of names of payers, search our online catalogue to series E 179 at **www.national archives.gov.uk/e179**.

What if you can't find your ancestor?

• Have you tried all variant spellings of your surname? Look also at records about families into which yours was married, or with which they were connected as tenants or fellow-residents. Wills of other contemporary inhabitants are especially useful in enabling you to pick up the trail again, if you are prepared to spend time searching those proved in all the relevant courts of the period. For wills proved in probate courts other than PCC, look in *The Phillimore Atlas and Index of Parish Registers*, edited by C.R. Humphery-Smith, to find out which courts had authority over property in the places where your ancestors lived, and then scour *Probate Jurisdictions: Where to Look for Wills*, by J. Gibson and E. Churchill to discover their whereabouts, any copies and indexes.

• Try researching at records created by or about prominent local landowners, whose tenants or part of whose workforce your ancestors might have been. Church memorials are a good source of information, as are printed local county, parish or manorial histories. Search the National Register of Archives for catalogue entries relating to family and estate papers and their whereabouts, at **www.nationalarchives.gov.uk/nra**. Local studies collections and county record offices may include promising early material.

• If you broaden your venture trawl through the taxation lists of other towns, villages and hamlets surrounding your forebears' places of residence, in series E 179, you may be able to pick up other entries of the surname.

• Consult *Texts and Calendars: An Analytical Guide to Serial Publications* and *Texts and Calendars II: An Analytical Guide to Serial Publications 1957–82,* both edited by E.L.C. Mullins, and visit **www.rhs.ac.uk** for later published material. These will reveal what has been transcribed, translated and printed for your ancestral area and era of interest. We hold copies of many serial publications.

Other medieval records in the National Archives

Details of enrolments of grants of land between private individuals may be located amongst Ancient Deeds, in a large variety of National Archives series. Often they took the form of deeds of enfeoffment by which local abbots or priors held an estate in trust. This was a device by which the law of primogeniture was circumvented. The deed might also provide for the transfer of specified land over several generations in a family. The Ancient Deeds are fully indexed, and you can search the catalogues online by personal- and place-name. Other enrolled deeds are on the Close Rolls in series C 54, which from 1536 onwards were used to formally record sales and grants of freehold estates.

Conveyances known as feet of fines, in series CP 25/1 and CP 25/2, and extending from 1182 until 1833, were designed to provide for the descent of land within a family for perhaps many future generations. The feet of fines are in Latin, but a number have been translated or published in county volumes by local historical societies. You can find out which these are from the sources listed above.

Early county militia muster rolls can prove valuable too, as liable male inhabitants in each Hundred and parish between the ages of 15 and 60 were listed for the lord lieutenant by the local constables at regular intervals. Their names and physical condition (for instance able-bodied, infirm or weak) may be given alongside the type of armed equipment each could provide. There is an excellent series of county musters for 1522 and some later years, in series E 101, and also in series E 36, E 315, SP 1, SP2, SP10–SP12, SP 14, SP 16 and SP 17. Look in *Tudor and Stuart Muster Rolls*, compiled by J. Gibson and A. Dell for a complete county-by-county outline of places and dates for which musters exist, together with their full National Archives document references.

To find out more, read our Research Guides:
Medieval and Early Modern Sources for Family History
Manorial Documents Register and Manorial Lordships
Manorial Records in The National Archives
Manor and Other Local Court Rolls, 13th century–1922
Inquisitions Post Mortem, Henry III-Charles I: Landholders and Their Heirs
Court of Wards and Liveries, 1540–1645: Land Inheritance
Dissolution of the Monasteries
Land Conveyances: Enrolment of Deeds and Registration of Title
Land Conveyances: Feet of Fines 1182–1833
Taxation Records before 1689

Tudor and Stuart Militia Muster Rolls
Outlawry in Medieval and Early Modern England; and
M. Ellis, *Using Manorial Records.*

Merchant Navy

Until 1853, the Royal Navy and the Merchant Navy Service recruited from the same labour pool, so your seafaring ancestor may have spent time in both. Records in the National Archives about merchant seamen are good from 1835 until 1857, and from 1918 until 1972. For masters, mates and engineers you can pick up service details between 1845 and 1969. Much of the material is indexed, and available on microfilm or microfiche.

In 1835, a registration scheme was instituted for merchant sailors, which lasted until 1857, and was reintroduced in 1913. The regulations applied to men employed in the coastal trade in home waters around the British Isles, and to those engaged in foreign and colonial commerce. A ticketing system for merchant seamen was introduced in 1845, but discontinued after October 1853. Certificates of service and of competency began to be issued to masters and mates in foreign-going ships in 1845, becoming mandatory in 1850, when it was extended to those on board vessels engaged in the home and coastal trade. From 1894, a certificate issued to the master or mate of a foreign-going ship entitled him to trade in home waters, but not the other way round.

A Royal Naval Reserve (RNR) was set up in 1859, comprised of ratings only until 1869, when officers were included. Recruitment of seamen and fishermen as reserves took place at shipping offices in UK ports. In 1911 the Royal Naval Reserve Trawler Section, composed of fishermen, and Royal Fleet Auxiliaries were established. The Mercantile Marine Reserve was made up of merchant seamen on merchant ships which had been requisitioned by the Admiralty for war service. Some of its members may have served in the RNR too.

Women seafarers can be traced in the seamen's records from 1921 onwards.

The Merchant Service is administered from the Registry of Shipping and Seamen, in Cardiff, which holds later records.

For more information, read *Records of Merchant Shipping and Seamen*, by K. Smith, C.T. Watts and M.J. Watts.

What will you find?

Merchant seamen 1835–1913

The registers of seamen in 1835 and 1836 are in series BT 120, on microfilm in the Microfilm Reading Room, at Kew, and are also accessible for hire in family history centres. The entries were compiled from crew lists and are arranged alphabetically under the first two letters of each surname. They record the age, birthplace and capacity (rank) of each mariner, his registration number, and ship. A new ticket was issued for every voyage. Though registration started only in 1835, the registers encompass seamen who had joined the service much earlier in the 19th century. Another series of filmed volumes, spanning the period 1835–44, is in series BT 112. This includes the names of all the seamen registered in series BT 120. Registers of seamen's tickets between 1845 and 1854 are in series BT 113, which is also on microfilm. These disclose the date of birth and a physical description of each man. Another microfilmed series, running from October 1853 to 1857, is in series BT 116, and this is arranged alphabetically by surname. The registers in series BT 112, BT 113 and BT 116 contain details of age and birthplace, plus cross-references to the crew lists of the ships in which they sailed, but series BT 113 adds the date and place of birth, a physical description of each mariner, and indicates his literacy level, as well as showing the year and in what capacity he first went to sea, any later capacities, any Royal Naval or foreign service, and his home address when not at sea. The seamen's registers in series BT 116 give from 1854, and for the first time, both the names of ships and their ports of registry, which you can then link to the agreements and crew lists in series BT 98 described on p. 135. If a merchant seaman had an earlier Royal Navy career then you can follow this up in our records. See **ROYAL NAVY**.

A selection of numerical service records of Royal Naval Reserve ratings between 1860 and 1946 is in series BT 164, and further service record cards, 1908–55, are in BT 377/7, to which there are personal-name indexes in BT 377/8–27 (for service dating from 1908 up to 1922), on microfiche, in our Microfilm Reading Room. The indexes include references to records which have been destroyed.

Merchant seamen
1913 onwards

Registration of seamen began again in 1913, but little material survives before 1920. However, our later records relate to the careers of men and women who joined the Merchant Navy long before 1913. Some may have once served in the Royal Navy, so the continuous engagement books, between 1853 and 1872 in series ADM 139, and the service returns of entrants from 1873 to 1923, in series ADM 188 are worth searching too. You can examine the indexed digital images of the service registers in series ADM 188 at **www.nationalarchives.gov.uk/documentsonline**. Expect to find the age, birthplace, service details and a list of ships and dates on board, of each rating and from 1873 onwards a physical description of his appearance, including any scars or tattoos. This series includes people whose service commenced as early as 1853.

Particulars about merchant seamen discharged after 1921 and up to 1941 occur in several series of records, all of which are available on microfiche in the Microfilm Reading Room. The first, a set of cards known as CR1, is in series BT 349, and concerns men leaving the Service between the above years, and is arranged alphabetically by name. The information consists of the full name, rating, discharge number, date and place of birth, accompanied by a short physical description of each mariner. Sometimes there is a photograph too. The second series of cards, called CR2, is in BT 348, and this provides similar information about men discharged during the same period, arranged in discharge number order, to which there are personal-name indexes in series BT 350. The cards in series BT 349 and BT 348 provide details of the official registration numbers of the ships on which they were crewmen.

The alphabetical cards, CR10, in series BT 350, cover discharges from 1918 until 1921, and contain similar personal details to series BT 349, plus a photograph. Finally, series BT 364, also on microfiche, appears to be a mixture of extracted CR1, CR2 and CR10 cards covering the years 1921 until 1941, making up three cards per person, and photographs may be found here too. It is similarly arranged numerically according to discharge number, and may include records earlier than 1918.

Later registers of merchant seamen, from 1973 onwards, are held by the Registry of Shipping and Seamen, in Cardiff.

Representative records of service of some Royal Naval Reserve ratings who served in World War I and up to 1946 can be traced in series BT 164, and service record cards, 1908–55, in BT 377/7, to which there are microfiche copies of indexes containing individual service numbers in BT 377/1–6 (for service beyond 1922 and as far as 1955), and BT 377/8–27 (relating to service up to 1922). The indexes include references to destroyed records. Information about the later service of Royal Naval Reserve ratings who are still alive can be obtained by writing to Naval Pay and Pensions (Accounts), in Gosport. Information about ratings who are now deceased is available from TNT Archive Service, in Swadlincote.

As a result of an Order in 1941, a Merchant Navy Reserve Pool was created. All those who had served at sea during the five previous years had to register, and a new Central Register of Seamen (sometimes called the Fifth Register of Seamen) was set up and continued until 1972. You can find out about merchant seamen available for war service between 1941 and 1972 from the docket books in series BT 382. The books include each reserve's name, age, discharge number, rank, rating or grade, qualifications, the names and official numbers of the ships on which served, and the dates of engagement and of discharge, extracted from ships' logs and crew agreements. They are arranged alphabetically in eight parts, and take in sailors of non-European origin too, particularly men from the Indian sub-continent and China. Search the catalogue of names online and then order the original document.

A major collection about merchant seamen serving between 1913 and 1972 is the set of seamen's pouches in series BT 372. These have to be examined in a special area under staff supervision. They are listed alphabetically, so you can hunt for their document references using our online catalogue and then order them as original items. The pouches furnish of personal identity cards giving the date and place of birth, a physical description, a photograph of each man or woman, his or her signature and a fingerprint, plus any official correspondence and final discharge papers. However, there is not a pouch for everyone, and it seems that the pouches for merchant mariners with discharge numbers below 5000 were destroyed. You can also delve through a set of seamen's pouches relating to the sea service of merchant seamen on Special Operations in 1944 and 1945 during the Liberation of Europe. These are in series BT 391, and are listed in our online catalogue by personal-name and date and place of birth.

MASTERS AND MATES, 1845 ONWARDS

The *Mercantile Navy List*, published annually since 1857, should provide an outline of your ancestor's career from the date he first became a mate through his various grades of seniority, until retirement or death in service.

An alphabetical register of masters between 1845 and 1854 is in series BT 115. The entries were extracted from the registers of seamen's tickets (in series BT 113) during this period. Beginning in 1845, intending masters and mates of foreign- and home-going British merchant ships could volunteer to sit an examination of competency. Indexed registers of copies of the certificates issued between 1845 and 1849, are in series BT 143, and disclose the year of birth as part of each entry. The registered copies of obligatory certificates of competency, introduced in 1850 and relating to the foreign trade, are in series BT 122 (1845–1906, including some earlier voluntary certificates), and series BT 123 for steamships (1881–1921). Copies of the compulsory certificates of long service, introduced in the same year, are in series BT 124 (1850–1922). For certificates of competency issued to masters and mates engaged in the home trade, consult series BT 125 (1854–1921), and series BT 126 (1854–88) for their certificates of service. These reveal date and place of birth, register ticket number if any, the rank at or for which examined, and the date and number of the resulting certificate. Colonial issues of certificates of competency supplied to masters and mates between 1833 and 1934 are in series BT 128. These are listed by colony (Bombay, Bengal, Canada, Newfoundland, Hong Kong, Malta, New South Wales, Queensland, South Australia, Victoria, Tasmania, and the Straits Settlements of Singapore and Mauritius) and by date range. The colonial certificates each yield the year and place of birth, date and port of the grant of a certificate, the rank at which examined or served, with details of retirement, injury or death, and up to 1888 they include details about the ships on which the masters or mates had sailed. All of these are accessible on microfilm in our Microfilm Reading Room.

Copies of the numbered mandatory certificates of competency awarded to engineers from 1861 up to 1921 are in series BT 139, and registers of their certificates of long service from 1862 to 1921 in series BT 142. Copies of colonial certificates of competency of engineers issued between 1870 and 1921 are in series BT 140. Finally, copies of the numerical certificates of competency granted to skippers and mates of fishing vessels from 1880 until 1921 are in series BT 129 and certificates of their long service issued between 1883 and 1919 are in series BT 130. All of these are on microfilm. They contain similar personal information to the masters' and mates' certificates described above.

Registers of passes and renewals of certificates of competency of masters and mates for home-trade and foreign-going vessels between 1913 and 1977 are to be found in series BT 317, which includes replacements of lost certificates. However no details of date of birth are included. A set of registers of passes and failures in the examinations of masters, mates and engineers between 1929 and 1984 is in series BT 318.

A self-indexed register of certificates of competency of all deck officers, from 1910 until about 1969, is available on microfiche in series BT 352. This covers both the home and foreign trade. Each person's entry gives name, date and place of birth, certificate number, rating, date of passing the examination for a certificate and the port where it took place. You can find out on which ships the men had previously sailed from the registers of seamen (in series BT 349, BT 348 and BT 364), which start in 1913, though as already mentioned, few survive from before 1920, and from the seamen's pouches for men still serving in 1941, in series BT 372, described above.

The names of Royal Naval Reserve officers can be elicited from the annual *Navy List* from 1862 onwards, and officers in the Royal Fleet Auxiliaries from 1911. Service records of officers in the Reserve between 1862 and 1964 are in series ADM 240, and these contain details of both Royal Naval and merchant service officers, engineers and paymasters, arranged by rank and dates of seniority and final record entry. For officers who were entrants from 1872 with notations up to 1964 service details are filed together regardless of rank in ADM 240/37–50, to which there are indexes in ADM 240/84–8. For details about RNR officers who were captured and held as prisoners of war, were casualties, died or reported missing between 1939 and 1946, look in BT 164/23, which also includes references to any awards.

Officers as well as ratings ashore belonged to the Merchant Navy Reserve Pool. You can discover about officers available for war service between 1941 and 1972 from the docket books in series BT 382. The docket books include date and place of birth, discharge number, rank and certificate number, and record the qualifications, names and official numbers of the ships on which served, their dates of engagement and discharge. The books are arranged alphabetically in eight sub-series, and take in seafarers of non-European origin.

Later registers of merchant naval officers from 1973 onwards, are kept by the Registry of Shipping and Seamen, in Cardiff.

For details about Royal Naval Reserve officers who are still alive, contact Data Protection Cell, in Portsmouth, and for those who are now deceased, write to TNT Archive Service, in Swadlincote.

Finding aids

Where the registers are integrally indexed (in series BT 120 and BT 116), they have been indicated above. Series BT 112 is arranged in two parts, the first of which, up to February 1840, is roughly indexed in numerical order according to the first two letters of the seaman's surname, and the second of which, from December 1841 until 1844, is mostly alphabetical. An index to the first part is in series BT 119, though surnames beginning with the letter 'K' are missing. Some parts of the index are interleaved in series BT 112 as well. You can find an alphabetical index of seamen's names from 1841 to December 1844 in BT 119/28. There is a finding aid in the Microfilm Reading Room to help you decode the various abbreviated voyage details outlined in BT 112. In order to locate your forebear's ticket number in series BT 113 (1845–54), and his given birthplace, search the filmed indexes in BT 114. However, some ticket numbers are missing, and the indexes are often sub-divided by forename, so use them warily.

To identify the relevant certificate number of a master or mate between 1845 and 1894, in series BT 122–BT 126, search the indexes in series BT 127, which will tell you the dates and places of birth as well. This also contains the certificate numbers of masters and mates engaged in the colonial trade from 1880 to 1917 in series BT 128. Series BT 141 is a set of indexes to the registers of certificates of competency and of service of engineers between 1861 and 1921 in series BT 139, BT 140 and BT 142. Series BT 138 consists of indexes from 1880 to 1917 to similar certificates awarded to skippers and mates of fishing vessels in series BT 129 and BT 130, and they indicate the dates and places of birth as well as certificate numbers.

The registers of passes and renewals of certificates of competency between 1913 and 1977, in series BT 317, are indexed from 1917 onwards in series BT 352.

What if you can't find your ancestor?

• Some of the index entries in series BT 119 and BT 114 do not match up with the numbered registrations of seamen in series BT 112 and BT 113 respectively. Ask staff at the Help Desk for advice on what to do.

• You have looked at the wrong set of seamen's registers, for instance those relating to home trade instead of colonial.

• Try searching the indexes or seamen's registers ignoring prefixes such as 'Mc' and 'Mac', for example, by looking under both 'McDonald' and 'Donald'.

• Try the continuous engagement books in series ADM 139 (1853–72) and service records in series ADM 188 (for service until 1928 of entrants from 1873 up to 1923) for merchant seamen who were Royal Naval ratings. The former series is indexed, and mostly available on microfilm in our Microfilm Reading Room. Indexed digital images of series ADM 188 can be viewed at **www.nationalarchives.gov.uk/documentsonline**. Some of the service records go back as far as 1853 and thus overlap the continuous engagement books, so pursue both series.

• Search the indexed *Trinity House Petitions 1787–1854*, for the names of disabled merchant seamen, their widows and dependants, who applied for financial support. The index is also available at **www.originsnetwork.com**. No pensions were paid out automatically to members of the Merchant Service, though Trinity House administered a charity. The petitions can provide a lot of detail about birthdays, marriages, dates and circumstances of death or disablement.

• After 1857, registration of seamen ceased, so you will have to rely on other sources, particularly ships' crew agreements and crew lists. Surviving musters, agreements and crew lists between 1747 and 1860 are in series BT 98. In 1747, masters of UK merchant ships were ordered to compile a muster of all those on board at the start of each voyage, in response to the Act for the Relief of Disabled Seamen, whereby each seaman's monthly pay was docked to build up a relief fund. From 1835, masters of merchant ships bound on foreign voyages and of British-registered vessels of 80 tons or more engaged in the coastal trade or in fishing were obliged to enter a written agreement with each of their crew on their conditions of service.

• Official ships' logs were required too after 1850. These were deposited with the crew agreements and lists after every foreign voyage, or half-yearly for the home trade. Usually only those containing details of any births and deaths on board have been preserved up to 1860 in series BT 98, and later ones up to 1990 in series BT 99, BT 380 (1939–50) and BT 381 (1939–45), except for the years between 1902 and 1919 when they are separately found in series BT 165.

• If you know the name of the vessel your ancestor crewed at a specific date and/or the port of departure, perhaps from the seamen's registers in series BT 116 (1854–7) you can go straight to our catalogue for series BT 98 and then order the relevant box of ships' muster rolls, crew agreements, lists and official logs. If you don't know the ship's name, then you could spend a lot of time with these records.

Musters	BT 98/1–139, 1747–1853	Arranged by year and port of filing on return, and often exclude crew names. There is no index to ships or crew.
Agreements and crew lists	BT 98/140–563, 1835–44	Arranged by ship's port of registry, then by initial letter of ship's name. Two types: Schedule C (Crew Lists (foreign), filed within 48 hours of return to a UK port). Schedule D (a half-yearly account of voyages and crew for the coastal and fishing trade, made within 21 days of the end of every June and December).
Agreements and crew lists	BT 98/564–4758, 1845–56	Arranged by year, port of registry, and by initial letter of ship's name. As well as Schedules C and D, there are Schedule A agreements (foreign trade, filed within 24 hours of return to a UK port), Schedule B agreements (home trade, half-yearly returns filed within 30 days of the end of June and December), and Schedule G agreements and register tickets of crew (listing crew and register ticket numbers, filed for foreign-going vessels on leaving port).
Agreements and crew lists	BT 98/4759–6944, 1857–60	Arranged by official ship's number.

There is a key to the port numbers at the front of the bound catalogue to series BT 98. An official number was assigned and retained by each ship throughout its commission. You can ascertain the numbers from the annual *Mercantile Navy List* and *Lloyd's Register of Shipping* in our Research Enquiries Room.

Until 1800, the muster rolls are confined to the ports of Shields, Dartmouth, Liverpool and Plymouth. They often don't include the names but merely the numbers of crew on board, except for those of the owner and master. If you do encounter a muster including their names, then not only are the date and port of departure and destination recorded, but also the names, addresses, dates of engagement and of discharge, and the name of the previous ship of each crew member, and from 1845 their ticket numbers. The crew agreements and lists from 1835 are arranged randomly in boxes. As well as the ship's name, they set out details of the port of registration and the official registration number as appropriate. Under headed columns were written in the name of each officer and rating, details of his registration or certificate number where relevant, age on joining the ship, birthplace, name of the last ship he crewed, date and place of joining the present vessel, at what rank or rate, and the date and place of death or leaving ship, and how disposed of.

From 1861 until 1938, and from 1951 until 1990, only 10 per cent of the crew agreements, lists and official logs of UK merchant ships are to be found in series BT 99, with those of famous liners such as RMS *Titanic* in series BT 100. Series BT 98 is arranged by year and ships' official number ranges. Information about the disposition of the remaining 90 per cent is available from our online Research Guide *Registrar General of Shipping and Seamen: Agreements and Crew Lists after 1861*. Some records are at the National Maritime Museum in Greenwich in south east London, but by far the majority of the crew agreements and lists went to the Maritime History Archive, based in the University of Newfoundland. These cover the years between 1863 and 1938, and 1951 and 1976. There are two guides to this Archive's 70 per cent sample, 1863–1912, and 1913–38, available on microfiche in our Microfilm Reading Room, and you can also consult the catalogue online at **www.mun.ca/mha/holdings/searchcrew.php**. Later agreements and crew lists from 1990 onwards are still in the care of the Registry of Shipping and Seamen, in Cardiff. The crew lists of fishing vessels under 80 tons between 1884 and 1929 are in series BT 144, and are also represented by a 10 per cent sample. They too are arranged by official ship's number range and by year. The crew agreements and lists in series BT 99 also contain a sample of those from fishing boats after 1930 under this tonnage, and all the lists of casualties and deaths between 1914 and 1918.

The ships' crew agreements and log books of ships trading round the UK and Irish Free State coasts from 1939 to 1945 are in series BT 381, and those of Allied and commandeered vessels between 1939 and 1950 are in series BT 380, and mainly relate to World War II. Some of the crew agreements which would otherwise have been in series BT 380 are located in series BT 99. You can search our online catalogue to ships included on the index cards in series BT 380 and BT 381 between 1939 and 1950 in series BT 385, which are listed by name range. The index cards prior to 1939 and after 1950 are now in the National Maritime Museum, in Greenwich. Series BT 387 consists of log books, crew agreements and crew lists of Allied foreign ships, which were requisitioned or chartered by the government during World War II, and span the years between 1939 and 1946. You can interrogate our online catalogue to this series by ship's name.

Other records about merchant seamen in the National Archives

Personal details about the crew on board ships in port on the nights of the ten-yearly census counts, or at sea and putting back to port within a prescribed period around the census dates survive from 1861 onwards. There is a microfiche index of names of crewmen on the night of the 1861 census (7 April) in the Family Records Centre; indexed digital images of these returns of the names, ages, ranks or rates, and birthplaces of crew on vessels in English and Welsh ports and on 2 April 1871, 3 April 1881, 5 April

1891 and 31 March 1901 or returning to port during the specified intervals are available online via **www.nationalarchives.gov.uk/census**. The Marine Returns for 1901 at least should relate to British shipping wherever it was throughout the world, though they are far from complete.

Deaths of merchant seamen were reported to the Registrar of Shipping and Seamen from 1850 onwards, and for information about these, look in series BT 153 (1852–81, and June 1888–September 1893) to which there is a personal-name index in series BT 154, BT 156 (monthly lists, 1886–90), BT 99 (1914–18), BT 380 (1939–50), BT 381 (1939–45), BT 385 (1939–50) and BT 387 (1939–46). Series BT 334 (1891–1964) holds discrete returns of deaths of seamen reported to the Registrars General of England and Wales, Scotland and Ireland after 1896 up to 1964, and embraces some who died whilst ashore. Rolls of Honour, commemorating the dead and those missing presumed dead from the ranks during both World Wars, in series BT 339, include the crews of fishing trawlers. The entries are arranged in alphabetical order of surname within each volume. You can obtain the names of Royal Naval Reserve officers killed between 1914 and 1920 in ADM 242/1–5, and of other ranks between 1914 and 1919 in ADM 242/15. There is a card index to the alphabetical entries in ADM 242/1–5 in our Research Enquiries Room, which will reveal the date and place of death, the last ship on which the officer served, any awards for gallantry or Mentions in Dispatches, and sometimes the name and address of his next of kin. The War Graves Roll in ADM 242/7–10 provides details of ratings' last rank, date and place of birth, cause and date of death and place of burial, plus the name, address and relationship of the next of kin. Microfiche copies of the General Register Office indexes to Marine Returns of deaths at sea since 1 July 1837, can be searched in our Microfilm Reading Room up to 1965, and then as part of the annual union indexes to Deaths Abroad until 1992. The index can also be trawled up to recent registrations at **www.1837online. com/Trace2web/LogonServlet**.

Indexes to the Mercantile Marine Medal, and British War Medal, from 1914 up to 1925 are in series BT 351, on microfiche, in the Microfilm Reading Room. They disclose the name, year and place of birth, officer's certificate number or seaman's discharge number. The registers of awards of the Albert Medal for gallantry at sea, 1866–91, and then those given to civilians up to 1913, are in series BT 97, and other gallantry awards made between 1856 and 1981 can be traced in series BT 261, which includes recommendations (citations). You will have to order these as original documents. You can also find awards of long-service medals to officers and men of the Royal Naval Reserve between 1909 and 1949, in ADM 171/70–72, which are available on microfilm, and are indexed. For details about seamen's medals and claims between 1946 and 2002, in series WO 395, relating to World War II issues, search the indexed digital images at **www.national archives.gov.uk/documentsonline**. The entries disclose each seaman's name, his medals, plus any ribbons and clasps, accompanied by a reference to the relevant medal papers file held by the Registry of Shipping and Seamen, in Cardiff, and the discharge book number, and date and place of birth.

Filmed indexes to registers of apprentices from 1824 until 1953 are in series BT 150. These constitute details of name, age, date and length of apprenticeship, the name of the master, and later the port of signing on, and on which ship. Five-yearly specimens of copies of these indentures between 1845 and 1950 are in series BT 151, and of apprenticeship indentures of fishermen between 1895 and 1935, in series BT 152.

You can search filmed copies of *Lloyd's Captains' Registers, 1851–1947*. They consist of pasted-in summaries of the qualifications and service up to 1869 of men still on the active list. Thereafter handwritten details state year and place of birth, date of issue of a master's certificate, any other special qualifications, the name and official number of each ship on which the officer served, the dates of engagement and discharge, the destination of each voyage, any casualties and receipts of special awards. The original volumes are in the Corporation of London Guildhall Library.

To find out more, read our Research Guides:
Merchant Seamen: Records of the RGSS, a Guide to Research Guides
Merchant Seamen: Registers of Service, 1835–1857
Merchant Seamen: Sea Service Records 1913–1972
Merchant Seamen: Interpreting the Voyages in the Registers of Seamen's Tickets and the Alphabetical Registers of Masters
Merchant Seamen: Interpreting Voyage Details in the Registers of Seamen, Series II
Merchant Seamen: Officers' Service Records 1845–1965
Merchant Seamen: Abbreviations Found in the RGSS Registers
Merchant Shipping: Registration of Ships, 1786–1994
Merchant Seamen: Interpreting Voyage Details in the Registers of Officers' Services Royal Naval Reserve
Merchant Shipping: Crew Lists and Agreements, 1747–1860
Merchant Shipping: Crew Lists and Agreements after 1861
Merchant Seamen: Medals and Honours; and
C.T. Watts and M.J. Watts, *My Ancestor was a Merchant Seaman: How Can I Find Out More About Him?*

Nonconformists

The religious census of churchgoers, undertaken in every parish in England and Wales on a single Sunday in 1851 (30 March), showed a high proportion of them to be nonconformists, who preferred to worship in chapels and other places outside the Established Church of England. The parish returns are in series HO 129.

Since the early part of the 17th century, groups of people dissatisfied with the official Anglican rites had begun to meet and form separate congregations according to their own religious beliefs. The Baptists, Congregationalists, Independents and Presbyterians were collectively known as Old Dissenters. As a result of the Act of Toleration in 1689, the Old Dissenting congregations were allowed to apply to the county quarter sessions or to the local bishop for a licence to erect their own meeting places. However, Roman Catholics were subject to heavy civil penal laws, and were forced to worship in secret, only being accorded legal recognition to worship openly in 1791 and full civil status in 1829.

The Religious Society of Friends (Quakers) was founded in the 1650s, and the Methodist Movement, starting in the early 1740s, won many converts in mining areas, especially in the southwest of England, and in the Welsh valleys.

Religious dissidents took their children to their own chapels and meeting places for baptism, or to register their births, were married and buried there according to their own rites, though where no special burying ground was available they might have been buried in the parish churchyard. Non-Anglican weddings were prohibited after 25 March 1754, and until civil registration began on 1 July 1837 only the Quakers and Jews were allowed to continue to perform and record their own marriage ceremonies. If you come across a church marriage register entry between those dates, particularly if it was by licence, which was not followed by the baptisms of any children, then this might well indicate that the couple was nonconformist.

In 1837, a special government Commission was set up to receive the registers of birth, baptism, marriage and burial from Protestant and Catholic congregations, so that they could be scrutinized and authenticated as legal documents and used in a court of law as proof of age and parentage. The deposited registers are in the National Archives, together with those surrendered in 1857 when there was a further round-up.

For more information, read *Protestant Nonconformity and Roman Catholicism*, by D. Shorney.

What will you find?

Those registers handed in as a result of the 1837 Commission are in series RG 4 (covering the years 1567 until 1858), and those collected up in 1857 or deposited later are in series RG 8 (with entries dating from 1646 until 1970). The latter includes records that were not authenticated, some cemetery registers, a variety of records from the Russian Orthodox congregation in London, and registers of admissions to the Lying-In Hospital, in Holborn, London, between 1749 and 1868 of pregnant wives of servicemen and poor but deserving married women. Their children's births and baptisms from 1749 until 1830 are recorded too. Both series are on microfilm.

Unlike parish church registers, which usually provide details of date of baptism, the child's name and those of both parents, chapel registers often add not only the date of birth, but the mother's maiden name, the parents' place of residence, and the father's occupation too. The burial entries generally disclose the date, name, last abode and occupation of the deceased, for married women the husband's name, and for children the names of both parents. Sometimes the family would follow a favourite priest on circuit, and entries of their baptisms will be found in the registers of the several chapels in his area. A family might have to travel up to 30 miles to attend a congregation meeting if there was no nearer place, so you may have to search the registers stretching over a wide radius. When the registers were finally deposited, it was the current denomination which was recorded by the Commissioners, and which will appear in our catalogue. Many congregations foundered and changed denomination over time, though using the same premises and register books, so don't ignore any books relating to the area where your ancestors lived, which seem to relate to a different sect.

You can also examine registers deposited by Protestant immigrant congregations in England, in series RG 4. These were often written in the vernacular, and the birth and baptism entries generally give the names of the baby's sponsors (godparents), whose own known origins abroad may be a valuable indicator of your ancestor's place of provenance.

Few Roman Catholic registers were surrendered. Those that were, in series RG 4, are written in Latin, and mostly relate to births and baptisms, the burials taking place in the Anglican churchyard. The names of the children's godparents are given as well as those of the parents, plus the parental place of residence.

The Quaker minute books of births, deaths and burials notified to the local monthly meeting, and registers of the marriage vows exchanged between bridal couples before their relatives and Friends, are available on microfilm in series RG 6. The entries cover the period from 1613 until 1841. The birth registrations disclose the natal date and place, the names of each child and his or her parents, and sometimes those of grandparents, as well as the father's occupation. The death and burial entries can be very informative, because both these dates and places were written in, together with the name, age, abode and occupation of the dead person, and frequently the names of both parents. The marriage entries supply the date of the meeting when vows were exchanged, the name, place of domicile and occupation of the groom, the name and residence of the bride, and the names and abodes of their fathers, followed by a list of the names of all their relations and Friends who were present as witnesses. Some of the books contain integral indexes.

For clandestine (secret) weddings before 25 March 1754, in series RG 7, see **MARRIAGES – 'FLEET' AND OTHER CLANDESTINE WEDDINGS IN LONDON.**

See **CEMETERY RECORDS** for information on series RG 37.

Finding aids All of the records in series RG 4 and RG 8 are catalogued by county, then by the name of the town, village or hamlet where each chapel was situated, and also cite the denomination at the time the registers were deposited. You can search our online catalogue by place-name. There are some indexes to the registers in series RG 8 of London cemeteries used largely by dissenters. The records in series RG 6 are listed in our catalogue by county, then by the monthly or quarterly meeting places. Some counties shared joint meetings.

The registers of foreign Protestant congregations in England, in series RG 4, have all been copied and published by the Huguenot Society of London. Some of the Roman Catholic registers have been transcribed and printed by the Catholic Record Society.

Extracts from the birth and baptism registers in series RG 4 and the Holborn Lying-In Hospital birth and baptism entries in series RG 8 have been incorporated into the International Genealogical Index, though burial entries are not.

You can obtain almost all the same details about Quaker births, deaths and burials contained in series RG 6 by searching the County Digests up to 1837 held in the Religious Society of Friends Library, in London. These are on microfilm and you can inspect them for a small fee. Each entry will record the monthly meeting to which the events were reported. The county marriage digests do not contain the names of the witnesses, so it is best to use these as a guide only, and then go to the filmed registers for full details.

What if you can't find your ancestor?

- The chapel registers don't go far enough back. Even though chapels and meeting houses were legalized from 1689, many books do not start from the specified year of foundation. Look at the registers of other chapels in the vicinity for that period. Explore the possibility that they have been deposited elsewhere, because many were not surrendered up in 1837 or 1857. You can do this by consulting the county-by-county volumes of the *National Index of Parish Registers* produced by the Society of Genealogists, and *Nonconformist Registers of Wales*, edited by D. Ifans. Both almost always list the type, date coverage and whereabouts of known registers, plus individual denominational chapel foundation dates, and the known existence of any copies or indexes. County record offices can also advise on the location of local chapel registers. The Society of Genealogists has published a useful series of denominational *My Ancestors were...* booklets, focusing on Baptists, Congregationalists, Presbyterians, Unitarians, Methodists and Quakers.
- In the early days of a Movement, many nonconformists still attended the Established Church of England for family baptisms, marriages and burials, only gradually pulling away completely, so don't overlook the registers of the local parish church. Conversely some dissenters later lapsed and returned to their Mother Church, received adult baptism and, when they died, were interred in the churchyard. Many Catholics had a public baptism of their children in the parish church to conform with the law, but then held a separate and private ceremony according to their own beliefs. You can find the known whereabouts of existing Catholic registers from *Catholic Missions and Registers 1700–1880*, by M. Gandy. *Catholic Parishes in England, Wales and Scotland, an Atlas*, by the same editor, will reveal their boundaries. When a nonconforming sect had no burying place of its own, its members were permitted to use part of the local churchyard to dispose of their dead, and the parish register entries normally allude to them as 'hurled' or 'tumbled' into the ground, in other words without benefit of the rites of the Anglican Church. Look in *The Phillimore Atlas and Index of Parish Registers*, edited by C.R. Humphery-Smith, for more information on their whereabouts, and of any copies. Some indexes to parish registers can now be searched online at **www.familyhistoryonline.net**. Try the most recent edition of the National Burial Index for burials recorded in parish churchyards, in denominational burying grounds and cemeteries. The date coverage is 1538–2001, though not every place is included, nor for the entire period. There is an accompanying place-name index to tell you the various date spans, the best being between 1812 and 1837, immediately prior to the introduction of civil registration of deaths.

• If you are hunting for a birth, examine the microfilmed indexed volumes once kept in Dr Williams's Library, London, and now in series RG 4. A registry was established there in 1742 in response to a growing recognition by nonconformist elders of the poorly kept registers of local chapels. People came from all over the country to register the births of their children at home and abroad, and in some instances, their own births too, so the earliest registration relates to a birth in 1717. The latest registration occurred in 1837 when the registry was closed with the onset of civil registration in England and Wales. The parents brought duplicate certificates to the registry, which had been signed by themselves and at least two witnesses to the birth. The certificates set out the date and place of birth, the names of the child and of both parents, their place of residence, the father's occupation, mother's maiden name and the name, abode and occupation of the child's maternal grandfather. The certificates were endorsed with the sequential entry number of the details copied up into the register itself, and the date of registration. One copy was retained by the registry, and the other handed back to the parents. The registry copies are in series RG 5, available on microfilm. You can search extracts from 80 per cent of these certificates in the British Isles Vital Records Index. The registered entries in series RG 4, extracted from the certificates, are omitted from the International Genealogical Index. Microfilmed and bound photocopies of the initial-alphabetical indexes to the registers in this series are available in our Microfilm Reading Room. The indexes are arranged in tranches of years, according to the year of registration, which might happen some years after birth, especially when a whole family's births were registered together under consecutive numbers. A similar Wesleyan Methodist Metropolitan Registry was set up in London in 1818. Microfilm copies of the registered births from 1777 to 1840 are in series RG 4. The registers are indexed. Indexed and numbered duplicate certificates, in series RG 5, are included in the British Isles Vital Records Index, though the entries in series RG 4 are excluded from the International Genealogical Index.

• The family and estate papers of notable Roman Catholic gentry in the area where your ancestors were known to be often turn up references to other recusants who were perhaps their tenants, estate workers, local craftsmen, neighbours, friends or associates. You can find them by searching the catalogues of the National Register of Archives in our Research and Enquiries Room or online at **www.nationalarchives.gov.uk/nra**. A printed county history will reveal which families were prominent in the district.

Other records about nonconformists in the National Archives

From 1625 onwards, convicted Papists aged 17 or more and parishioners over the age of 21 who had failed to take Holy Communion during the previous year attracted double taxation or were forced to pay a poll tax. This penalty was extended in 1640 to embrace indicted, but not yet convicted suspected Catholics. See TAX LISTS for more information, particularly about those prior to 1689, in series E 179, and later listings up to 1830 in series E 182. Appeals made by Roman Catholics after 1828 for relief against payment of double Land Tax are preserved in IR 23/122–6. The papers frequently track the descent of landownership and occupancy over several generations of a family as claimants sought a refund for overpayment.

You can unearth information about participants in the failed Jacobite Rebellion of 1715 by studying the material relating to registered and forfeited estates of Roman Catholics between 1716 and 1724, in series FEC 1, and the resulting claims and appeals in series FEC 2. Particulars about estates forfeited after the 1745 uprising is in series T 64. Follow up summaries of the trials of captured Jacobites in series KB 8, to which there is a printed nominal index, including the names of informers. Other details of trials after 1745 are in series TS 20 and TS 11.

To find out more, read our Research Guides:
Catholic Recusants
Jacobite Risings, 1715 and 1745; and
G.R. Breed, *My Ancestors were Baptists: How Can I Find Out More About Them?*
D.J.H. Clifford, *My Ancestors were Congregationalists in England and Wales: How Can I Find Out More About Them?*
W. Leary, *My Ancestors were Methodists: How Can I Find Out More About Them?*
E.H. Milligan and M.J. Thomas, *My Ancestors were Quakers: How Can I Find Out More About Them?*
A.R. Ruston, *My Ancestors were English Presbyterians or Unitarians: How Can I Find Out More About Them?*
D.J. Steel, *National Index of Parish Registers, vol. II: Sources for Nonconformist Genealogy and Family History*
D.J. Steel and E.R. Samuel, *National Index of Parish Registers, vol. III: Sources for Roman Catholic and Jewish Genealogy and Family History.*

Police: London Metropolitan Police and Royal Irish Constabulary

From early times responsibility for keeping law and order rested on each local community, relying on officers appointed through the manorial, borough or sheriff's court. By the 16th century, the parish had begun to usurp the authority of the manor, and annually elected parish constables were confirmed in office by and answerable to the county magistrates sitting in quarter sessions. Two Acts of Parliament, in 1829 and 1839, provided for the setting up of a professional police force. By 1857, every county in England and Wales had its own Police Constabulary. Consult *The Local Historian's Encyclopaedia*, by J. Richardson, for their start-dates. Many of the older staff records are still held in the relevant county headquarters or police museum, but some have been deposited in county record offices.

The London Metropolitan Police (the Met) was established in 1829 to maintain law and order within an area of about 7 miles' radius of Charing Cross, excluding the City of London which has its own force. In 1839 the Met's jurisdiction was extended to a radius of 15 miles. The Met is regulated by central government and is made up of Divisions. Recruits were assigned the letter representing their own particular Division plus a unique personal number. If they transferred to another Division, a new letter and number was allocated. From 1860 to 1934 the Met's jurisdiction extended over the royal dockyards and military stations at Portsmouth, Chatham, Devonport, Pembroke, Rosyth and Woolwich. Some of the Met personnel records are in the National Archives, and other documentation is kept in the Metropolitan Police Museum, London. Although women began to be recruited by the Met in 1919, no service records survive.

If your ancestor was employed in the colonial police, you will need to apply to the country concerned, unless he was in the South African Constabulary between 1902 and 1908, for which the National Archives holds some material in series CO 526 (Original Correspondence, arranged chronologically by date), CO 639 (registers logging the daily correspondence) and CO 640 (a register briefly recording the dated out-letters).

For enquiries about the British Police in Palestine during the British mandate between 1920 and 1948, write to The Middle East Centre, St. Antony's College, Oxford, which holds the staff service index cards. The service files themselves are kept in the British Empire and Commonwealth Museum, in Bristol.

The Irish Constabulary was set up in 1836 to police all of Ireland except the city of Dublin, which from 1786 possessed its own Metropolitan Force. Before this, as in England and Wales, public law and order in Ireland was maintained by a number of local unpaid forces. Renamed the Royal Irish Constabulary in 1867, it ceased to exist from August 1922, when Ireland was divided up into the Republic of Ireland and Ulster. Service records of Irish constabularymen up to 1922 are in the National Archives too.

For more information, read *My Ancestor was a Policeman: How Can I Find Out More About Him?* by A. Sherman.

What will you find?

The deposited records about members of the Metropolitan Police are fragmentary, and none exist for the period between May 1857 and February 1869. The main series in which to look for biographical information about personnel is MEPO 4.

Registers of joiners between September 1830 and April 1857, and from 1878 until 1933 are in MEPO 4/333–38. Some of these are available on microfilm in our Microfilm Reading Room. They usually disclose the rank, warrant number, Division, dates of appointment and removal, and include the names and addresses of referees. Attestation ledgers from February 1869 until May 1958, in MEPO 4/352–60, carry the signatures of both the new recruit and a witness. The registers of leavers between March 1889 and January 1947, in MEPO 4/339–51, are easier to use, because each volume is indexed. They bear the same details as the registers of joiners.

An unindexed service register relating to the Bow Street Foot Patrol, 1821–9, in MEPO 4/508, contains the name of each policeman, his place of abode, age, birthplace, height, marital status, number of children, the identity of the person recommending him for employment, any military service and date of appointment, plus the date and reason for discharge. The certificates of service of policemen between 1889 and 1909, in MEPO 4/361–477, are bound in volumes, and arranged by warrant number. They record the examination of each candidate, endorsed with a brief summary of his career, including any promotions, demotions, postings to different divisions, any disciplinary action taken against him, cause of his dismissal, or his resignation or death in service. The dated examination sheet gives the person's full name, age, date and place of birth, a physical description, his current address and occupation at the time of the application to join, as well as his married status, number of children, name of his last employer and address where he last worked. If the person had already seen public or military service, details regarding length of service and when discharged were inserted as well. A surgeon's certificate of fitness for police duty completed the examination. Returns of deaths of Metropolitan policemen in service between 1829 and 1889 can be found in MEPO 4/2, to which there is an index in MEPO 4/448. The entries give the cause of death.

The prime source about Royal Irish Constabulary personnel between 1836 and 1922 is series HO 184, which is available on microfilm. The entries are arranged by service number, and will tell you the policeman's name, age at recruitment, height, religious denomination, native county, former trade, marital status, native county of any wife (but not her name), date of appointment and counties where he served, his length of service, and the date of his retirement or death. The series also comprises the auxiliary forces (the Black and Tans).

Finding aids

There is an alphabetical register of Metropolitan policemen from 1829 until 1836 in HO 65/26, which you will have to order as an original document. This will divulge their warrant numbers, rank, division, dates of promotion and removal, which might enable you to track down your man more easily in series MEPO 4.

The Royal Irish Constabulary: A Complete Alphabetical List of Officers and Men 1816–1922, compiled by J. Herlihy, includes brief service details about them, with HO 184 document references where appropriate. Look at **http://ancestry.co.uk** for online biographical extracts for the same period.

What if you can't find your ancestor?

• The records haven't been deposited. Approach the Metropolitan Police Museum.

• If you cannot find your ancestor as a joiner, try the records of leavers, and the certificates of service for the duration of his time in the police.

• He was in a different police force. If it was the City of London rather than the Metropolitan Police, contact the City of London Police Record Office. It holds full staff records from 1832 onwards. For county police forces, write to the archivist at the relevant police headquarters.

Other records about police in the National Archives

Records about pensioners retired from the Met between 1852 and 1932 are in series MEPO 21. This series includes some widows' pensions too. The latest entry is in 1993. There is an incomplete card index of names in our Research Enquiries Room, but otherwise you will have to have a rough idea of when your forebear retired so that you can find the original document references in our catalogue, or consult the lists of leavers between March 1889 and 1932 in series MEPO 4. Before 1890, pension awards were discretionary, but thenceforward they were granted after 25 years' service and a modified pension/gratuity was awarded to men discharged as medically unfit. The records will provide you with a physical description of the former policeman at the time of going to pension, together with his date and place of birth, marital status, parentage and next of kin as well as a summary of his service. Up to 1923, they also yield information on any promotions and postings, the intended place of residence, the names of parents and of next of kin. After 1923, the pensioner's date and place of marriage, wife's date and place of birth and a physical description of her are recorded too. The entries are arranged by pension number. A register of pensions paid to widows of officers killed on duty between 1840 and 1858 is in MEPO 4/33.

Series PMG 25 contains records of pensions paid between 1867 and 1894 to members of the Met who once served in the Admiralty Dockyard Police.

Details about railway policemen can be located amongst staff records of the appropriate railway company (see **RAILWAY WORKERS BEFORE NATIONALIZATION**).

To find out more, read our Research Guides:
Metropolitan Police (London): Records of Service
Royal Irish Constabulary Records
Police, Transport; and
J. Herlihy, *The Royal Irish Constabulary: A Short History and Genealogical Guide with a Select List of Medal Awards and Casualties.*

Railway workers before nationalization

Before central government brought the railways under the wing of British Railways in 1948, there were hundreds of railway-operating companies. The privately owned enterprises of the early and mid-19th century often evolved out of canal, dock and mining companies. Some of the smaller ones didn't last long and were taken over by or merged with other companies. Hundreds of thousands of men and women were employed by the railway companies at any one time, especially when the lines were under construction and during World War I (1914–19). Many former farm labourers and rural workers took local jobs on the railways. When nationalization occurred, British Railways inherited a labour force of 641,000 men and women.

The railway companies often provided special housing for their employees close to their workplace, and you can often recognize the typical architectural style of the former railway cottages, terraced houses and station hotels dotted around our countryside. The records of nearly all of the companies have been deposited in the National Archives, though the survival rate of staff registers is uneven.

For more information, read *Railway Records, a Guide to Sources*, by C. Edwards.

If you already know it, you can search our online catalogue by keying in the name of a specific railway company, or study the bound copies of the catalogues in our Research Enquiries Room. The department code for our railway records is RAIL; you will need to find both the series number assigned to the records of a particular company, and then the individual document references, so that you can order up the original material.

Railway company staff registers vary in content from merely listing the names of employees, their job titles, an assessment of their performance, their wages, dates of appointment, age on recruitment or date of birth, to full-blown service records, noting moves, any disciplinary action, and the dates and reasons for transfer or cessation of employment. An entire career might thus be traced through a sequence of different company records, showing migration around a particular region or further afield. Between October 1915 and February 1916, and leading up to conscription in January 1916, the surviving staff registers record the names of men aged between 19 and 41 who were willing to join up to serve in World War I.

Our online catalogue should be sufficient, or consult *Tracing Your Ancestors in the Public Record Office*, by A. Bevan, for an alphabetical list of our holdings of railway company staff records, giving their department code and series numbers, start- and end-dates.

If you are not sure which railway company your ancestor worked for but know the station or area where he or she was based, consult *British Railways Pre-grouping Atlas and Gazetteer*, by W.P. Connolly and U.A. Vincent, which lists every company prior to their amalgamation into the four big companies. This book contains details about canal and dock companies too.

• There are gaps in the records, or they haven't been deposited. Unfortunately, the start- and end-dates given in the catalogues may mask missing years and may be misleading. Peruse *Railway Ancestors, a Guide to the Staff Records of the Railway Companies of England Wales 1822–1947*, by D.T. Hawkings, for the known whereabouts of other railway company records elsewhere, the online catalogue of the National Register of Archives, at **www.nationalarchives.gov.uk/nra**, or bound copies of the NRA catalogues in our Research Enquiries Room.

• The indexed digital images of the ten-yearly census returns between 1841 and 1901 should enable you to locate your railway ancestor and his immediate family or workmates at a particular address, and thus identify the railway company which employed him at that time (see **CENSUS RETURNS**).

• If your ancestor belonged to a union, there may be branch records of members recording their movement from one branch to another. Search the catalogues of the National Register of Archives for more information about these. Membership records, branch minutes and journals of the Amalgamated Society of Railway Servants (ASRS) from 1875 until 1913, of the United Pointsmen's and Signalmen's Society (UPSS) from 1908 until 1912, and the UPS Mutual Aid and Sick Society 1892–1908, the General Railway

What will you find?

Finding aids

What if you can't find your ancestor?

Workers' Union (GRWU) from 1890 until 1913, the Association of Stokers, Locomotive Engineers and Firemen (ASLEF) from 1914 until 1989, the National Union of Railwaymen (NUR) from 1913 until 1974, and the NUR Orphan Fund between 1913 and 1980 are held in the Modern Records Centre at the University of Warwick, in Coventry.

Other records about railwaymen in the National Archives

Deposited monthly pay books, minute books of railway company board, committee and shareholders' meetings, disciplinary report books, reports on railway accidents, and on staff sicknesses, railway timetables and journals, are identified in our catalogue under the appropriate company titles. The minutes may record recruitment drives, new appointments, promotions, prizes and awards, staff moves and retirements, deaths in service, superannuation and pensions, reports on staff misconduct and any disciplinary action taken. These are worth examining just to see what matters preoccupied the directors and shareholders at the time your forebear was an employee. Railway company staff magazines and journals, issued monthly, refer to retirement presentations, staff moves, promotions and deaths as well as special events and activities and general company news.

The Railway Benevolent Institution granted annuities and gratuities to needy subscribing staff past and present, and their families. The applications chronicle each petitioner's age, family circumstances, railway and any subsequent employment, current earnings and reason for the request (illness or death) together with the decision and details of any award. The date of death of the recipient is recorded too. The application papers are in series RAIL 1166, and cover the period 1858 to 1982. Each volume is indexed by personal-name.

To find out more, read our Research Guides:
Railways: An Overview
Railways: Staff Records; and
T. Richards, *Was Your Grandfather a Railwayman? A Directory of Railway Archive Sources for Family Historians.*

Royal Air Force

The Royal Air Force (RAF) was formed on 1 April 1918 from the Royal Flying Corps (RFC) and the Royal Naval Air Service (RNAS). Founded in May 1912, the RFC comprised Military and Naval Wings, the Central Flying School and the Royal Aircraft Factory, for which the War Office was responsible. In July 1914, the Naval Wing was hived off to form the RNAS, under the control of the Board of Admiralty. The minimum age for recruitment to the Royal Flying Corps was 17, and 18 for the Royal Naval Air Service. In 1914 the Royal Flying Corps numbered merely 1,900 men, but by the end of 1918, 293,522 had been enlisted into the Royal Flying Corps and Royal Air Force. After World War I former RNAS officers and men joined the Royal Air Force or returned to the Royal Navy. The remaining naval RAF squadrons became the Fleet Air Arm (FAA) on 1 April 1924. Service records of ratings joining the Fleet Air Arm from 1924 until 1938 are kept by TNT Archive Service, in Swadlincote, and those from 1939 are held by Data Protection Cell (Navy), at HM Naval Base, in Portsmouth, to whom you should write in both instances for information.

By 1917, to ease the labour shortage, the RFC was already employing all-women companies. The Women's Auxiliary Air Force (WAAF) was created at the same time as the RAF in 1918, but was formally disbanded in 1920. It was re-formed on 28 June 1939, changing its title to the Women's Royal Air Force (WRAF) on 1 February 1949. Their personnel were engaged as clerks, fitters, drivers, cooks, armourers, radio operators, parachute packers, balloon operators, flight mechanics and pigeon women. The women were divided into two sections: those who were only able to work locally owing to duties at home, and 'mobiles', who were sent to France and Germany to replace demobilized airmen. Records relating to personnel from 1939 onwards are kept by the Ministry of Defence at RAF Innsworth, Gloucester.

Service records only about those airmen and women who left the Royal Air Force or its predecessors, or were killed or reported missing in action before 1928 and details of officers' careers up to 1920 have so far been transferred to the National Archives. Write to RAF Innsworth, Gloucester for subsequent information and about later personnel.

For more information read *Air Force Records for Family Historians*, by W. Spencer.

What will you find?

If you aren't sure if your relative was an officer or airman or woman, search the indexed annual, half-yearly, quarterly and monthly *Army Lists* up to 1919 for commissioned officers of the Royal Flying Corps, and the yearly *Navy Lists* to the same year for officers of the Royal Naval Air Service, and then the annual *Air Force Lists* from April 1918 onwards. If you can locate the officer's name after 1921, then his service records will still be at RAF Innsworth. The *Lists* reveal the present rank, and date of latest commission. Copies of the *Lists* are available in our Microfilm Reading Room. The *Confidential Air Force List*, published every year between 1939 and 1954, is in series AIR 10.

AIRMEN AND AIRWOMEN

If your relative was in the Royal Flying Corps, but died or left before the RAF was instituted, investigate the service records in series WO 363 and pension papers in series WO 364 (see pp. 44–6), both of which are available on microfilm. Unfortunately, more than 60 per cent of the service records in series WO 363 were destroyed by fire in 1940; the surviving series is therefore made up of 'burnt documents'. If your relative transferred to the Royal Air Force, the RFC papers were removed and filed with those for the new service, in series AIR 79 (1918–28), which you will have to order as original documents. The files of loose service documents of men with service numbers up to 329,000 are arranged by consecutive RAF number. You can also find service records of Special Reservists and the South African Aviation Corps in this series. The files contain the name, date and place of birth, residence and former occupation of the airman, his rank on recruitment, the date and place of enlistment, level of education, religious denomination, and a physical description, plus details of his service, and the date of his discharge or death, together with reports on his conduct and a medical sheet. Any campaign or other medals or awards are noted, as are any Mentions in Dispatches, and the files are completed by the name, relationship and address of the next of kin, and details of any wife and children. Records relating to service numbers higher than this, and to those of airmen with service numbers between 1 and 329,000 who remained in the RAF and flew during World War II are held by the Ministry of Defence, at RAF Innsworth, which will release information to the person himself, his next of kin, or to someone with his permission.

A small series of service records about women employed in the Women's Auxiliary Air Force (WAAF) between 1918 and 1920 is in series AIR 80. These mainly microfilmed documents are arranged in alphabetical blocks. They encompass details of age, home address, a physical description, married status, how and where employed, number of dependants, appointments and promotions, and the unit to which each woman had been attached, and whether her service was part-time (immobile, meaning that she was willing to work in her own town or district, and thus lived at home) or full-time (mobile, indicating that she was living in camp or in lodgings and was working at home or abroad).

If your relative was in the RNAS, his service records would have been preserved in series ADM 188, each individual's service number being prefixed by the letter 'F'. These are available on microfilm and indexed digital images of them searchable at **www.nationalarchives.gov.uk/documentsonline**. Because the details were written up in a book the RNAS entries remained intact, the relevant entries being stamped with the date of any transfer to the RAF.

Finding aids   For RFC personnel, the filmed service records in series WO 363 run alphabetically by surname and forename. The catalogue is arranged by surname ranges. There is also a separate and similar index to misfiled papers in this series. There are two sets of surname range indexes to series WO 364 (see p. 46).

The RNAS service records are organised by rating number, which can be obtained from the microfilmed personal-name indexes to series ADM 188 or by name in the online indexes.

To find the RAF service number of your relative, search the nominal indexes in series AIR 78, which are available on microfilm in our Microfilm Reading Room, and then consult the catalogue of the original service documents in AIR 79 for the number range including his. This series also contains an index to the service records of WAAF personnel in series AIR 80.

OFFICERS

For career outlines of officers, refer to the annual editions up to 1919 of the *Army List* for members of the RFC, and the *Navy List* for members of the RNAS, and the *Air Force List* for April 1918. *Air Force Lists* after March 1919 give RAF rather than Army and Royal Navy ranks as before. The printed *Army List, Navy List and Air Force List* will help you to pinpoint the dates of commissions and promotions of officers. The 'War Services' sections give information about operations officers were involved in, and any medals and awards they received. From April 1920 until March 1939, the *Air Force List* gives the location and names of officers arranged according to unit. For the period between 1939 and 1954 there is a *Confidential Air List*, in series AIR 10. This harbours information omitted from the standard *List*. Retired lists began to be included in early 1949, which record each former officer's date of birth, qualifications, honours and awards, dates of first commission and of retirement and the date he commenced at his highest rank. Series AIR 10 *Lists* have to be ordered as original documents.

Royal Flying Corps officers who left or became casualties before the RAF was established in 1918 may be traced in the army service records of officers in series WO 339 and WO 374 (see p. 49). However, fewer than 86 per cent of the original files survive.

Officers in the Royal Naval Air Service, who similarly did not serve or survive long enough to transfer to the Royal Air Force, may be tracked down in the earlier microfilmed records of service in series ADM 196 (see p. 161). Service records of RNAS officers from July 1914 until March 1918 are in indexed volumes in series ADM 273. The entries are arranged by consecutive service number, and usually provide information on the officer's date of birth, marital status, the name and address of his next of kin, his date of entry into the RNAS, any previous service in the Forces or former civilian occupation, RAC (Royal Aero Club) certificate number and date and place where it was obtained and on whose recommendation, the dates and nature of appointments, his dates of seniority and ranks, an account of his naval service, reports of any accidents, meritorious service and flights, accompanied by confidential reports on his character and an assessment as to his suitability for promotion.

Records concerning commissioned RAF officers who did not see service beyond 1920 are in series AIR 76, and these are arranged alphabetically by name, making it relatively easy to find the correct reference from the name ranges given in the catalogue. The documents are accessible on microfilm, and include some relating to RFC officers killed before the RAF was formed. The papers disclose each officer's name, date and place of birth, residence, former occupation or profession, rank(s) and date(s) of commission(s), units in which he served and where, and the name, relationship and address of the next of kin.

Finding aids

You can search for an RFC officer's name using our online catalogues to series WO 339 and WO 374, and then order up the original documents. Series WO 338 (1870–1922), available on microfilm in our Microfilm

Reading Room, is a personal-name index to service files created for commissioned officers and refers to long number papers which no longer exist. The catalogue is arranged by surname range and dates each file was opened and closed. The entries in this series may give more information than the catalogues to series WO 339 and WO 374.

What if you can't find your ancestor?

- The records may no longer survive. If he was killed or reported missing in action, search the Debt of Honour Register (see p. 46). You could also probe the General Register Office indexes of war deaths for army other ranks and for officers between 1914 and 1921, and a similar set of indexes for all Royal Navy personnel during the same period on microfiche or at **www.1837online.com/Trace2web/LogonServlet**. Study our indexed digital images of *The Times* for listings of casualties.
- He may have continued in the RAF beyond 1920. For airmen and airwomen you will need to write to PMA (CS) 2a(2), at RAF Innsworth. For officers, the annual *Air Force List* should establish if this was the case, and a series of *Lists* give you a career outline, and then you can write to RAF Innsworth as described above. The Debt of Honour Register extends to Second World War victims too. Consult the General Register Office indexes to war deaths of RAF officers and men between 13 September 1939 and 30 June 1948, to army chaplains' returns of births and marriages to 1955, and to deaths overseas to 1950, including those of RAF personnel and their families from 1920 onwards, and the combined Service Department indexes to births, and to marriages between 1956 and 1965, and to deaths abroad from 1951 until 1965, and thereafter the annual indexes to Births, Marriages and Deaths Abroad up to 1992. The indexes can also be searched up to recent registrations at **www.1837online.com/Trace2web/LogonServlet**.
- The RAF Museum, at Hendon, holds photographs, log books, other records and personal memorabilia deposited about officers, as well as examples of the planes they flew.

Other RFC/RNAS/RAF records in the National Archives

For biographical information about the first 1,400 other ranks to join the Royal Flying Corps between 1912 and August 1914, read *A Contemptible Little Flying Corps,* by I. McInnes and J.V. Webb.

There is a complete muster of RAF airmen (but excluding the names of officers) at its formation on 1 April 1918, in AIR 1/819/204/4/1316, AIR 10/236 and 237, with addenda and supplements for 1918 and 1919 in AIR 10/232–35. This divulges each individual's rate of pay, trade, date of last promotion, and whether on an open engagement or signing on merely for the duration of the war. Nominal rolls of officers at the same date are in AIR 1/116/204/5/2516–21.

The unit records in series AIR 1 often include RFC and RAF officers' services, biographies, and reports on their ability.

Many of the Squadron Operations Record Books, between 1911 and 1977, in series AIR 27, are available on microfilm in our Microfilm Reading Room. These list the crew, their ranks and log the times they took off and landed again, and give an account of every flight and bombing campaign, with combat reports, and details of crashes and casualties. Most start from the mid-1930s onwards, and also embrace squadrons from the Dominions, and Allied air force squadrons under British command. For other Squadron RFC and RAF Operations Record Books, try series AIR 1 (Reports on Overseas Commands, 1916–78), AIR 23 (Middle East, 1916–78), AIR 25 (Groups, 1914–75), AIR 28 (RAF Stations, 1913–77) and AIR 29 (miscellaneous units, 1912–77). For RNAS operational reports look in ADM 116/1352 and 1353 (1914–18). Apart from series AIR 217, these have to be ordered as original documents.

For the Second World War you can examine Operations Record Books as original documents in various AIR series: for Commands in AIR 24 (including the WAAF); for Groups in AIR 25; for Wings in AIR 26; for Squadrons in AIR 27 (which continues beyond 1945, until 1977); for Stations in AIR 28; for other units in AIR 29.

First World War campaign medals sent to members of the Royal Flying Corps or their next of kin are in series WO 329. Digital images of the card indexes to these, in series WO 372, can be inspected at **www.nationalarchives. gov.uk/documentsonline**. They reveal the individual airman's service number, rank, squadron, any date of casualty and theatre of war. Officers are included only if they or their next of kin had applied to the War Office for the appropriate medals. The actual medal rolls themselves rarely add anything extra, and you will need to convert the coded references contained in the index to find the correct document reference. You can do this using the key book linked to the index volume (WO 329/1) for series WO 329, in our Microfilm Reading Room. Most of the Silver War Badges, introduced for military personnel discharged because of sickness or wounds who were in service after 4 August 1914, were awarded to RFC men. For RNAS campaign medals, in ADM 171/78–88, trawl the catalogue for the name range including your relative's surname, and then help yourself to the correct microfilm. There were no Silver War Badges for RNAS personnel.

All gallantry and meritorious service awards are announced in the *London Gazette* (see p. 29). You can search for these online for both the First and Second World Wars at **www.gazettes-online.co.uk/index**.

Details about pensions and gratuities paid to airmen who were disabled during World War I are in PMG 42/1–12, which are arranged alphabetically. Pensions paid to the dependants of deceased officers from 1916 to 1920 are recorded in series PMG 44.

Royal Naval Air Service officers who were casualties during World War I are listed alphabetically in ADM 242/1–5, which covers the period 1914–20 There is a card index of officers' names in our Research Enquiries Room, giving the dates, places and causes of death. The War Graves Roll, in ADM 242/7–10 (1914–19), notes the rank or rating, date of birth, date and place of death and the name and address of the next of kin of each casualty. You can find out about deceased RFC officers and men by searching *Soldiers Died in the Great War*, and *Army Officers Died in the Great War*, both of which databases are available in our Online Publications and Electronic Resources Archive. From these you can discover their dates and places of birth, last place of residence, rank, when and where they died or were killed. Registers of killed and wounded members of the Royal Naval Air Service are embedded in ADM 104/145–9 (1914–18), which are indexed in ADM 104/140–3. *Airmen Died in the Great War*, by C. Hobson, is worth checking too.

To find out more, read our Research Guides:
RAF, RFC and RNAS: First World War, 1914–1918: Service Records
Royal Air Force: Second World War, 1939–1945: Service Records
Women's Military Services, First World War
Royal Air Force: Operational Records
Medals: British Armed Services: Campaign, and Other Service Medals
Medals: British Armed Services: Gallantry
Medals: British Armed Services: Gallantry, Further Information.

Royal Marines

Marines were first raised as the Lord Admiral's Regiment in 1664. They were really land soldiers on board ship, though they sometimes served onshore as infantrymen. They were borne on the ships' books, so their names appear in the Royal Navy muster books and pay lists. Further Marine regiments began to be raised for war service after 1690. They were under the control of the Army and were organized like foot regiments, using army ranks.

A new Corps of Marines was created in 1755, which was responsible to the Board of Admiralty. When under military control the Marines followed military discipline; otherwise they were responsible to the Admiralty. In 1855 the Corps adopted the title of the Royal Marine Light Infantry (Red Marines), and in 1859 a new Division of the Royal Marine Artillery (Blue Marines) was created. The two were merged in 1923 to form the Royal Marines.

Until the 20th century, Royal Marines provided detachments for ships. During the 1930s the Marines became part of the Mobile Naval Base Defence Organization, and from 1942 provided Commando Units specializing in raids on enemy coasts. This became their principal duty after 1945.

Marine artillerymen manned the mortars carried by bomb vessels. In 1804, they were formed into companies, and from 1859, the newly established Division of the Royal Marine Artillery (Blue Marines) was based at Eastney, near Portsmouth.

For more information read *Records of the Royal Marines*, by G. Thomas.

What will you find? Each depot kept its own attestation and discharge papers, description books and service records, which were similar to those of army regiments, whilst detachments at sea were written up on ships' musters and pay lists.

Was your ancestor an officer or in the ranks? Look for his name in the index of commissioned officers in the annual printed *Navy List* from 1797, annual *Army List* from 1779, and the *List of the Officers of H.M.'s Royal Marine Forces on full and half-pay (The Marine List)* from 1755. If his name is not there, then you can assume he was in the ranks.

OTHER RANKS

There are three sets of service records for Marines. They are all arranged by Division, and a man usually stayed in the same one throughout his career. The attestation forms completed by recruits on enlistment, expressing a willingness to serve wherever required, are in series ADM 157, and cover the years from 1790 to 1925. This series includes attestations of Royal Marine engineers on short service between 1914 and 1919, attestation and discharge books of the Royal Marine Labour Corps at Chatham and Deal from 1914 to 1922, and certificates of service of the Royal Marine Artillery running from 1899 to 1923. As well as details of enlistment and attestation, the forms set out the age on enlistment, the date and place of birth, former trade, a physical description, and a service summary of each new Marine, and sometimes add the name of his next of kin.

The description books, in series ADM 158, start in about 1750 and end in 1940. They are organized by date of enlistment, and by the first letter of the Marine's surname. From these you can discover the Marine's age on enlistment, his birthplace, a short physical description and other details as given in series ADM 157, but without any information about his career. The service registers, in series ADM 159, run between 1842 and 1936, and are closed for 75 years. These give the date and place of birth of each Marine, his previous trade, religious affiliation, date and place of enlistment, a physical description at the time of re-engagement and discharge, plus a full service record and comments on his conduct, details of any promotions or any disciplinary action taken against him. This series embraces men who served up until the Second World War.

Some Marines' attestation and discharge papers between 1873 and 1882 are in WO 97/2170, which are arranged alphabetically. These disclose details of age and birthplace, former trade, date and place of enlistment and discharge, Division, rank and number, and service record, to which were added medical and conduct sheets.

For service records of men joining after 1925, write to DPS(N)2, in Portsmouth. Information can only be released to the rating himself or his next of kin with his consent.

Finding aids

There is a card index up to 1883 in our Microfilm Reading Room for the attestation forms in series ADM 157. Try this to identify the Division when you want to search series ADM 158 and ADM 159 too. In 1884, divisional numbers were assigned retrospectively to each Marine then in service. If you don't know this number, but know the Division to which he belonged, search the indexes to the attestation papers in series ADM 157 and service registers in series ADM 159 in series ADM 313 (1834–1936), which is available on microfilm in the Microfilm Reading Room. There are also some nominal indexes to the service registers in series ADM 159 for Chatham, Plymouth and Portsmouth in the Research Enquiries Room.

What if you
can't find your
ancestor?

156

The
Records
A to Z

• Search the campaign medal rolls in series ADM 171 (on microfilm), which are arranged by campaign and then alphabetically by name to 1913, and for the First World War, 1914–20, again arranged alphabetically by the names of recipients, as these disclose each man's Marine Division. If you have a Company number and a date, look in Appendix 1 of *Records of the Royal Marines*, by G. Thomas, for details of the Division to which it belonged.

• If your relative died or was killed during the two world wars, exploit the Debt of Honour Register (see p. 46). Read our indexed digital images of *The Times* for details of casualties, which were sometimes published some time after the event.

• If you know a Marine's address from a birth, marriage or death certificate or from the ten-yearly census returns from 1841 until 1901, he is likely to have belonged to the local Division. Divisional barracks should be easy to locate, and from 1861, if your man was at sea, he might be traced in the shipping returns. Indexed digital images of all the foregoing censuses are accessible via **www.nationalarchives.gov.uk/census**.

• If you know the name of the ship and approximately when your Marine ancestor was on board, try the bi-monthly or monthly musters in series ADM 36 (1688–1808), ADM 37 (1792–1842), ADM 38 (1793–1878), ADM 39 (1667–1798), for hired armed vessels in series ADM 41 (1794–1815), and for hospital ships' musters in series ADM 102 (1740–1860).

OFFICERS

Some Marine officers went on to buy army commissions. Applications for army commissions between 1793 and 1870 are in series WO 31, and officers' service records from 1828 onwards may be located in series WO 25 or WO 76. You can find the names of Marine officers in *English Army Lists and Commission Registers, 1661–1714*, by C. Dalton, the annual *Navy List* from 1797, *Army List* from 1779, and *Marine List* from 1755. Starting in 1846, the *New Navy List* contains short statements of service going back to the 1790s. You can also find an outline of an officer's career from the yearly *Marine List*, copies of which from 1757 to 1850 are in ADM 118/230–336, and from 1760 to 1882 in series ADM 192. The latter series is indexed from 1770 onwards.

Many warrant officers later became commissioned. Service records of officers who were warranted between 1904 and 1912, and the latest of whom was discharged in 1923, are in ADM 196/67, and those relating to both commissioned and warrant officers, which run from the first date of entry in 1793 until 1923, with the latest recorded service in 1966, are in ADM 196/58–65, 83, ADM 196/97 and 98, and ADM 196/106–16. Most of the volumes from 1884 onwards (that is, ADM 196/106–16) are integrally indexed and disclose the date of birth, rank, order of seniority, date of appointment and a career summary of each officer.

Details of commissions and appointments of officers between 1703 and 1713, and 1755 and 1814 are in ADM 6/405. You can also consult the results of surveys undertaken in 1822 and 1831 in ADM 6/73–83, and 409, and in ADM 6/84 and 85 respectively, for the ages and an account of the previous service of officers currently in the Marines. Occasionally the father's name and occupation can be found among these papers.

There are separate service registers for officers entering the Royal Marine Artillery from 1798 to 1855 in ADM 196/66, final recorded discharge being in 1870.

For information about officers commissioned after 1925, write to TNT Archive Service, in Swadlincote.

There is a personal-name index of warrant officers attached to the ADM 196 bound catalogue. For the names of officers appointed from 1834 up to 1883, in ADM 196/58–67, 83, 97 and 98 consult the index in series ADM 313, which is available on microfilm in our Microfilm Reading Room.

• You've got the wrong Division. Examine each of the three sets of records in series ADM 157, ADM 158 and ADM 159.

• Try the General Register Office indexes. Those to Royal Navy War deaths 1914–21 include Royal Marines of all ranks, and there are separate indexes to names of deceased Royal Naval officers and deceased other ranks, both between 3 September 1939 and 30 June 1948. The indexes to Service Departments' registers of births, marriages and deaths betweeen 1959 and 1965, and the subsequent annual indexes to returns of Births Abroad, Deaths Abroad and of Marriages Abroad of British citizens include Royal Marine service personnel and their families (see p. 56). You can search all these indexes up to recent registrations at **www.1837online.com/ Trace2web/LogonServlet**.

• The personal-name index in series ADM 313 for ADM 196, and running up to 1883, is incomplete. Find the register in the latter series covering the date of the officer's commission, which if you don't know it already can be extracted from the annual indexed *Army List, Navy List* or *Marine List*.

Registers of births, marriages and deaths of Royal Marines and their families for the Chatham Division between 1830 and 1913 are in ADM 183/114–120, and for the Plymouth Division, 1862–1920 in ADM 184/43–54. Registers of marriages of Royal Marines in the Portsmouth Division, 1869–81, are in ADM 185/69, and for the Woolwich Division between 1822 and 1869 in ADM 81/23–25. Baptism and marriage records for the Royal Marine Artillery Division at Portsmouth from 1810–53 are in ADM 193/9, and details of baptisms performed between 1866 and 1921 at Eastney Royal Marine Barracks, are in ADM 6/437. They each show the Marines' current ranks and details of postings to a specific ship or station. You will need to order these as original documents.

Registers noting the names of killed and wounded Royal Marines from 1854 to 1911 are in ADM 104/144, and from August 1914 until 1929 in ADM 104/145–9. First consult the indexes to the registers between 1915 and 1929 in ADM 104/140–3. Registers of reports of deaths from July 1900 until October 1941 are in ADM 104/122–6. Each man's rank, service number, Division, ship's or unit name, date and place of birth, cause and date of death and place of burial are recorded, together with the name, address and relationship to the deceased of the next of kin, who was informed of the death. The

War Graves Roll, covering the years from 1914 to 1919, in ADM 242/7–10, gives the name, last rank, service number, ship's name, date and place of birth, date and cause of death, where buried and the name of the next of kin of each Marine. ADM 242/1–5 is an alphabetical card index to the names of commissioned and warrant officers who died between 1914 and 1920. This is available in our Research Enquiries Room, and contains references to any Mentions in Dispatches or gallantry awards, as well as the date of death, ship's name, place of death and interment and sometimes the name and address of the officer's next of kin. You can also find details about casualties in *A Register of Royal Marine Deaths, 1914–19*, and *A Register of Royal Marine Deaths, 1939–1945*, both by J.A. Good, and don't forget to visit the Debt of Honour Register (see p. 46) for details about Royal Marine casualties in both wars.

Awards of medals to Royal Marines are encased in series ADM 171. Many Marines also received army gallantry medals, which were announced in the *London Gazette* (see p. 29).

To find out more, read our Research Guides:
Royal Marines: Other Ranks' Service Records
Royal Marines: How to Find a Division
Royal Marines: Officers' Service Records
Royal Marines: Further Areas of Research
Medals: British Armed Forces: Campaign and Other Service Medals
Medals: British Armed Services: Gallantry
Medals: British Armed Services: Gallantry, Further Information.

Royal Navy

The foundations of our modern English Navy were laid during the reign of King Henry VIII, when the Navy Board was established in 1546. It began to be called the Royal Navy during the reign of King Charles II, reflecting its growing professionalism.

The Navy Board had charge of the civil administration of the Navy, shipbuilding, maintenance of ships and supplies, stores, contracts and auditors' accounts for the dockyards at Portsmouth, Chatham and Plymouth. By the late 17th century, other administrative boards began to evolve: the Sick and Hurt Board, founded in 1653, provided medical care, paid out pensions and gratuities to wounded men, and was responsible for the exchange of prisoners of war, the Victualling Board, set up in 1683, provisioned ships and oversaw the distribution of food by the pursers, and the Transport Board, established in 1686, supervised the ferrying of troops overseas. In 1832, the Navy Board's functions were transferred to the Board of Admiralty, which in 1964 became the Admiralty Board of the Defence Council of the Ministry of Defence.

The Royal Navy consisted of ratings (able seamen, ordinary seamen, petty officers, leading seamen, stokers, midshipmen and master's mates) and warrant officers (men with specialist skills, like carpenters, cooks, boatswains, engineers up to 1846, and gunners, masters, surgeons up to 1842, and pursers), all accountable to the ship's captain. Finally came the commissioned officers (ranging from lieutenants up to admirals, and after the above dates, surgeons and engineers), who commanded the ships, fleets, and stations. Qualifying examinations for commissions as lieutenants were introduced in 1677, when the minimum age for candidates was 20.

Recruitment was originally for the length of a ship's commission, usually four to six years. Wars gave rise to the urgent temporary need for a large sea force and dockyard staff to construct and service its ships. One of the ways this could be achieved up to 1835 was by impressment. It has been estimated that one in 48 men was employed by the Royal Navy in 1811.

In 1853, a system of continuous service engagement for Royal Naval seamen was introduced, guaranteeing a pension after 20 years' service. This meant that there was a standing Navy, whose personnel had a secure career. In 1903, the Admiralty introduced a short-service scheme of 12 years, 5 or 7 of which were spent in the Navy and the rest in the Royal Fleet Reserve.

The Royal Naval Volunteer Reserve (RNVR) was made up of officers and ratings who underwent naval training in their own time, but unlike the Royal Naval Reserve (RNR), they were not professionally employed at sea. During the First and Second World Wars, Reserve officers entered the Royal Navy only for the duration of hostilities. In 1958, the RNVR was merged with the RNR.

Using Navy Records, by B. Pappalardo, is an excellent general introduction.

What will you find?

If you don't know whether your ancestor was a commissioned officer, check the annual *Navy List*, published from 1782 onwards. The surnames and initials of officers are listed according to their dates of seniority (commission or promotion) at each rank, and by ship. From the outset both commissioned officers and masters are included, to which were added the names of surgeons from 1794, pursers after 1796, chaplains from 1815, mates from 1841, clerks from 1846, engineers from 1853, and boatswains, carpenters and gunners from 1870. If you can't find your forebear's name, then look for him among our records about ratings.

RATINGS

The continuous service engagement books, in series ADM 139, run from 1853 until 1872. The contents are arranged by service number, and disclose the full name of each rating, his date and place of birth, a physical description, his date of entry to the Royal Navy, career to date, including the names of ships on which he had served, and at what rates. Since the books encompass men who joined the Navy before 1853, reference is made to careers which commenced much earlier in the century.

From 1873, the registers of seamen's services, in series ADM 188, furnish career details up to 1928, of men entering the Royal Navy before 1923. They are set out chronologically by date of entry to the Royal Navy, and by official rating number, and give the full name, date and place of birth, date and period of continuous service engagement, a physical description, former trade or occupation of each rating, together with the names of ships in which he had served, at what dates and rates, when, where and why he was discharged or if he died in service. These records are now available as indexed digital images at **www.nationalarchives.gov.uk/documentsonline**.

Finding aids

Indexes to series ADM 139 in ADM 139/1019–27 bear the continuous service numbers (CS). Because ratings could sign on for further engagements, they might be assigned several CS numbers during their careers.

What if you can't find your ancestor?

• He joined after 1924 and before 1938, or his service continued beyond 1928. For particulars about ratings who joined the Royal Navy after 1924 and who have died, and for service records between 1928 and 1938, contact TNT Archive Service (Navy Search), at Swadlincote. Information about men joining after 1924 and who are still alive, and details of careers running beyond 1938, can be obtained from the Data Protection Cell (Navy) in Portsmouth.

• He left the Navy before 1853. If you know the name of the ship and approximate date he was on board, search the monthly muster books in series ADM 36 (1688–1808), ADM 37 (1792–1842), ADM 38 (1793–1878), ADM 39 (1667–1798), and ADM 41 (1794–1815). Those of hospital ships between 1740 and 1860 are in series ADM 102. You can also examine the bound catalogues to each of the above series, which are arranged alphabetically by the name of each vessel and then chronologically by the dates of the musters. The muster books identify everyone on board, including Royal Marines (see that section) and any prisoners of war. They list name, rank or rate, date of entry to the ship, and if the person left during the course of the voyage, when, where and why. The entries are annotated with references to transfers to other ships, hospitals, or deaths on board. Starting in 1764, ages and birthplaces of crew are recorded too. The muster books are surname-indexed from 1797.

• You can track a sailor's career from ship to ship using the muster books. If you don't know the ship's name, but know one of the ports his ship called at and the date, glean the list books, in series ADM 8, which are the monthly returns of ships at home and abroad between 1673 and 1909, and then inspect the musters of each ship until you find your ancestor's name.

• Another possible source is series ADM 29, which elicits the dates of entry to and discharge from named ships of pensioners between 1802 and 1894, though prior to 1834 they deal mostly with payments made to warrant officers. There is an online personal-name index to this microfilmed series.

• Try the indexed tickets and registers of merchant seamen between 1835 and 1857, in series BT 120, BT 112, BT 113 and BT 116, since there was much crossing-over between one Service and the other (see **MERCHANT NAVY**).

COMMISSIONED OFFICERS AND WARRANT OFFICERS

You can trace an outline of your ancestor's career in the annual *Navy List*, the first edition appearing in 1782. After 1810, the *Lists* identify each ship and the names of officers on board. Surname indexes were added in 1847.

Confidential editions of the volumes for the First and Second World Wars have to be ordered as original documents in series ADM 177. These carry details of where each officer was serving, including the identities of their ships or establishments. Editions of the *New Navy List* from 1841 until 1856 disclose information on the war service of officers. There are surname indexes after 1846.

You can delve into various printed biographies about naval officers in our Library and Resource Centre. Look out especially for *A Naval Biographical Dictionary*, by W.R. O'Byrne, which embraces all those commissioned officers alive on 1 January 1845; *Naval Biography*, by J.W. Marshall, which focuses on all those commissioned officers of the rank of Commander and above alive on 1 January 1823; and *Biographia Navalis, 1660–1794*, by J. Charnock.

Enrolled copies of lieutenants' passing certificates, in series ADM 6 (issued by the Admiralty, 1744–1819), series ADM 107 (granted by the Navy Board, 1691–1832) and series ADM 13 (1851–1902), provide details of each successfully examined candidate's name, age, current rank, date of his examination, degree of competency, the names of vessels on which he had served, for how long and at what rates. From 1761, as proof of the minimum qualifying age of 20, a copy of the candidate's birth or baptism certificate might be attached, certified by the parish priest. It is a good idea to check the original church registers, because some of these 'certificates' were forgeries to raise younger men's ages.

Similar passing certificates for competency were introduced for midshipmen, boatswains, pursers, masters, clerks, carpenters, surgeons, engineers and gunners. You can find those for midshipmen from 1857 to 1866 in series ADM 13; for boatswains between 1810 and 1813 in series ADM 6, and for 1851–87 in series ADM 13; pursers' passing certificates from 1813 until 1820 are in series ADM 6, and from 1851 until 1889 in series ADM 13; masters' passing certificates from 1660 to 1830 are in series ADM 106, from 1851 up to 1863 in series ADM 13; clerks' and assistant clerks' certificates from 1852 to 1899 are in series ADM 13; those issued to carpenters between 1851 and 1887 are in series ADM 13; to surgeons from 1700 to 1800 in series ADM 106; and engineers' and gunners' certificates from 1731 to 1812 are in series ADM 6, and from 1856 to 1887 and 1863 and 1902 respectively in series ADM 13. The certificates record the name, date of certification of competence, names of ships previously sailed in, and length of each voyage.

Signed returns of officers' services for both commissioned and warrant officers between 1817 and 1822, and in 1846, can be found in series ADM 9. Others, spanning 1741–1869, are in series ADM 11, and still more, from 1756 until 1931, are in series ADM 196. The first two series are original documents, but you can help yourself to the microfilm copies of ADM 196 references. The returns in series ADM 9 and ADM 11 contain details of the various ranks held, the names of ships in which served and the names of the captains, where they were stationed, and the various dates of entry to and of discharge from each vessel.

From the mid-19th century, series ADM 196 usually includes the officer's birthplace, name of any wife, his date of death, as well as all his promotions

ADM 107/6: The passing certificate of Lieutenant Horatio Nelson, 1777, confirming he had complied with the necessary qualifications of age, capacity and time at sea. The voyage lengths are noted for each ship, and he produced journals kept on four of them. One of his commanders was his uncle, Captain Suckling.

and any awards. The entries in ADM 196 cover some naval careers which continued up to 1966, and between 1893 and 1943 they contain the commanding officers' confidential reports on each officer's character, performance and suitability for promotion. Similar reports on some warrant officers are included between 1881 and 1939.

You can discover when your forebear was commissioned and the relevant document references by searching the published index of names of candidates successfully examined to be lieutenants, and giving the dates of their commissions, extracted from series ADM 6, ADM 107 and ADM 13. The index was compiled by B. Pappalardo as *Royal Naval Lieutenants: Passing Certificates 1691–1902*.

For the officers' service returns in series ADM 9, you will need to scour the indexes in series ADM 10. There is a card index to entries in series ADM 196 up to 1883, but this is not fully comprehensive. The entries from 1884 onwards are self-indexed.

• He wasn't a commissioned officer. Bear in mind that some of the indexes mentioned above are not always complete, so double-check the original documents for the period in question.

• He was described as a 'Captain'. Try the army records (see **ARMY SERVICE RECORDS**).

• He was commissioned after May 1917. For information about officers who have died, write to TNT Archive Service (Navy Search) at Swadlincote, and for information about officers who are still alive, and aged between 61 and 100, write to the Data Protection Cell (Navy) at Portsmouth. Information about warrant officers whose service commenced after 1931 can be obtained in the same way as for commissioned officers.

You can find personal information about Royal Naval personnel who were ashore or in port on the nights of the ten-yearly census counts between 1841 and 1901. The 1861 census returns were the first to include details of those on board ships on voyages in home waters or overseas over a longer fixed period, the completed ships' schedules being handed in by the commanding officers to the customs office at the return ports. The returns provide details about each named person's age, current marital status, rank or rate, and birthplace, as well as the name of the vessel. Similar returns were filed for subsequent census years, though like the returns for 1861, they are far from an overall record of all naval shipping. You can search indexed digital images of the returns between 1841 and 1901 (see **CENSUS RETURNS**).

The original daily log books kept during voyages from 1667 until 1965 are in series ADM 50 (1702–1916), ADM 51 (1669–1852), ADM 52 (1672–1840), ADM 53 (1799–1976, though some of these are not open to the public for 75 years, and after early 1940 they appear to be confined to vessels of cruiser-size upwards), ADM 54 (1808–71), and ADM 55 (1757–1904). Log books for submarines between 1914 and 1965 are in series ADM 173. The entries indentify any casualties on board.

The names of recipients of naval campaign medals up to the end of the First World War are preserved on microfilm in series ADM 171. The earliest medals date from the China Medal, awarded in 1842. The Naval General Service Medal was introduced in 1847 and made retrospective to 1793. The series is listed by medal title. No long-service or good conduct medal records survive before 1912; these are in series ADM 171 too. For gallantry medals and Mentions in Dispatches, try the *London Gazette* (see p. 29).

We hold a register of marriages which took place on Royal Naval vessels between 1842 and 1889, in RG 33/156, which is available on microfilm. The index to this is in RG 43/7, also on microfilm. Copies of marriage certificates of officers from 1806 to 1866 can be tracked down in ADM 13/70 and 71, from 1866 until 1902 in ADM 13/186–92, and for boatswains, gunners and carpenters from about 1891 to 1902, in ADM 13/191 and 192. They are arranged alphabetically by year. You will have to order these items as original documents.

Admissions of ratings as in-pensioners to the Royal Hospital at Greenwich between 1764 and 1865 will be found in series ADM 73. The entry books include the date of entry, at what age, a physical description, details of wounds and the last ship on which each inmate served, as well as his marital status, number and age of any children. Entry books relating to warrant officers admitted as pensioners between 1748 and 1873 are also in series ADM 73. Selected disablement pension files concerning service prior to the First World War, are in series PIN 71. They cover applications ranging from 1854 up to the final payouts (the latest being in 1979), and contain medical records, the disabled person's own account of what happened, a conduct sheet setting out age, birthplace, parents' names and those of siblings, religious denomination, a physical description and marital and parental status. You can search our online catalogue to the applications by personal-name. This series carries applications by widows too.

For details about naval casualties among officers and ratings between 1854 and 1957, search the volumes in series ADM 104, which encompass registers and reports of deaths due to causes other than enemy action from July 1900 until October 1941 in ADM 104/122–26, and from September 1939 until June 1948 in ADM 104/127–39. The indexes to the names of naval ships between 1893 and 1950, in ADM 104/102–08, provide references to the registers and reports of death on board up to 1946, in ADM 104/109–18. The indexes disclose the name, rank, vessel, report page and year of death of each man. The registers of names of officers and ratings killed or wounded in action between 1854 and 1929, in ADM 104/144–9, are indexed by surname ranges from 1915 to 1929 in ADM 104/140–3. The entries themselves are arranged chronologically by date within each letter of the alphabet, and these reveal the full name, date and place of birth, date and cause of death, place of burial, rate and official number, ship's name, branch of service, and the name, address and relationship to the deceased of the next of kin who was informed of the death. Ratings who lost their lives between 1914 and 1919 are similarly recorded on the War Graves Roll in ADM 242/7–10, which is organized alphabetically. There is a personal-name card index in our Research Enquiries Room to commissioned, warrant officers and midshipmen who were killed, 1914–20, giving document references in ADM 242/1–5. Details of their births and deaths, and the names and addresses of their next of kin, are included, as well as of their last ship and rank. You can learn about naval casualties in both world wars in the Debt of Honour Register (see p. 46). Deaths of naval men are traceable in the General Register Office indexes of Marine Returns from 1 July 1837 to 1965, and from 1959 until 1965 in the indexes to the Service Departments' Returns of births, marriages and deaths, and then in the annual indexes to Births Abroad, Marriages Abroad and Deaths Abroad. For deaths of all ranks in the Royal Navy from 1914–21, as a result of hostilities, for ratings, 3 September 1939 to 30 June 1948, and for officers between the same dates, there are separate General Register Office indexes. You can search the General Register Office indexes up to recent registrations at **www.1837online.com/Trace2web/LogonServlet**. Have a look at the indexed digital images of *The Times* for death announcements and obituaries of men killed or reported missing in action.

Widows of naval men who had been killed in action or who had died of wounds, could apply for the Royal Bounty. This was equal to a year's pay, and each child likewise received a third of his or her deceased father's pay. Widowed parents aged over 50 qualified for a bounty for unmarried sons who were casualties. The application papers, in series ADM 106, span 1675–1821. They contain marriage and baptism certificates and letters from applicants setting out the circumstances of death and the applicant's home address. There is a personal-name index to these in our Research Enquiries Room. Details about pensions, allowances and charitable relief distributed to widows of officers are in series ADM 22, which covers the period 1734–1835, and in series ADM 23, for the years 1830–78. Their applications for financial assistance, accompanied by certificates of birth, marriage and death in support of the claims, are in series ADM 6. There is a card index to personal-names of applicants for Greenwich Hospital pensions between 1737 and 1840, citing document references in ADM 6/223–47, in our Research Enquiries Room. Further papers of claimants between 1809 and 1820 are in series ADM 22.

To find out more, read our Research Guides:
Royal Navy: Ratings' Service Records, 1667–1923
Royal Navy: Officers' Service Records
Royal Navy: Officers' Service Records, First World War, and Confidential Reports, 1893–1943
Women's Military Services, First World War
The Royal Naval Volunteer Reserve
Royal Navy: Log Books and Reports of Proceedings
Royal Navy: Operational Records 1660–1914
Royal Navy: Operational Records, First World War, 1914–1918
Medals: British Armed Services: Campaign, and other Service Medals
Medals: British Armed Services: Gallantry
Medals: British Armed Services: Gallantry, Further Information
Royal Navy: Pay and Pension Records: Commissioned Officers
Royal Navy: Pension Records: Warrant Officers
Royal Navy: Pension Records: Ratings; and
B. Pappalardo, *Tracing Your Naval Ancestors*; and
N.A.M. Rodger, *Naval Records for Genealogists.*

State tontines and life annuities

A largely unexplored and potentially genealogically rewarding set of 18th-century records are those generated by the three state tontines of 1693, 1766 and 1789, and the five life annuities of 1745, 1746, 1757, 1778 and 1779. Irish state tontines were also set up in 1773, 1775 and 1777.

In 1693, central government urgently needed to reduce the National Debt, so it introduced the first of a series of state tontines and life annuities. A tontine was a scheme whereby a group of investors clubbed together to buy a financial stake at a fixed price. They each nominated someone or several people during the rest of whose lives a six-monthly dividend was to be paid out. The tontine was extinguished when the last nominated life ended. In contrast, a life annuity was bought for the enjoyment of a single person during the lifetime of named nominee(s). When the nominee(s) died, so did the dividends. The assignments of dividend entitlements were recorded in books kept by the Bank of England, which supervised the schemes.

The proprietors entitled to collect the dividends were required to produce a life certificate to the National Debt Office every six months, to prove their nominees' continued existence. Annual lists of the surviving nominees were then published.

For more information read *A Guide to the Records of the British State Tontines and Life Annuities of the Seventeenth and Eighteenth Centuries,* by F. Leeson.

What will you find?

For people with Huguenot or immigrant ancestry, with Dutch or German connections, or with a middle-class, trading, professional or landed background, these records are well worth delving into.

The original list of contributors to the first state tontine at Easter 1693 is in E 401/2274. This is written in Latin. The register gives the names, addresses and status or occupations of the purchasers, how much they each invested, the annual percentage yield, the names of the intended beneficiary or beneficiaries and the nominated lives. In 1698, a 96-year annuity was offered to existing tontine-holders. A roll setting out the names of purchasers, the amounts they subscribed, the pledged annual percentage yields and the names of their nominees is in E 403/2379, which is also written in Latin.

The books and bundles of material in series NDO 1–NDO 3 are a goldmine for family historians. Not only do they include full details of who contributed and the names of people entitled to receive the dividends, but they also tell you what happened to them and the nominees until the final payout, listing all sorts of personal information.

The 1766 state tontine divided the proprietors into classes, according to the date of purchase, and in 1789 the classes were determined by the ages of the nominees, starting with those under 20. The 1766 and 1789 registers of contributors, proprietors and nominees, in series NDO 2, give the names and addresses of each numbered investor, those of the proprietors, how much had been invested, the amount of the annuity to be paid out, plus the names, addresses, and ages of the nominees, annotated with their subsequent dates of death and the names of any proprietors' assignees.

A full list of subscribers to the 1766 state tontine is in NDO 2/1, the last nominated life becoming extinct in 1859. Lists of deaths of proprietors, nominees and defaulters failing to make returns of certificates of existence for the 1766 state tontine are in NDO 2/3.

You can study the ledgers of all six classes of contributors' annuities for the 1789 state tontine in NDO 2/10–14. The printed lists of their nominees (arranged by class) survive for 1792 in NDO 2/15 and 16, and are annotated with their dates of death or default of return of a certificate of existence. There is an index of the contributors' nominees in NDO 2/31. Further printed lists of nominees who were still alive in 1818, 1852, 1865, 1873 and 1878 are in NDO/26–30 and some during the years between 1790 and 1854 in NDO 2/60. These set out name, parentage, current age and address, to which were later added notifications of date and age at death.

Copies of marriage and death certificates of proprietors and nominees between 1803 and 1884, mostly relating to the 1789 state tontine are in NDO 2/48–51, and birth certificates are included in NDO 2/49 for the period 1820–39. The bundles of Dead Orders, in NDO 1/128–50, relate to the 1789 state tontine, the last surviving nominee dying in 1887. Certificates of death of the contributors' nominees between 1833 and 1888 are in NDO 2/47A. You can examine the relevant parts of wills and administration grants of proprietors of the 1789 state tontine between 1802 and 1828 in NDO 2/53 and a register of wills between 1835 and 1855 in NDO 2/55. The authorized assignments of dividends are recorded from 1802 until 1820 in NDO 2/56, and from 1836 until 1878 in NDO 2/58.

The first three state life annuities offered in 1745, 1746 and 1757 were linked to lotteries. For the names of the proprietors and nominees of all three state life annuities consult NDO 1/1–3. The ledgers record the consecutive numbers, dates of purchase, and the name and address of each of the intended proprietors, how much was invested by the named contributors (not always the same as the proprietors), the number of lottery tickets bought, the annual yield or dividend, and the names, addresses and ages of the nominees. The entries were updated to record their dates of death or the date of the last payment of the dividend. An index of nominees for the 1745 state annuity has been published in *Blackmansbury*, vol. 5, nos 1 and 2 (April and June 1968). No names of contributors survive for 1746, but for 1757 the ledgers, in NDO 1/3, identify the nominees' parents' names too.

Details of assignments, copies of marriage settlements, deeds, extracts from wills and administration grants authorizing the transfers of dividends accruing from these three annuities between 1746 and 1767 are in NDO 1/4. These are arranged in chronological order and cite the original debenture (stockholder) numbers.

The 1778 state life annuities offered an investment based on a nominated life or a 30-year term, to which a lottery ticket was attached, whilst the 1779 state annuities were for a life or 29 years, plus a lottery. The registers of proprietors and nominees, in NDO 2/4 and 6 respectively, provide details of all dividend assignments during the lifetimes of the various nominees, and of nominees' deaths. A book of endorsements for the 1778 and 1779 annuities, in NDO 2/8, includes similar information.

The papers relating to the Irish state tontines of 1773, 1775 and 1777 are in series NDO 3, which covers the period 1773–1871, the last nominee having died in 1870. A register of subscribers to the 1773 and 1775 state tontines, their nominees, executors and administrators, people given powers of attorney, and assignees is in NDO 3/5, with an identical register for 1777 in NDO 3/6. Each of the registers is arranged by all three classes. A further list of 1773 subscribers and their nominees is in NDO 3/26, for 1775 in NDO 3/27, and of 1777 subscribers and their nominees in NDO 3/25 and 28. Ledgers recording the sums received from contributors in Ireland, and the half-yearly payments to the 1773 debenture holders from Christmas 1775 until Christmas 1798 are in NDO 3/1, with similar information from Midsummer 1779 until Christmas 1798 relating to the 1775 tontine in NDO 3/2, and from Christmas 1778 until Christmas 1798 for the 1777 tontine in NDO 3/3. There is a list of subscribers to the 1777 state tontine who were based in England, including their receipts for dividends paid out in 1779, in NDO 3/51. Original lists of nominees of the 1773 tontine, where the dividends were payable in London are in NDO 3/29, and similar lists for all three tontines, indicating if the dividends were payable in London or Dublin, are in NDO 3/32 and 33.

Certificates proving the continued existence of nominees for all three Irish state tontines are included in NDO 3/17, and NDO 3/34 consists of printed lists of subscribers giving the names and abodes of clergy and others signing certificates of existence of the various nominees in 1819 and 1820. Certificates of marriage and death and declarations of identity of proprietors of all three state tontines are in NDO 3/46 and 47. For printed half-yearly lists of deaths, forfeitures of dividends and names of surviving nominees of these tontines between Midsummer 1802 and Midsummer 1869, consult NDO 3/36–8. Half-yearly accounts of deaths and forfeitures of dividends between Midsummer 1812 and Christmas 1848 are to be found in NDO 3/12–14, and from Christmas 1856 until Midsummer 1871 in NDO 3/16 and 50. Forfeitures between Christmas 1829 and Midsummer 1862 are in NDO 3/15.

Finding aids

Frank Leeson has compiled an index to the names of all the purchasers, beneficiaries and nominated lives for all but the first state tontine. This is now in the library of the Society of Genealogists. The Society has published a list of the nominees for the 1745 and 1757 state tontines on microfiche.

What if you can't find your ancestor?

• If he or she was described in a document as an annuitant, this may refer to a private annual income received in return for the loan of a lump sum. Such annuities became popular during the 18th century, when financial speculation, gambling and personal indebtedness reached a peak. Under the Grants of Life Annuities Act 1776, enrolment of private annuities was made compulsory. This was not repealed until 1861. Some enrolled copies of memorials of annuity deeds between 1777 and 1812 are on the Close Rolls, in series C 54, and memorial rolls of annuities in series C 63 contain abstracts between 1814 and 1854. There are special indexes to the names of the grantees between 1777 and 1842 in IND 1/1316–21, and to the names of the grantors from 1777 to 1814 in IND 1/1296–1303, and from 1812 until 1854 in IND 1/1303–15. The indexes are arranged by regnal year, and then by legal term.

• An annuitant might also be a beneficiary of an investment in the consolidated funds (known as consols) of the Bank of England. You can search an index to assignments of dividends made between 1717 and 1845 at **www.originsnetwork.com**, which offers a subscription service. The original ledgers of transfers are held in the library of the Society of Genealogists.

• The Death Duty registers, from 1796 to 1903, in series IR 26, furnish details of annuities too (see **DEATH DUTY REGISTERS**).

• From 1810, the Bank of England only accepted probates in the chief church court (the Prerogative Court of Canterbury) as authorization for assignments of its consolidated funds (see **WILLS AND OTHER PROBATE RECORDS**). Other banks and public and limited companies sold or offered shares in return for half-yearly dividends. If you know which one (a will, family tradition or family papers such as share certificates may help here), contact the relevant bank or company, or its successor. Consult the *Banker's Almanack* or trawl the companies and business catalogue at **www.nationalarchives.gov.uk/nra** to see if you can trace the present whereabouts of their archives.

Other investment records in the National Archives

In 1695, the Million Bank was founded as a result of a Million Lottery, announced in the previous year to raise capital to pay for the wars with France. It paid out half-yearly dividends to stockholders and to their legal heirs and successors, until the fund was wound up in 1796. The registers of names of original subscribers are in C 46/1. The entries give their addresses, details of how much each invested, and the names of their nominees for the duration of whose lives the dividends continued to be paid. Ledgers recording the payment of dividends between 1696 and 1795 in C 114/9–23, and C 114/153, note details of any marriages of female beneficiaries, changes of address, deaths and stock transfers throughout the period. There are printed lists of names and addresses of the remaining proprietors in 1793 and 1795, giving details of the final distribution in 1796. The lists are initial-alphabetically indexed by surname.

During the early 18th century, several state lotteries were run. The names of purchasers of lottery tickets for the 1711 Adventure for Two Million (pounds), are preserved in E 401/2600, and for the Classis Lottery of 1712, in E 401/2599. The documents contain both their names and addresses, arranged in five classes according to the date when they bought the numbered tickets, and the sum invested towards an annuity.

To find out more read:
S. Colwell, *Family Roots, Discovering the Past in the Public Record Office.*

Tax lists

Until the abolition of feudal tenure in 1660, the monarch's main source of income was derived from his position as supreme landlord, nominal head of the judiciary, and as the grantor of rights, offices and privileges. To make up any shortfall, the king had to rely on heavy borrowing and the levying of feudal aids. On the death of a landowner holding an estate directly from the Crown as a tenant-in-chief, it claimed a fine before the next legal heir could take possession (see pp. 125–7 for details about Inquisitions post mortem). People owning a certain amount of land were automatically qualified to become knights, and thus subject to military service, but they could pay 'scutage' to avoid it. Crown tenants paid tallage, and a type of land tax called hidage and carucage was imposed on property not liable to military knight service.

Tax collection became more widespread in the late 13th century, with the introduction of a regular levy on a fraction (usually a fifteenth) of the capital value of a person's movable personal goods in the shires, and a tenth in towns and cities. After 1334, these lay subsidies became a fixed quota from each community. In 1523, Parliament voted for an extra tax, based on a person's capital wealth in goods, annual wages, or yearly income from land, whichever was of the greatest value over a minimum amount. It was regularly charged, and either collected in instalments over a set number of years, or paid repeatedly over a prescribed period. By the reign of Queen Elizabeth I wages were excluded.

Between 1642 and 1660, Parliament imposed weekly and monthly assessments on householders or individuals, and drew further income from the fines and seizures of land and property belonging to known and suspected supporters of King Charles I. This was done by county committees, acting on the advice provided by informers (see p. 71).

Lay subsidies, begun in the 13th century, continued to be levied up until 1663/4, when they were replaced by a series of grants and by the Hearth Tax. From Michaelmas (late September/October) 1662 until Lady Day (25 March) 1689, this tax became payable on the number of chimneys (fireplaces) in each house.

The Hearth Tax was succeeded by assessed personal taxes on windows, land, public office, silver and plate, wheeled vehicles, horses, dogs, male and female servants, coats of arms, hairpowdered wigs, shops and so on. Surviving records of these later taxes are usually to be found in county record offices, though some lists are in the National Archives. Look in *Land and Window Tax Assessments,* by J. Gibson, M. Medlycott and D. Mills, for a county-by-county list of their dates and whereabouts.

From 1625, convicted Roman Catholics aged 17 or more, and people aged over 21 who had not taken Holy Communion within the previous year were subject to double taxation, or to pay a poll tax if their wealth fell below the minimum threshhold. Aliens and denizens (granted limited status as English subjects by the Crown) were regularly subject to special taxation, especially from 1439 until 1487, and like Roman Catholics had to pay double tax or a poll tax.

From time to time a poll tax was levied on everyone over a certain age. Occasionally too, the Crown or Parliament requested a loan, grant of an aid or invited a 'contribution' for some specified cause, and lists of their subscribers exist too.

The dated lists of householders or inhabitants subject to tax are specially helpful when you want to know their whereabouts at a certain time, how the surname was spread out over a geographic area, or over a number of years. They will not indicate family relationships, except perhaps status as a widow, 'senior' or 'junior', 'elder' or 'younger'.

Because no-one was taxed twice for the same levy, the lists can help resolve whether or not there were two or more individuals of the same name in a community at the same date. A person was taxed where he or she actually resided. The assessments and return reveal a person's current financial status compared with that of neighbours, at different dates, and the family's relative prosperity or reduced circumstances in previous and later generations. If a person's name disappears from a list, it does not always indicate death or migration, because his or her income or capital might have fallen beneath the minimum tax level, or the individual had somehow avoided paying tax. It is a good idea to check parish registers of burials, and to examine the indexes to local wills and administration grants to see if death is the explanation.

The lay subsidy assessments and returns from 1290 to 1663/4, in series E 179, are arranged by regnal year, by county, then by administrative division, and then by its constituent towns, villages or hamlets.

The assessments and returns for each named administrative division were written in Latin on parchment membranes. Up to 1332, the 'particulars of names' for each place record the names of assessed residents, together with how much they were to pay or had paid. Because surnames were by no means yet hereditary or fixed, such lists usually serve merely as a pointer to the use of certain surnames in a locality at a specific date.

In 1523, an additional lay subsidy was introduced. The new lists continued to be arranged in the same way as before, but they now indicated whether the taxpayer was subject to tax on goods, wages or income from land.

In 1662, the lay subsidies on individuals were superseded by the Hearth Tax, which in turn was abolished in 1688. The dated half-yearly tax returns to the Exchequer, starting with Michaelmas 1662, are in series E 179. They are arranged by county, administrative division and then by parish, and are written either in Latin or in English. Instead of the amount to be paid, they may depict the number of hearths for which the named householder was liable, so you can contrast the relative house size of your ancestor with that of his or her neighbours, detect transfers of property ownership over time, the changing number of hearths possessed by a person which might point to a move to a different property, a building shared by more than one household, the addition of extra rooms or hearths, or demolition, and to learn how the surname was distributed in a locality.

Chadlington Hundred

Sarsden

Sir William Walter — xxiiij
George Farmer — iij
Edmund Chamberlaines
ffrancis Mansell — iij
William Bradford — j
Arthur Wittell — ij
Sampson Adall — j
Thomas Hampton — iij

William Board — iiij
Margarett Church widd — ij } ditch by powrty
William Box — ij

Kiddington

E 179/164/513, m51r: Sir William Walter was liable to pay tax on 24 hearths in his house at Sarsden, in Oxfordshire, in 1665. Three householders were discharged from payment because of their poverty. They were probably his tenants, as he was lord of the manor.

From 1663 the returns also show the names of people in arrears of payment and householders who were granted exemption. Exemption certificates, certified by the parish priest, churchwardens, overseers of the poor and two local magistrates, were necessary to avoid liability. Many of the printed exemption certificates from 1670 onwards are arranged in county order in E 179/324–51, the remainder of them usually being filed with the parish returns. The reason for non-chargeability may be included too.

From Michaelmas 1666 until Lady Day 1669, and from Michaelmas 1674 onwards, the Hearth Tax was farmed out to local county commissioners, so only the total receipts are conveyed. Surviving lists of names are purely incidental and sometimes turn up among family and other local archives, many of which are now in county record offices.

Householders with property in several places required a certificate of residence as proof of payment where they actually lived, thus avoiding double liability. There is a series of such certificates, including some relating to the earlier lay subsidies from the reign of King Edward VI onwards until that of King Charles II, in series E 115. This is catalogued alphabetically by name. The certificates stated where each householder resided, the amount of tax paid, and were signed by the county commissioners. A personal-name index to these is available on the open shelves in our Map and Large Document Room.

In 1377, 1379 and 1381, everyone above the age of 14, 16 and 15 respectively, except beggars, had to pay a poll tax, but there was widespread evasion and resentment, so the lists are not reliable. The lists of names, in series E 179, are, like those for the lay subsidies, written in Latin, and are organized by county, administrative division, and then by town, village or hamlet. Occasionally they reveal family relationships between inhabitants, or their occupations. The lists have been published in *The Poll Taxes of 1377, 1379 and 1381*, edited by C.C. Fenwick. Poll taxes were revived in 1640 and levied at infrequent intervals between 1660 and 1698. Surviving nominal parish lists of payers over the age of 16, excluding paupers, are preserved in series E 179. These are written in English.

Other 17th-century poll tax lists are in county record offices. You can find out which these are from *The Hearth Tax, Other Later Stuart Tax Lists and the Association Oath Rolls*, by J. Gibson.

Finding aids

Some early feudal aids and lay subsidies have been published. For feudal aids, look in the index to *Feudal Aids 1284–1431*, and for published lay subsidies search *Texts and Calendars, an Analytical Guide to Serial Publications*, by E.L.C. Mullins, in two parts, and for those printed after 1982, consult **www.rhs.ac.uk**.

Use the online E 179 database at **www.nationalarchives.gov.uk/e179** to see what dated lists have survived for the places in which you are interested, and what their document references are.

At least one published transcription of the names of householders instead answerable to the Hearth Tax in the 1660s is now available for most counties. You can find out about most of these in *The Hearth Tax, Other Later Stuart Tax Lists and the Association Oath Rolls*.

What if you can't find your ancestor?

• There is no extant list. Many of the assessments and returns of actual payments are fragmentary, undecipherable or in a poor condition. Widen your scope in case you can pick up other entries of the surname in the same district. Use a map to mark up which places you have examined, found references to your surname or drawn blanks, and to show for which places lists are missing. Search lists for earlier and later years for evidence of surname continuity. Scrutinize the wills of other inhabitants during the period your last known forebear was there in case there might be references to your family as kinsfolk, neighbours or friends. Many published nominal indexes to wills include discrete indexes to places of abode, especially those produced by the British Record Society Index Library.

• Your ancestor's name is missing but you know he or she lived there. His or her wealth might have been insufficient to attract tax. He or she might have been a tax evader, belonged to someone else's household, died, moved away, or suffered temporary financial loss or fall in wages. Try the tax lists of surrounding years. Scour the tax lists of contiguous places, because you might find other liable members of the family nearby. Consult other sources, such as parish registers and wills.

Other tax lists in the National Archives

Records of the various weekly and monthly assessed taxes collected between 1642 and 1660 are in SP 28/196–204, and between about 1680 and 1689 in series E 179. The lists in series SP 28 are listed alphabetically county by county. The parish lists in series E 179 can be individually identified from the database at **www.nationalarchives.gov.uk/e179**.

The contribution for the relief of the king's distressed subjects in Ireland, in 1642 was 'voluntary', so the names of many other people besides householders are included in the returns in SP 28/191–5 and in series E 179, alongside the sums they contributed. The former series is listed alphabetically only by county. For document references to the Hundreds and parishes in series SP 28, you will need to find the bound paper catalogue and consult the typescript list at the front for original document references. You can extract document references for individual parishes in series E 179 from the above online database. The parochial lists of names of contributors to the 'free and voluntary present' to King Charles II in 1662, are also in series E 179.

The myriad taxes gathered in almost yearly after 1689 and up to 1830 seem to have merited few preserved name lists other than those in series E 182. This series largely consists of the names of exempt people, certificates drawing attention to those in arrears or default of payment, with a possible explanation ('gone away', 'died') and indicating whether their goods had been seized and sold to recover the due sums (a practice known as 'distraint'). Roman Catholics, aliens and denizens with only partial rights as British citizens, were subject to double taxation, so lists of their names may survive too, in series E 182. Sometimes, names of taxpayers surface in this series for particular dates for counties such as Middlesex, and a few receipts of the names of people in arrears of payment of Income Tax in 1799, 1803–16, and of the Land Tax are included. Sadly, the bundles of papers in E 182 remain to be catalogued in depth, but their potential is huge.

Some early personal-name lists of Land Tax payers are in series E 182. The earliest date from 1689, and specify exactly on what source of wealth (to 1698 on public offices, annual wages or income from land) each person was taxed. In 1798, owners of land in England and Wales ceased to be chargeable if it was worth less than a pound a year in rent. In 1798, too, it became possible for a landowner to exonerate himself from future liability for the tax by paying a lump sum equalling 15 years' tax, or to redeem any further payment by the purchase of 3 per cent consols in government stock, which yielded an annuity exceeding the calculated tax by a fifth. Nominal lists of landowners and occupiers, setting out their individual tax assessments in that year, are in series IR 23. The lists are arranged by county, Hundred and Land Tax parish (which does not always coincide with ecclesiastical or Tithe boundaries). You can use our online catalogue to find original document references only for each county. Written against the names of people exonerating or redeeming themselves from any future claims are the registered contract numbers and dates, which can then be matched up with the registered copies of the contracts signed between 1799 and 1963, in series IR 24. The catalogue for IR 24 is organized by contract number. The contracts themselves often reveal far more than the mere list of taxpayers compiled in 1798. You can find details about redemptioners' names and those of occupiers of relevant property, the amount of tax which was redeemed and the contract registration numbers from the parish books of redemptions between 1799 and 1953, which are listed alphabetically under each English and Welsh county, then by Land Tax parish, in series IR 22.

Following an Act of 1794, Roman Catholics paying double tax were able to appeal against overpayment, and the paperwork relating to allowed and disallowed claims after 1828 is in IR 23/122–6. The appeals are listed by county. Some certificates of Land Tax returns relating to Catholics are also included in the registrations of Papists' Estates, 1723–1725, in series E 174.

For details about the tax on apprenticeship indentures between 1710 and 1811, see **APPRENTICESHIP RECORDS**.

There are a few lists in series T 47 of names of taxpayers assessed on their ownership of wheeled vehicles between 1753 and 1766, on silver plate from 1756 to 1762, and on the number of their male servants in 1780. The lists are arranged alphabetically by county or county borough, then by initial-alphabetical index of surname, giving the residence, basis of liability and the amount of tax paid by each householder.

For Death Duties 1796–1903, see **DEATH DUTY REGISTERS**.

To find out more, read our Research Guides:
Taxation Records before 1689
Roman Numerals, How to Read Them
Hearth Tax, 1662–1689
Apprenticeship Records as Sources for Genealogy
Death Duty Records, From 1796; and
M. Beresford, *Lay Subsidies and Poll Taxes*
R.W. Hoyle, *Tudor Taxation Records*
M. Jurkowski, C.L. Smith and D. Crook, *Lay Taxes in England and Wales 1188–1688*.

Wills and other probate records

Continuous runs of formally approved English wills stretch back to the 13th century. Most of the surviving early ones belong to the nobility, magnates and rich merchants, but by the 19th century wills were being made by all ranks of society.

Strictly speaking, a will deals with a person's real estate (realty) and a testament with his or her personal property (personalty). Probate courts have authority only over personalty, but for convenience, the two documents are combined together. Before 1858, there were hundreds of probate courts, where wills were taken by executors (usually appointed in the will) for approval so that they could carry out the deceased testators' instructions concerning the final distribution of his or her possessions. If there was no will, then the next of kin or chief creditor of the deceased could apply to the court for a grant of letters of administration to authorize the disposal of the personal estate. In cases of intestacy, the dead person's land automatically passed to the next heir under civil law. The heir-at-law was the nearest blood relative, beginning with the son, whereas the next of kin, who was entitled to the personal estate on intestacy, started with the spouse.

The chief church courts in England and Wales were the Prerogative Court of York (PCY), covering the northern dioceses, and the Prerogative Court of Canterbury (PCC), responsible for dioceses south of the River Trent, and for property held in Wales or by people overseas, including that of soldiers and sailors dying on active duty and leaving property over a certain value. After 1815, only the probate records of seamen who were owed £20 or more in pay arrears will be found in the PCC. Wills of people of small means tended to be proved in one of the local courts. It is important to check which courts will be relevant, from the lowest to the highest court.

To discover which courts served the places where your ancestors lived and had property, look at the county maps in *The Phillimore Atlas and Index of Parish Registers*, edited by C.R. Humphery-Smith, and then consult *Probate Jurisdictions: Where to Look for Wills*, by J. Gibson and E. Churchill, to learn their whereabouts and those of any indexes, some of which are available online. Original and registered office copies of PCY wills and administration grants from 1389 until 1858 are held in the Borthwick Institute of Historical Research, in the University of York. You can search the indexes to PCY wills between 1389 and 1500 at **www.originsnetwork.com**, which offers a subscription service. Original wills in PCC from about 1600, and registered office copies from 1384 until 1858 are in the National Archives, along with registered grants of letters of administration from 1559 to 1858.

Since 11 January 1858, when the church and other probate courts were abolished, wills have been approved and administration grants made either in the Principal Probate Registry (originally called the Court of Probate), in London, or in local District Probate Registries (see p. 26).

Before 1882, a wife could only make a will with her husband's written consent. Thenceforward, until 1892, any will made by a woman married after 1 January 1883 had to be re-executed on her husband's death. A way of circumventing the earlier restriction was to bestow some property on a new wife for her sole benefit by means of a marriage settlement, to which her husband was a party and one of the trustees. His own will might then refer to the date and contents of this settlement. The settlement provided for what would happen on the wife's death or remarriage, so that she might actually have no personal rights over its future ownership. Surviving copies of such settlements may be located in family and estate papers, among or cited in legal proceedings (see **LEGAL PROCEEDINGS: CIVIL ACTIONS**), and in local record office collections. For the whereabouts and dates of listed family and estate papers visit **www.nationalarchives.gov.uk/nra** and key in the family name or that of the estate in which you are interested.

For more information, read K. Grannum and N. Taylor, *Wills and Other Probate Records, a Practical Guide for Researching Your Ancestors' Last Documents.*

What will you find?

Wills only take effect after a person's death. They are made to ensure the testator's possessions go to the people he or she wants, and often express a wish for burial in a particular parish churchyard, and for gifts to be made to specific charities. Wills can tell us a lot about our ancestors' emotional lives and attitudes at the time they were drawn up. From the date of the will we can learn which beneficiaries were then alive, which might not be the case when the will was proved. Conversely, the testator might refer to relatives who were already dead. A will might record the date, terms and conditions of a marriage settlement, the inheritance or purchase of a freehold estate or occupancy of copyhold land which after 1540 and 1815 respectively could be devised to someone other than the next legal heir. Freehold and copyhold land did not need to be mentioned in a will, as freeholds otherwise passed to the nearest blood relative (sons and male descendants first), and copyholds according to the custom of the relevant manor.

Wills made by people resident or absent overseas or settlers in the New World with connections in England or Wales, merit scrutiny to see to whom they left their property. Refer to *American Wills and Administrations in the Prerogative Court of Canterbury, 1610–1857,* by P.W. Coldham for indexed abstracts, and *American Wills proved in London, 1611–1775,* by the same compiler, for abstracts of wills in the London probate courts.

You can read indexed digital images of the registered copies of PCC wills and appended probate grants in series PROB 11, at **www.nationalarchives. gov.uk/documentsonline**.

Each will begins with the testator's name, any alias, current place of residence, status or occupation, the date when it was drawn up, revoking any previous will and expressing his or her soundness of mind, and, occasionally, present state of physical health. It was signed or marked at the end by the testator, and by at least two witnesses in his or her presence. It was the latest dated will which was acted upon. There might, however, be any number of dated, similarly signed and witnessed codicils (modifications or additions), but each of these had to be attached to the original will and clearly refer to it and the date it was made.

Appended to the end of the will is the probate grant, giving its date, where and by whom the grant was issued, the name, last abode and occupation of the deceased, and the executors' names, addresses and any family relationship to the deceased. Sometimes the court had to intervene and make an appointment if an executor was already dead, absent abroad, unwilling to act, under the age of 21, or the testator had failed to nominate anyone. Such a person was usually the residuary legatee, who received the balance of the estate once all the debts and legacies had been paid. The documentation was then called an administration with will annexed ('A with W annexed'). In such cases, the Probate Acts were written up into the Probate Act Books, in series PROB 8 (1526–1858), or in the Limited Probate Act Books in series PROB 9 (1781, 1800, 1802–04, and 1806–58), and the will itself was registered in series PROB 11. Up to 1650, and from 1661 to 1733, the probate details are recorded in Latin.

It was possible for a person to dictate instructions on the disposal of his or her estate if death was imminent or they could not be written down. Such nuncupative wills required at least two credible witnesses, who repeated them to the court. A nuncupative will begins with the words 'Memorandum quod…'.

Original wills filed in PCC from 1620 to 1858 are in series PROB 10, which also includes wills proved in Oxford between 1643 and 1646 during the period of civil unrest, and other wills that were not registered.

When a will had been written by the testator himself or herself, rather than by a lawyer or scrivener, this was known as a holograph. If this happened and the will had not been properly witnessed or there was some other legal irregularity, friends and associates of the deceased would be called upon by the probate court to identify his or her handwriting, and to testify to the length of their acquaintanceship. The will, and the registered copy of it, in series PROB 11, was then endorsed with details of the sworn declarations.

Because the law on intestacy was very strict, you can quickly find out from the grants of letters of administration made by the probate courts who was the closest living relative to the deceased. The wife was deemed to be the nearest next of kin. She was entitled to a third of the personal estate and the deceased's legitimate children shared the rest in equal portions. If there was no widow, then the children received the personal estate in equal portions, grandchildren taking any deceased child's share. If there were none of these, next in line came the parents of the deceased, then uncles and aunts (or their descendants if any were already dead), then grandparents, then great-uncles and -aunts (or their descendants if already dead), then the chief creditor.

Registered microfilmed copies of grants of letters of administration, also called 'admons', authorized by the PCC between 1559 and 1858, are in series PROB 6. The grants were written in Latin until 1733, except for the period 1651 until 1660, when, like later grants, they were composed in English. Each grant delivers the date, intestate's name, last place of residence, occupation and marital status at the time of death, followed by the name, address, occupation and relationship to him or her of the next of kin appointed to act as administrator, and who was entitled to the personal possessions remaining once all the debts had been settled. From 1792, a personalty valuation was added, because of the introduction of a tax on deceased's estates, which eventually became Legacy Duty in 1796. The valuation was based on the submission by the administrator of an inventory of the

PROB 1/20: Part of the original will of Thomas Gainsborough, the artist, made in May 1788. It was signed at the bottom of each page, as required. He died in August the same year, and the will was proved in the Prerogative Court of Canterbury later that month.

deceased's assets and a set of final probate accounts showing how much remained to be distributed once all the bills and debts had been paid. This documentation was filed separately in the PCC. From 1719 until 1743, the registered entries are arranged successively by month, for people whose surnames start with the same letter of the alphabet, then under the name of the clerk of one of five regional Seats, but from 1744 onwards the arrangement is by Seat, then successively by month, and under the names of people whose surnames start with the same letter of the alphabet. Entries recorded in the Registrar's Seat, at the beginning of each yearly volume, relate to grants made after litigation, and to estates of people dying outside the jurisdiction of the PCC.

An adminstration grant *de bonis non* ('admon. d.b.n.') means that another administrator had been appointed by the court to distribute goods left unadministered by the previous administrator owing to his or her death.

Limited or special grants of administration in the PCC were recorded up to 1809 in the Administration Act Books in series PROB 6. Limited grants applied to a certain part of a person's estate, whereas special grants might have certain conditions attached. Microfilmed copies of later limited and special grants up to 1858 are in series PROB 7, and are arranged by year and Seat like the grants in series PROB 6.

Finding aids   Search the free online indexes to the digital images of registered copies of Prerogative Court of Canterbury wills in series PROB 11 at **www. nationalarchives.gov.uk/documentsonline**, then go straight to the digital image. A copy of the probate grant is appended at the end of each will.

There are also printed indexes to the registered copies of PCC wills in series PROB 11 and Probate Act Books in series PROB 8. The volumes have been produced by the British Record Society as part of its Index Library publications. They cover the period 1384–1700 and are widely available. The printed indexes give the testator's name, status or occupation and place of abode at the time the will was made, and when the will was proved, the date of probate, plus the register volume's given name for that probate year, and its quire reference in series PROB 11. A quire is a gathering of 16 pages, or 8 folios.

To locate a PCC administration grant earlier than 1701, consult the printed Index Society indexes from 1559 to 1660, then the microfilmed annual manuscript initial-alphabetical indexes in series PROB 12 to 1700. There are microfiche indexes to both PCC wills and administration grants for the years 1701 to 1749, which give full PROB 11 and PROB 6 references. For the years between 1750 and 1800 you can search the index to wills either on microfiche or online at **www.originsnetwork.com**. At present there is only one typescript index to PCC administration grants for this latter period, which is kept on the open shelves in the Family Records Centre. You will need to search the annual manuscript initial-alphabetical indexes in series PROB 12 from 1751 to 1858 on microfilm in our Microfilm Reading Room or the bound copies of this series from 1801 up to 1858 on the open shelves in the Family Records Centre. The indexes include the limited and special grants in series PROB 6 and PROB 7.

Be careful when studying the indexes in series PROB 12, because it is easy to confuse the lists of wills with those of administration grants, which follow. Remember as well that the entries are not strictly alphabetical, but are arranged sequentially by month of probate or administration grant within each year, then chronologically by surnames beginning with the same letter. The admon entries supply the intestate's name, county of death, and month when the grant was made.

What if you can't find your ancestor?

• It has been reckoned that less than 10 per cent of the population left wills that were taken to court for probate. See if there was an administration grant instead of a will. Even then, not everyone's personal estate was distributed with formal court approval. Until relatively recently the most valuable possession a person had was the house he or she occupied, but this might be merely rented.

• You didn't search a long enough period. Wills were not always proved within the first six months after death. If you are relying on a burial date for someone as your starting point, work forwards from this for up to 15 years.

• You didn't check any addenda for surnames beginning with certain letters of the alphabet which were inserted at the end of the annual main lists in series PROB 12.

• Don't forget, that until 1 January 1752, the first day in the year was 25 March, so any probate or administration before this listed as say in 1740 and falling between 1 January and 24 March, will actually be in 1741 New Style.

• The will might have been proved in a different court. Look at Gibson and Churchill's *Probate Jurisdictions: Where to Look for Wills* for guidance. You could also try the microfilmed annual indexes in series IR 27 to the Death Duty registers from 1796 to 1903 in series IR 26 for abbreviated details of when and where probate occurred. See **DEATH DUTY REGISTERS**. All the wills and administration grants approved in England and Wales from 11 January 1858 onwards are filed in the Principal Probate Registry in London.

• Women did not often leave wills before 1882, because of the law affecting the status of married women and their property. However, wills of unmarried females in your family can shed light on the numerous relatives they frequently wished to benefit.

• Remember to look for the wills and administration grants of maternal kinsfolk too, as they were related to your family as equally as the paternal line.

• Not all of a person's children might be mentioned in his or her will – if earlier provision had been made, offspring might be given a token legacy of maybe a shilling, which thus didn't invariably indicate disfavour. Wills often made financial provision for a capital sum to be invested and the interest spent on the maintenance and education of infants under the age of 7, minors and single daughters until the age of 21 or marriage. Sometimes children as yet unborn were provided for too. If the will was proved between 1796 and 1903, then see **DEATH DUTY REGISTERS**.

• You can't locate the administration grant. Have you looked at the correct Seat? The catalogue from 1744 onwards gives the folio references for each one, plus a list of counties and the number of the Seat each belonged to. If the grant was limited or special after 1810, it will be found in series PROB 7, though listed in series PROB 12. The arrangement of the entries in series PROB 7 is by year, then by Seat.

Other probate records in the National Archives

Try the Death Duty registers from 1796 to 1903 for extra information. The National Archives holds a series of Army, Royal Navy and Royal Marine wills too. These concern assets of too small a value to be dealt with by the PCC and examples of soldiers' wills are placed amongst the army casualty returns from the early 19th century onwards in WO 25/1359–2410, and WO 25/3251–3471, which list the debts, personal effects and credits owing to the estates of the deceased. They are catalogued by regiment, and cover the period 1841 to 1968. For wills and administration grants found amongst the personal papers of army officers between 1755 and 1881, consult WO 42/1–51 (arranged alphabetically). Naval men could make arrangements for the disposal of their outstanding pay after death, so there are many surviving wills and administration grants for ordinary seamen as well as officers. These are to be discovered among records of the relevant probate courts (see p. 175). Other naval wills for the period 1800–60 are in series ADM 44 and relate to the estates of ratings. They are indexed in series ADM 141. Details about probates on the estates of deceased naval officers between 1830 and 1860 are in series ADM 45, to which there is an incomplete set of index cards in our Research Enquiries Room. Probate registers relating to the estates of Royal Naval ratings, other ranks in the Royal Marines and warrant officers between 1836 and 1915, and which affected the payment of pensions, are listed by date order in series PMG 50. Wills of naval ratings and other ranks in the Royal Marines, and warrant officers from 1786 to 1882 are in ADM 48/1–107 to which the registers between 1786 and 1861, in ADM 142/1–14, serve as personal-name indexes. These were lodged with the Navy Pay Office to prevent fraudulent claims relating to their personal effects and wages. Registers of Naval law wills from 1862 until 1909 are in ADM 142/15–9. The indexes are arranged according to the first letter of a surname, then the first vowel (including 'y' under 'i'), and finally, by the first consonant. A register of wills and administration grants of Royal Marines between 1740 and 1764 is in ADM 96/524. Other seamen's wills were taken for probate to the Commissary Court of London, whose records are in the Corporation of London Guildhall Library.

Probate inventories were prepared by at least three relatives or neighbours very soon after death, to protect the deceased's personal estate from theft and fraud, and to defend the executors or administrators from false claims. Inventories were required by the probate court by a specified date so that the estate could be quantified. They are obviously a useful pointer to when and where a person died and was probably interred. The appraisors itemized and assigned a probate value to all the household goods, domestic utensils, work tools, contents of barns and outbuildings, crops and livestock belonging to the deceased, drew up a list of debts owing, estimated the value of any leasehold property and counted up the total amount of loose cash. The assets were then totted up. Surviving PCC inventories are preserved in several series: PROB 2 includes those filed between 1417 and 1660, PROB 3 contains inventories for the year 1702, and others filed between 1718 and 1782, PROB 4 covers the period 1661 to 1720, PROB 5 (1643 to 1836, though most date between 1661 and 1732), PROB 31 (among court exhibits in cases where wills were disputed) from 1722 up to 1858, and PROB 32 (in files of court exhibits) from 1658 to 1723. These all have to be ordered as original documents. There are online personal-name indexes to PROB 2, PROB 3, PROB 4, PROB 5 and PROB 32, which also furnish the place, county and date of the inventory. For series PROB 31 references, consult the indexes in PROB 33/2–36, which are listed by date ranges. There is also a card index in our Research Enquiries Room up to about 1840 for series PROB 31. This is arranged in two parts: by personal-name, and by place-name. The place-name index is by English county, and then for places in Wales, Scotland, Europe, Africa, America, Asia and by ships' names.

Probate inventories are not a true guide to the exact final value of someone's personal estate, because the executors or administrators subsequently prepared and lodged probate accounts with the court by a given deadline. The accounts set out all their necessary disbursements such as the settlement of any debts or financial claims against the deceased, payments of medical bills, funeral costs, outstanding rent and/or rates and taxes, plus the receipts of moneys into the estate, and the deceased's capitalized or valued investments, and recorded the payment of the various legacies to achieve an ultimate residual estate value. They reveal who actually was still alive and received their legacies. You can find some PCC probate accounts filed with the inventories in series PROB 2 (1417–1660) and PROB 5 (1643–1836), and as court exhibits in series PROB 31 (1722–1858) and PROB 32 (1658–1723), described above, and among the cause papers in series PROB 37 (1783–1858), outlined below.

The card index to inventories in series PROB 31 also provides references to the probate accounts in series PROB 37, and runs up to about 1840.

If there was a lawsuit (called a cause) involving a person's will, the indexes in PROB 12 will carry a note against the relevant entry to say it was proved 'by sent' (by sentence of a church court), or 'by decr' (by decree of the Court of Chancery). The registered copy of the will should bear a brief marginal summary specifying the names of the litigants and the court's decision, together with the date. There may be a great deal of documentation to read through, often casting valuable insight into the circumstances under which a particular will was drawn up, and highlighting family relationships and tensions. All of the PCC lawsuits are written in Latin before 1733, except for the period 1651 to 1660, when English was used. The libels (allegations) of the plaintiffs, in series PROB 18 (1661–1858), and the answers of the respondents, in series PROB 25 (1664–1854), the cause papers from 1641 to 1722, in series PROB 28, and from 1783 to 1858 in series PROB 37, give you full details about each case as it unfolded. You can search the card indexes in our

Research Enquiries Room to the titles of causes, which are cross-referenced to the names of testators and intestates, and the indexes to the names of the deceased, which are included in the libels in series PROB 18. The volumes in series PROB 25 are self-indexed by cause title up to 1718 and between 1765 and 1787, and by the name of the respondents from 1726 to 1764. The catalogue to this series merely sets out date coverage. For PROB 28, there is a published list of cause titles and the names of the deceased, in *List and Index Society*, volume 161, a copy of which is available in our Library and Resource Centre. You can search the online catalogue to the cause papers in series PROB 37 for the personal-names of all the parties and of the deceased, and by place-name and date. An outline of each cause can also be constructed from the Acts of Court Books, in series PROB 29, which relate to the years 1536 to 1819, and the Acts of Court between 1740 and 1858, in series PROB 30, though the entries from 1740 to 1818 are duplicated by those in series PROB 29. There are integral indexes to PROB 29, arranged by the name of the plaintiff, rather than that of the deceased. For later court decisions and judgements up to 1858, in PROB 30/251–440, you will need to thread your way through the monthly bundles which are arranged alphabetically according to the name of the deceased.

The written sworn evidence extracted from witnesses (called depositions or cause papers) are usually the most interesting items. These will be found between 1657 and 1809 in series PROB 24, and from 1826 until 1858 in series PROB 26. Series PROB 26 is listed online by cause title and date. Court exhibits produced between 1653 and 1721 are in series PROB 36, and those between 1722 and 1858 are in series PROB 31. The online catalogue to series PROB 36 lists the name and last abode of each of the deceased, the cause title and its date, whereas series PROB 31 is catalogued merely by cause number and date. To match these numbers up with the cause titles you will need to seek out the annotated copies of the yearly indexes to this series on the open shelves in our Map and Large Document Room. These are arranged by the names of the testators and intestates, and bring together all the exhibits relating to each disputed estate.

Appeals against probate court decisions went to the Court of Arches, whose records are held by Lambeth Palace Library, in London. For brief abstracts of appeals see *Index of Cases in the Records of the Court of Arches at Lambeth Palace Library 1660–1913*, edited by J. Houston. Further appeal lay to the High Court of Delegates, until this was replaced by the Judicial Committee of the Privy Council in 1834. We hold records of appeals in the High Court of Delegates and the resulting probate grants prior to 1834 in series DEL 1 (starting in 1609), DEL 7 (from 1796), and DEL 2 (from about 1600). Series DEL 1 is indexed online, outlining the names of the parties to each case, the type of litigation initiated and the date, whilst series DEL 7 is indexed in date order in IND 1/10323. Series DEL 2 is listed online by case title and date. Probate inventories produced as exhibits to the court between 1665 and 1771 are in DEL 8/60, and are listed online by deceased's name, place of abode, type of case and date. The cause papers from 1624 to 1766 are in DEL 8/74–8, which are listed online by case title. All of the foregoing series were written in Latin up to 1733, and you will need to order them as original documents. Appeals to the Privy Council can be tracked down in series PCAP 1 (1834–80) and PCAP 2 (1833–78). You can search the online catalogue to PCAP 1 for the appellants' names and addresses, plus those of the respondents, and the dates of appeals.

Litigation might be instigated both in the church and civil courts, so it is worth trawling the records of each. See **LEGAL PROCEEDINGS: CIVIL ACTIONS** for how to find Chancery proceedings. For 17th-century cases, consult *Indexes to Disputed Wills in Chancery*, compiled by P.W. Coldham. This is also searchable online at **www.originsnetwork.com**.

To find out more, read our Research Guides:
Probate Records
Wills before 1858: Where to start
Wills and Death Duty Records after 1858.

Some general comments and advice

This guide is not designed for you to read from cover to cover, though congratulations if you have! It is a dip-book, an introductory and practical overview of the major family history sources in the National Archives, at Kew. I have ranged over a series of subject areas, showing how you can find those records which will be genealogically most productive, get to them quickly and easily, understand and interpret what they are trying to convey, and then move on. Since there are rarely swift and ready answers I have suggested other resources you might try, have outlined other research avenues you can pursue, and further reading to help you to expand your knowledge and think of new ideas on where to look next.

It would be impossible for this book to capture the vast body of other material in our archives which contains the names, activities and movements of people in the past, though generally not their births, marriages and deaths. For example, I have excluded references to our sources about the institution of beneficed Anglican clergy to their livings, some of our holdings relating to lawyers, our records about nurses, teachers, members of the Royal Household and Royal Warrant-holders, the Women's Land Army, bankrupts, patents of invention, New Poor Law records after 1834, registered designs and trademarks, and a host of other topics. Because the release of government documents to the public is a continuing programme, the best way of keeping abreast of newly accessible material is to check our monthly online newsletter at **www.nationalarchives.gov.uk/enewsletter**, search our online catalogue at **www.nationalarchives.gov.uk/catalogue**, and read (or better still, subscribe to) *Ancestors*, our monthly magazine. Don't neglect **www.nationalarchives.gov.uk/documentsonline** for newly accessible indexed digital images of some of the records of most value to you as a family historian, the special catalogues and databases at our website, and the indexed transcriptions and/or digital images at other websites, all work in progress and regularly updated as new ones are completed. Our online and on-site Research Guides, and our interactive 'How to...' leaflets are frequently reviewed and updated and essential reading.

In this fast-moving electronic age, it is easy to forget that we are engaged in the gentle art of patient original historical research. Not everything you will need to search is available on the internet, on CD-ROM or on microform. There are still millions of original records you will have to hunt down and wade through. You will struggle with unfamiliar handwriting styles, strange legal phrases, Latin abbreviations, curious dating schemes, and bizarre filing and 'indexing' systems. You will have to understand how the various government departments worked, and the frameworks of the different law courts. None of this can be achieved in a day, a week or a month, but is part of the excitement and challenge of family history. It is exacting work, so take it easy and don't demand too much of yourself each time you visit us. You will find yourself coming back again and again, gently easing yourself into the evolving National Archives system and familiarizing yourself with its treasure trove of historical material. Stick at it, don't get flummoxed, for you will be richly rewarded by your patience.

Further reading

Annal, D., *Using Census Returns* (PRO Publications, 2000)

Asplin, K.J. (comp.), *The Roll of the Imperial Yeomanry, Scottish Horse and Lovat's Scouts, Second Boer War, 1899–1902* (2 vols, Salisbury, 2000)

Atherton, L., *Never Complain, Never Explain: Records of the Foreign Office and State Paper Office, 1500–1960* (PRO Publications, 1994)

Atkins, P.J., *The Directories of London 1677–1977* (London, 1990)

Aylmer, G.E. and Morrill, J.S., *The Civil War and Interregnum* (London, 1979)

Bateson, C., *The Convict Ships 1788–1868* (Glasgow, 2nd edn 1969)

Baxter, C.J. (ed.), *General Muster and Land and Stock Muster of New South Wales, 1822* (Sydney, 1988)

Baxter, C.J. (ed.), *General Muster of New South Wales, 1814* (Sydney, 1987)

Baxter, C.J. (ed.), *General Muster of New South Wales, 1823, 1824, 1825* (Sydney, 1988)

Baxter, C.J. (ed.), *General Musters of New South Wales, Norfolk Island and Van Diemen's Land 1811* (Sydney, 1987)

Baxter, C.J. (ed.), *Musters of New South Wales and Norfolk Island, 1800–1802* (Sydney, 1988)

Baxter, C.J. (ed.), *Musters of New South Wales and Norfolk Island, 1805–1806* (Sydney, 1989)

Beech, G. and Mitchell, R., *Maps for Family and Local History, The Records of the Tithe, Valuation Office and National Farm Surveys of England and Wales, 1836–1943* (The National Archives, 2nd edn 2004)

Beresford, M.W., *The Lay Subsidies ... and the Poll Taxes of 1377, 1379 and 1381* (Canterbury, 1963)

Bevan, A., *Tracing your Ancestors in the Public Record Office* (PRO Publications, 6th rev. edn 2002, and new edn pending)

Blatchford, R. (ed.), *The Family and Local History Handbook* (Nether Poppleton, 9th edn 2005)

Breed, G.R., *My Ancestors were Baptists: How Can I Find Out More About Them?* (London, 4th edn 2002)

Burn, J.S., *History of the Fleet Marriages* (Rivington, 2nd edn 1834)

Butlin, N.G., Cromwell, C.W. and Suthern, K.L. (eds), *General Return of Convicts in New South Wales, 1837* (Sydney, 1987)

Cale, M., *Law and Society, an Introduction to Sources for Criminal and Legal History from 1800* (PRO Publications, 1996)

Calendar of the Committee for Advance of Money 1642–1656 (3 vols, HMSO, 1888)

Calendar of Proceedings of the Committee for Compounding 1643–1660 (5 vols, HMSO, 1889–93)

Charnock, J., *Biographia Navalis* (6 vols and index, London 1794–98)

Cheffins, R.H.A., *Parliamentary Constituencies and their Registers since 1832* (London, 1998)

Cheney, C.R., rev. by M. Jones, *A Handbook of Dates for Students of English History* (Cambridge, 1945, 2000)

Christian, P., *The Genealogist's Internet* (The National Archives, 3rd expanded edn 2005)

City Livery Companies and Related Organisations, a Guide to their Archives in Guildhall Library (Guildhall Library, 3rd edn 1989)

Clifford, D.J.H., *My Ancestors were Congregationalists in England and Wales: How Can I Find Out More About Them?* (London, 2nd edn 1997)

Coldham, P.W., *American Wills and Administrations in the Prerogative Court of Canterbury, 1610–1857* (Baltimore, 1989)

Coldham, P.W., *American Wills proved in London, 1611–1775* (Baltimore, 1992)

Coldham, P.W., *The Complete Book of Emigrants in Bondage 1614–1775* (Baltimore, 1987, Supplement, 1992)

Coldham, P.W., *Emigrants from England to the American Colonies 1773–1776* (Baltimore, 1988)

Coldham, P.W., *The Lives, Times and Families of Colonial Americans, who Remained Loyal to the British Crown* (Baltimore, 2000)

Colwell, S., *Dictionary of Genealogical Sources in the Public Record Office* (London, 1992)

Colwell, S., *The Family Records Centre, a User's Guide* (PRO Publications, 2002)

Colwell, S., *Family Roots, Discovering the Past in the Public Record Office* (London, 1991)

Connolly, W.P. and Vincent, U.A., *British Railways Pre-grouping Atlas and Gazetteer* (Shepperton, 5th edn 1967, repr. 1997)

Crowder, N.K., *British Army Pensioners Abroad, 1772–1899* (Baltimore, 1995)

Dalton, Sir C., *English Army Lists and Commission Registers, 1661–1714* (6 vols, London, 1892–1904)

Dalton, Sir C., *George I's Army, 1714–1727* (2 vols, London, 1910, 1912)

Edwards, C., *Railway Records, a Guide to Sources* (PRO Publications, 2001)

Ellis, M., *Using Manorial Records* (PRO Publications, 1997)

Fenwick, C.C. (ed.), *The Poll Taxes of 1377, 1379 and 1381 Pt I: Bedfordshire–Leicestershire; Pt II: Lincolnshire–Westmorland; Pt III: Wiltshire–Yorkshire* (British Academy, 1998, 2001, 2005)

Feudal Aids 1284–1431 (6 vols, HMSO, 1899–1921)

Fidlon, P.G. and Ryan, R.J. (eds), *The First Fleeters* (Sydney, 1981)

Filby, P.W. and Meyer, M.K. (eds), *Passenger and Immigration Lists Index, 1538–1900* (Detroit, 1981, with Supplements, 1982 onwards, P.W. Filby with various co-editors)

Fowler, S. and Spencer, W., *Army Records for Family Historians* (PRO Publications, 2nd rev. edn 1998)

Gandy, M., *Catholic Missions and Registers 1700–1880: vol. 1: London and the Home Counties; vol. 2: The Midlands and East Anglia; vol. 3: Wales and the West of England; vol. 4: North east England; vol. 5: North West England; vol. 6: Scotland* (London, 1993, vol. 5 rev. edn 1998)

Gandy, M., *Catholic Parishes in England, Wales and Scotland, an Atlas* (London, 1993)

Gibson, J., *The Hearth Tax, Other Later Stuart Tax Lists and the Association Oath Rolls* (Birmingham, 2nd edn 1996)

Gibson, J., *Quarter Sessions Records for Family Historians: A Select List* (Birmingham, 4th edn 1995)

Gibson, J. and Churchill, E., *Probate Jurisdictions: Where to Look for Wills* (Birmingham, 5th edn 2002)

Gibson, J. and Dell, A., *Tudor and Stuart Muster Rolls* (Birmingham, 1991)

Gibson, J. and Hampson, E., *Marriage and Census Indexes for Family Historians* (Birmingham, 8th edn 2000)

Gibson, J., Langston, B. and Smith, B.W., *Local Newspapers 1750-1920, England and Wales, Channel Islands, Isle of Man: A Select Location List* (Birmingham, 2nd edn 2002)

Gibson, J. and Medlycott, M., *Local Census Listings, 1522–1930: Holdings in the British Isles* (Birmingham, 2nd edn 1992)

Gibson, J. and Medlycott, M., *Militia Lists and Musters, 1757–1876* (Birmingham, 4th edn 2000)

Gibson, J., Medlycott, M. and Mills, D., *Land and Window Tax Assessments* (Birmingham, 2nd edn 1998)

Gibson, J. and Rogers, C., *Electoral Registers since 1832; and Burgess Rolls* (Birmingham, 2nd edn 1990)

Gibson, J. and Rogers, C., *Poll Books and Lists, c. 1696–1872: A Directory of Holdings in Great Britain* (Birmingham, 3rd edn 1994)

Gibson, J. and Rogers, C. (eds), *Poor Law Union Records: Pt 1: South-East England and East Anglia* (with C. Webb, Birmingham, 2nd edns 1997); *Pt 2: The Midlands and Northern England; Pt 3: South-West England, The Marches and Wales* (Birmingham, 2nd edn 1997)

Gibson, J. and Youngs, F.A., Jr, *Poor Law Union Records: Pt 4: Gazetteer of England and Wales* (Birmingham, 1993)

Giuseppi, M.S., *Naturalizations of Foreign Protestants in the American and West Indian Colonies, 1740–1772* (Huguenot Society of London, vol. XXIV, 1921)

Good, J.A., *A Register of Royal Marine Deaths, 1914–1919* (Royal Marine Historical Society, 1991)

Good, J.A., *A Register of Royal Marine Deaths, 1939–1945* (Royal Marine Historical Society, 1991)

Grannum, G., *Tracing your West Indian Ancestors* (PRO Publications, 2nd rev. edn 2002)

Grannum, K. and Taylor, N., *Wills and Other Probate Records, a Practical Guide to Researching your Ancestors' Last Documents* (The National Archives, 2004)

Grenham, J., *Tracing your Irish Ancestors: The Complete Guide* (Dublin, 2nd edn 1999)

Grieve, H.E.P., *Examples of English Handwriting 1150–1750* (Essex Record Office, 1954, 5th impression 1981)

Guildhall Library Research Guide 2: *The British Overseas: A Guide to Records of Births, Baptisms, Marriages, Deaths and Burials available in the UK* (London, 1995)

Hawkings, D.T., *Criminal Ancestors: A Guide to Historical Criminal Records in England and Wales* (Stroud, rev. edn 1996)

Hawkings, D.T., *Railway Ancestors, a Guide to the Staff Records of the Railway Companies of England and Wales 1822–1947* (Stroud, 1995)

Herber, M., *Clandestine Marriages in the Chapel and Rules of the Fleet Prison, 1680–1754* (3 vols, London, 1998–2001)

Herlihy, J., *The Royal Irish Constabulary: A Complete Alphabetical List of Officers and Men 1816–1922* (Dublin, 1999)

Herlihy, J., *The Royal Irish Constabulary: A Short History and Genealogical Guide with a Select List of Medal Awards and Casualties* (Dublin, 1997)

Hobson, C., *Airmen Died in the Great War* (Polstead, 1995)

Horwitz, H., *A Guide to Chancery Equity Records and Proceedings 1600–1800* (PRO Publications, 2nd edn 1998)

Horwitz, H., *Exchequer Equity Records and Proceedings 1649–1841* (PRO Publications, 2001)

Houston, J., *Index of Cases in the Records of the Court of Arches in Lambeth Palace Library, 1660–1913* (London, 1972)

Hoyle, R.W., *Tudor Taxation Records* (PRO Publications, 1994)

Hughes, R., *The Fatal Shore: A History of Transportation of Convicts to Australia, 1787–1868* (London, 1987)

Humphery-Smith, C.R. (ed.), *The Phillimore Atlas and Index of Parish Registers* (Chichester, 3rd edn 2003)

Ifans, D. (ed.), *Nonconformist Registers of Wales* (National Library of Wales and Welsh County Archivists Group, 1994)

Johnson, K.A. and Sainty, M.R. (eds), *Genealogical Research Directory, National and International* (Sydney, annual 1981–)

Joseph, A., *My Ancestors were Jewish: How Can I Find Out More About Them?* (London, 3rd edn 2002)

Jurkowski, M., Smith, C.L. and Crook, D., *Lay Taxes in England and Wales 1188–1688* (PRO Publications, 1998)

Kain, R.J.P. and Oliver, R.R., *The Tithe: Maps of England and Wales, Cartographic Analysis and County by County Catalogue* (Cambridge, 1995)

Kemp, T.J., *International Vital Records Handbook* (Baltimore, 4th edn 2000)

Kershaw, R., *Emigrants and Expats, a Guide to Sources on UK Emigration and Residents Overseas* (PRO Publications, 2002)

Kershaw, R. and Pearsall, M., *Immigrants and Aliens, a Guide to Sources on UK Immigration and Citizenship* (The National Archives, 2nd edn 2004)

Kirk, R.E.G. and Kirk, E.F. (eds), *Returns of Aliens Dwelling in the City and Suburbs of London from the Reign of Henry VIII to that of James I* (Huguenot Society of London, vol. X, 4 pts and index, 1900–8)

Kitzmiller, J.M., II, *In Search of the 'Forlorn Hope': A Comprehensive Guide to Locating British Regiments and their Records* (1640–WWI) (2 vols, Salt Lake City, 1988)

Leary, W., *My Ancestors were Methodists: How Can I Find Out More About Them?* (London, 2nd rev. edn, 1999)

Leeson, F.L., *A Guide to the Records of the British State Tontines and Life Annuities of the Seventeenth and Eighteenth Centuries* (Shalfleet Manor, 1968)

List of Officers of the Royal Regiment of Artillery, 1716–June 1914 (3 vols, London, 1899–1914)

Litten, J., *The English Way of Death: The Common Funeral since 1450* (London, 1991, repr. with corrections 2002)

Lumas, S., *Making Use of the Census* (PRO Publications, 4th rev. edn 2002)

McInnes, I. and Webb, J.V., *A Contemptible Little Flying Corps* (London, 1991)

Marshall, H., *Palaeography for Family and Local Historians* (Chichester, 2004)

Marshall, J.W., *Naval Biography* (12 vols and index, London, 1823–30)

Martin, C.T., *The Record Interpreter, a Collection of Abbreviations, Latin Words and Names used in English Historical Manuscripts and Records* (London, 1910, repr. 1994)

Mead, H. (ed.), *Change of Name* (London, 15th edn 1995)

Meller, H., *London Cemeteries, an Illustrated Guide and Gazetteer* (Brookfield, Vermont, 3rd edn 1994)

Milligan, E.H. and Thomas, M.J., *My Ancestors were Quakers: How Can I Find Out More About Them?* (London, 2nd edn 1999)

The Morton Allan Directory of European Passenger Steamship Arrivals (Baltimore, 1931, repr. 2001)

Mullins, E.L.C., *Texts and Calendars: An Analytical Guide to Serial Publications* (Royal Historical Society, 1958, repr. with corrections, 1978)

Mullins, E.L.C., *Texts and Calendars II: An Analytical Guide to Serial Publications 1957–82* (Royal Historical Society, 1983)

Newton, K.C., *Medieval Local Records, a Reading Aid* (London 1971, repr. 1986)

O'Byrne, W.R., *A Naval Biographical Dictionary* (Hayward, 1849, repr. 1986)

Outhwaite, R.B., *Clandestine Marriage in England 1500–1850* (London, 1995)

Page, W., *Denization and Naturalization of Aliens in England, 1509–1603* (Huguenot Society of London, vol. VIII, Lymington, 1893)

Pappalardo, B., *Royal Naval Lieutenants: Passing Certificates 1691–1902* (List and Index Society, vols 289 and 290, 2002)

Pappalardo, B., *Tracing Your Naval Ancestors* (PRO Publications, 2003)

Pappalardo, B., *Using Navy Records* (PRO Publications, rev. edn 2001)

Parry, G., *A Guide to the Records of Great Sessions in Wales* (Aberystwyth, 1995)

Peterkin, A., Johnston, W. and Drew, Sir W.R.M., *Commissioned Officers in the Medical Services of the British Army, 1660–1960* (2 vols, London, 1968)

Phillimore, W.P.W. and Fry, E.A., *An Index to Changes of Name, under Authority of Act of Parliament or by Royal Licence, and Including Irregular Changes, from I George III to 64 Victoria, 1760–1901* (London, 1905, repr. 1986)

Pugh, R.B., *The Records of the Colonial and Dominions Office* (London, 1964)

Raymond, S.A., *Monumental Inscriptions on the Web* (Bury, 2002)

Richards, T., *Was your Grandfather a Railwayman? A Directory of Railway Archive Sources for Family Historians* (Bristol, 4th edn 2002)

Richardson, J., *The Local Historian's Encyclopaedia* (New Barnet, 2nd edn 1989, repr. 1993)

Robson, L.L., *The Convict Settlers of Australia* (Carlton, Victoria, 2nd edn 1994)

Rodger, N.A.M., *Naval Records for Genealogists* (PRO Publications, 2nd edn 1998)

Roll of Officers of the Corps of Royal Engineers from 1660 to 1898 (London, 1898)

Ruston, A.R., *My Ancestors were English Presbyterians or Unitarians: How Can I Find Out More About Them?* (London, 2nd edn 2001)

Ryan, R.J., *The Second Fleet Convicts* (Sydney, 1982)

Sainty, M.R. and Johnson, K.A. (eds), *Census of New South Wales: November 1828* (Sydney, 1980)

Sharp, H., *How to Use the Bernau Index* (London, 2nd edn 2000)

Shaw, G. and Tipper, A., *British Directories: A Bibliography and Guide to Directories Published in England and Wales (1850–1950) and Scotland (1773–1950)* (London, 2nd edn 1997)

Shaw, W.A. (ed.), *Letters of Denizen and Acts of Naturalization for Aliens in England, 1603–1800* (Huguenot Society of London, vol. XVII, Lymington, 1911, vol. XXVII, Manchester, 1923, and vol. XXXV, London, 1932)

Sherman, A., *My Ancestor was a Policeman: How Can I Find Out More About Him?* (London, 2000)

Shorney, D., *Protestant Nonconformity and Roman Catholicism* (PRO Publications, 1996)

Smith, G., *Something to Declare: 1000 Years of Customs and Excise* (London, 1980)

Smith, K., Watts, C.T. and Watts, M.J., *Records of Merchant Shipping and Seamen* (PRO Publications, 1998)

Society of Genealogists, *The Trinity House Petitions* (London, 1987)

Spencer, W., *Air Force Records for Family Historians* (PRO Publications, 2000)

Spencer, W., *Army Service Records of the First World War* (PRO Publications, 3rd expanded edn 2001)

Spencer, W., *Records of the Militia and Volunteer Forces 1757–1945* (PRO Publications, 1997)

Steel, D.J., *National Index of Parish Registers, vol. II: Sources for Nonconformist Genealogy and Family History* (London, 1973)

Steel, D.J. and Samuel, E.R., *National Index of Parish Registers, vol. III: Sources for Roman Catholic and Jewish Genealogy and Family History* (including an index to vols I–III, London, 1974)

Steel, D.J. and various later editors, *National Index of Parish Registers* (London, 1966–)

Stone, L., *Road to Divorce: England, 1530–1987* (Oxford, 1995)

Stuart, D., *Latin for Local and Family Historians* (Chichester, 1995)

Tate, W.E., ed. M.E. Turner, *A Domesday of English Enclosure Acts and Awards* (Reading, 1978)

Thomas, G., *Records of the Royal Marines* (PRO Publications, 1995)

Thurston, A., *Records of the Colonial Office, Dominions Office, Commonwealth Relations Office and Commonwealth Office* (2 vols, London, 1995)

Watts, C.T. and Watts, M.J., *My Ancestor was a Merchant Seaman: How Can I Find Out More About Him?* (London, 2nd edn 2002)

Webb, W., *Coastguard: An Official History of H.M. Coastguard* (London, 1976)

Whitaker's Almanack (London, annual, 1869–)

Whyte, D., *A Dictionary of Scottish Emigrants to the U.S.A.* (Baltimore, 1972)

Willing's Press Guide (3 parts, Chesham, 2003)

Winder, R., *Bloody Foreigners, the Story of Immigration to Britain* (London, 2004)

Wise, T. and Wise, S., *A Guide to Military Museums and Other Places of Military Interest* (Knighton, 10th rev. edn 2001)

Wolfston, P.S., rev. by C. Webb, *Greater London Cemeteries and Crematoria* (London, 6th edn 1999)

Wrottesley, Sir G., *Pedigrees from the Plea Rolls 1200–1500* (London, *c.* 1900)

Useful addresses

Army Personnel Centre, Historic Disclosures, Mailpoint 400, Kentingern House, 65 Brown Street, Glasgow G2 8EX; tel: 0141 224 2023/3303

Association of Genealogists and Researchers in Archives, Joint Secretaries, 29 Badgers Close, Horsham, West Sussex RH12 5RU; website: *www. agra.org.uk*

Borthwick Institute of Historical Research, University of York, Heslington, York YO10 5DD; tel: 01904 321166; website: *www.york.ac.uk/inst/bihr*

British Empire and Commonwealth Museum, Clock Tower Yard, Temple Meads, Bristol BS2 6GH; tel: 0117 925 4980; website: *www.empiremuseum. co.uk*

The British Library, 96 Euston Road, London NW1 2DB; tel: 020 7412 7677 (reader admissions), 020 7412 7676 (reader information), 020 7412 7513 (manuscripts), 020 7412 7873 (Asia, Pacific and Africa Collections); websites: *http://catalogue.bl.uk* (printed books and other material), *www.bl.uk/ catalogues/manuscripts, www.bl.uk/collections/orientaloffice.html*

British Red Cross Society, Archive Section, Bamett Hill, Wonersh, Guildford, Surrey GU5 0RF

City of London Police Record Office, 26 Old Jewry, London EC2R 8DJ

College of Arms, Queen Victoria Street, London EC4V 4BT; tel: 020 7248 2762; website: *www.college-of-arms.gov.uk*

Corporation of London Guildhall Library, Aldermanbury, London EC2P 2EJ; tel: 020 7332 1868/1870 (printed books), 020 7332 1863 (manuscripts); website: *www.history.ac.uk/gh*

Court Funds Division, Chancery/Family Division, 22 Kingsway, London WC2B 6LE

Data Protection Cell (Navy), Building 1/152, Victory View, HM Naval Base, Portsmouth PO1 3PX; tel: 02392 727 381

DPS(N) 2, Building 1/152, Victory View, PP36, HM Naval Base, Portsmouth PO1 3PX; tel 02392 727 531

The Family Records Centre, 1 Myddelton Street, Islington, London, EC1R 1UW; tel: 020 8392 5300; website: *www.familyrecords.gov.uk/frc*

Federation of Family History Societies, PO Box 2425, Coventry, West Midlands CV5 6YX; email: *Info@ffhs.org.uk*; website: *www.ffhs.org.uk*

General Register Office (England and Wales), Certificate Services Section, PO Box 2, Southport, Merseyside PR9 2JD; tel: 0845 603 7788; fax: 01704 550013; website: *www.gro.gov.uk/gro/content*

General Register Office (Overseas Section), Smedley Hydro, Trafalgar Road,

Birkdale, Southport, Merseyside PR8 2HH; tel: 0151 471 4801; fax: 01633 652 988; website: *www.gro.gov.uk/gro/content*

General Register Office (Ireland), Government Offices, Convent Road, Roscommon, Eire; tel: 090 6632 900; fax: 090 6632 999; website: *www.groireland.ie*

General Register Office (Northern Ireland), Oxford House, 49–55 Chichester Street, Belfast BT1 4HL; tel: 02890 252000; website: *www.groni.gov.uk*

General Register Office for Scotland, New Register House, 3 West Register Street, Edinburgh EH1 3YT; tel: 0131 314 4433; website: *www.gro-scotland.gov.uk*

Guards Regimental Headquarters, Wellington Barracks, Birdcage Walk, London SW1E 6HQ

Home Office, Departmental Records Officer, Information and Record Management Services, 4th Floor, Seacole Building, Marsham Street, London SW1P 4DF

House of Lords Record Office, House of Lords, London SW1A 0PW; tel: 020 7219 5316; website: *www.parliament.uk/parliamentary_publications_and_archives/parliamentary_archives.cfm*

Immigration and Nationality Directorate, India Buildings, Water Street, Liverpool L2 0QN; tel: 0151 237 5200

Imperial War Museum, Lambeth Road, London SE1 6HZ; tel: 020 7416 5342; website: *www.iwm.org.uk*

International Council of the Red Cross, Archives Division, 19 Ave de la Paix, CH-1202, Geneva, Switzerland

Lambeth Palace Library, Lambeth Palace Road, London SE1 7JU; tel: 020 7898 1400; website: *www.lambethpalacelibrary.org*

The Law Society, 113 Chancery Lane, London WC2A 1PL; tel: 020 7242 1222; website: *www.lawsoc.org.uk*

Library and Archives Canada, 395 Wellington Street, Ottawa, ON K1A ON4; website: *www.collectionscanada.ca*

London Metropolitan Archives, 40 Northampton Road, London EC1R 0HB; tel: 020 7332 3820; website: *www.cityoflondon.gov.uk/Corporation/leisure_heritage/libraries_archives_museums_galleries/JAS/lma/lma.htm*

Maritime History Archive, Memorial University of Newfoundland, St John's, Newfoundland, Canada A1C 5S7; website: *www.mun.ca/mha*

Metropolitan Police Museum, c/o Room 1334, New Scotland Yard, Victoria Street, London SW1 0BG

The Middle East Centre, St. Antony's College, Oxford OX2 6JF

Ministry of Defence, PMA (CS) 2a(2)a (RAF officers) or PMA (CS) 2a(2)b (airmen), Building 248a, HQ RAF PTC, RAF Innsworth, Gloucester GL3 1EZ

Modern Records Centre, University of Warwick Library, Coventry, West Midlands CV4 7AL; tel: 024 7652 4219; website: *http://modernrecords.warwick.ac.uk*

The National Archives, Kew, Richmond, Surrey TW9 4DU; tel: 020 8876 3444; fax: 020 8878 8905; website: *www.nationalarchives.gov.uk*

National Archives of Ireland, Bishop Street, Dublin 8; tel: 003531 4072300; website: *www.nationalarchives.ie*

National Archives of Scotland, HM General Register House, Edinburgh, EH1 3YY; tel: 0131 535 1314; website: *www.nas.gov.uk*

National Council of Voluntary Child Care Organisations (NCVCCO), Unit 4, Pride Court, 80–82 White Lion Street, London N1 9PF; tel: 020 7833 3319; website: *www.ncvcco.org*

National Library of Wales, Department of Manuscripts and Records, Aberystwyth, Dyfed SY23 3BU; tel: 01970 632 800; website: *www.llgc.org.uk*

National Maritime Museum, Romney Road, Greenwich, London SE10 9NF; tel: 020 8858 4422; website: *www.nmm.ac.uk*

Naval Dockyards Society, c/o 44 Lindley Avenue, Southsea, Hampshire PO4 9NV; website: *www.hants.gov.uk/navaldockyard*

Naval Pay and Pensions (Accounts), 1F Centurion Building, Grange Road, Gosport, Hampshire PO13 9XA; tel: 02392 702 174

Newspaper Library, British Library, Colindale Avenue, London NW9 5HE; tel: 020 7412 7353; website: *www.bl.uk/catalogues/newspapers*

Principal Registry of the Family Division, Probate Searchroom, First Avenue House, 42–49 High Holborn, London WC1V 6NP; tel: 020 7947 7022 (probates); website: *www.hmcourts-service.gov.uk/cms/wills.htm*

Principal Registry of the Family Division; tel: 020 7947 6971 (divorces); website: *www.hmcourts-service.gov.uk/HMCSCourtFinder*

Public Record Office of Northern Ireland, 66 Balmoral Avenue, Belfast BT9 6NY; tel: 028 9025 5905; fax: 028 9025 5999; website: *www.proni.gov.uk*

Registry of Shipping and Seamen, PO Box 165, Cardiff CF4 5JA; tel: 029 2074 7333

Religious Society of Friends Library, Friends House, Euston Road, London NW1 2BJ; tel: 020 7663 1135; website: *www.quaker.org.uk*

Royal Air Force Museum, Department of Aviation Records (Archives), Hendon Aerodrome, Aerodrome Road, London NW9 5LL; tel: 020 8205 2266; website: *www.rafmuseum.org.uk*

Royal Courts of Justice, Room 81, Strand, London WC2A 2LL; tel: 020 7947 6656

Society of Genealogists, 14 Charterhouse Buildings, Goswell Road, London EC1M 7BA; tel: 020 7251 8799; website: *www.sog.org.uk*

TNT Archive Service (Navy Search), Tetron Point, William Nadin Way, Swadlincote, Derbyshire DE11 0BB; tel: 01283 227 911/913

York Probate Sub-Registry, The Chief Clerk, Postal Searches and Copies Department, 1st Floor, Castle Chambers, Clifford Street, York YO1 9RG abroad: births, marriages and deaths 60–3, 66, 96

Access to Archives (A2A) 9

accounts: probate 183; residuary 86–7

Act for the Relief of Disabled Seamen 134

Act of Toleration 1689 138

Acts of Court Books 184

Administration Act Books 180

administration grant *de bonis non* (admon d.b.n.) 180

administration grants (admons) 59, 84, 85, 86, 124, 178–81, 182

administration with will annexed (A with W annexed) 178

Admiralty Board of the Defence Council of the Ministry of Defence 158

Admiralty Dockyard Police 146

Advance of Money Committee 71, 72

advance ordering of documents 8, 16, 21

Adventure for Two Million 169

Adventurers for Lands in Ireland 71, 72

affidavits of due execution 34

Air Force Lists 149, 151, 152

Albert Medal 137

aliens 170, 174; declarations of alienage 103, 105; registration of 109

Aliens Act 1793 109

Aliens Act 1905 110

aliens' arrival certificates 107

Aliens Office 109

Aliens Order 1960 109

Aliens Registration Act 1914 109

Amalgamated Society of Railway Servants (ASRS) 147

American Loyalist Claims Commission 97

American Revolutionary War 97, 106

American wills 177

Ancestors 186

Ancient Deeds 128

Annual Criminal Registers 79, 81

annuities 85, 166–9

annulment 88

appeals (applications for mercy) 82

application forms (army officers) 49

apprenticeship records 32-5, 138

Arches, Court of 89, 112, 184

Army Lists 36, 41, 42, 50, 53, 149, 151, 156, 157

Army Officers Died in the Great War 50, 153

Army Personnel Centre, Glasgow 44, 46, 49, 50, 51, 54

Army Returns 40, 43, 48, 52

Army Roll of Honour 52

army service records 12, 22, 35–55; emigrants 99; First World War and later 43–51; immigrants 106; men and women in the army since 1921 51–2; militia, Yeomanry, Volunteers, Rifle Volunteers, Fencibles and Home Guard 52-5; 17th century to 1913 36–41; officers before 1914 41–3; officers in First World War 48–51; officers since 1 April 1922 51–2; soldiers 1914–20 44–8; soldiers' children 34–5; wills 182

articles of clerkship 34

Assize courts 77, 79, 87–8, 111

Association of Genealogists and Researchers in Archives (AGRA) 31

Association of Stokers, Locomotive Engineers and Firemen (ASLEF) 148

attestation forms (Marines) 154, 155

attorneys 34

Australia 68; emigrants to 98; transportation to 80–2

Australian Vital Records Index 62, 81, 96

Bank of England 166, 169
Banker's Almanack 169
baptism certificates (army officers) 42-3
baptisms 157; children born at sea 59; Nonconformists 138–42; parish registers 23–5
Baptists 138
beaded and leather weights 20
Belfast Gazette 29, 70
Belgian refugees 108
Bermuda 92
Bernau Index 114, 115
Bethnal Green Protestant Dissenters' Burying Ground 64
Big Brother Scheme 100
births 157; abroad 60–3, 96; Ireland 22; Nonconformists 138–42; Scotland 22; at sea 55–9, 93
Bishop of London 55, 60
Blackmansbury 167
Board of Admiralty 90, 154, 158
Board of Customs 73
Board of Ordnance 35
Board of Stamps 84, 87
Board of Trade 55, 56–7, 59, 66
Boer War 40, 54
borough record offices 31
Borthwick Institute of Historical Research, University of York 176
Bow Street Foot Patrol 144
Boyd's London Burials Index 25, 65
Boyd's Marriage Index 25, 121
British Citizenship 102
British Columbia 62
British Dependent Territories Citizenship 102
British Empire and Commonwealth Museum 144
British Isles Vital Records Index 24–5, 96, 122, 142
British Library 27, 44, 60, 63, 100, 122; Newspaper Library 30, 60, 76, 89, 99
British Nationality Act 1948 103
British Nationality Act 1981 102
British Overseas Citizenship 102
British Protected Person 102

British Railways 146
British Record Society Index Library 174, 180
British Subject 102
British War Medal 47, 50, 137
bulletin boards 107
Bunhill Fields Burial Grounds 64
burials: cemetery records 63–6; churchyard 63; Nonconformists 138–42; parish registers 23–5
Burma Office 100

cameras 19, 21
campaign medals *see* medals
Canada 62; emigrants to 99, 100
Capital Transfer Tax (Inheritance Tax) 84
Caribbean 60, 68
carucage and hidage 170
casualty returns 39
catalogues 8, 13, 21, 186; searching the catalogue 14–16
Catholic Record Society 140
cause papers 184
causes 183–5
cemetery records 63–6
Census of New South Wales 81
census returns 66–8, 95, 105, 107, 118, 147, 163; from colonies 68; Ireland 22–3
Central Criminal Court 77, 79, 121
Central Register of Seamen 131
certificates of arrival of aliens 107
certificates of competency: dockyard employees 90; Merchant Navy 129, 132–3, 134; Royal Navy 161, 163
certificates of residence 173
certificates of service: dockyard employees 90, 91; Merchant Navy 129, 132, 134; police 144–5
Chambers, J.M. 81, 99
Chancery, Court of 72, 115, 183, 185; civil proceedings 112–14, 115–17; entry books of decrees and orders 115–16; medieval ancestors 124, 125, 126
Chancery Masters' Exhibits 115
change of name 39, 69–70, 106

chapel registers 65, 138–43
Charter Rolls 126, 127
Chatham Chest 91
Chelsea Royal Hospital: Burial
  Ground 65; pensioners 36–7
Chester, Palatinate of 77, 79, 111
Child Migrant Central Information
  Index 100
children 11; apprenticeship records
  32–5; emigrants 92, 99–100;
  naturalization 101; wills and
  provision for 181–2
Children's Overseas Reception Board
  100
China Medal 164
Church of England: abolishment of
  70; *see also* church courts, parish
  registers
church courts 87, 89, 111–12, 183, 185
Church of Jesus Christ of Latter-day
  Saints 9
church memorials 127
City of London livery company
  records 33
City of London Police Record Office
  145
civil actions 111–17, 122
Civil War 70–3
clandestine marriages 120–2
Classis Lottery 169
Clergy Lists 28
clergy notebooks/registers 121
cloakroom 20
Close Rolls 69, 126, 127, 128
closure dates 18
Coast Life Savings Corps 75
Coast Prevention Force 74
Coast Watching Force 74
Coastguard 73–7
codicils 177
College of Arms 69, 122
colonial certificates of competency
  132
Colonial Office (CO) 60–1
colonial police 144
colonies, census returns from 68
Commander-in-Chief's Memoranda
  41–2

Commando Units 154
Commissary Court of London 182
commissioned officers: army 41–3,
  48–51, 51–2; Royal Marines 156–8;
  Royal Navy 159, 160–5
common law courts 111, 114
common repute 69, 70
Commonwealth Immigrants Act 1962
  102
competency certificates *see* certificates
  of competency
Compounding with Delinquents
  committee 71, 72
computer terminals, public access 19
Confidential Air Force List 149, 151
Congregationalists 138
conscription 43–4, 53
Consistory Court of London 87
consolidated funds (consols) 169, 175
consular returns 60–1
continuous service engagement books
  134, 159
continuous service number (CS) 160
convicts 79–80
copies of documents 11, 21
copyhold land 124, 177
Corporation of London Guildhall
  Library *see* Guildhall Library
Corps of Marines 154
Corps of Royal Military Artificers 35
'country wills' 86
county calendars 79
county committees 71–2, 170
county courts 87–8
county militia 35, 52–5, 128
county Quarter Sessions 33, 77, 79
county record offices 13, 24, 31
Court of Arches of the Archbishop of
  Canterbury 89, 112, 184
Court for Divorce and Matrimonial
  Causes 87
Court of Exchequer 115, 124, 125
court exhibits 184
Court of King's Bench (Crown Side)
  89
court leet 30, 124
Court of Requests 114–15, 124
Court of Star Chamber 115

Court of Wards and Liveries 126
courts: church courts 87, 89, 111–12,
    183, 185; civil courts 111–12,
    114–15; criminal courts 77–9;
    manorial courts 30, 77, 112, 124; *see
    also under individual courts*
crew lists 59, 134–6
crime 77–82; convicts 79–80;
    transportation 80–2; trials 77–9
criminal conversation (crim. con.) 89
Crockford's Clerical Directory 28–9
Crown Loyalists 97
Crown manors 30, 122–3, 124–5,
    170
Crown Minute Books 78, 79
Current Order Status screens 19
customs officers 83
Czech refugees 108

Data Protection Cell (Navy),
    Portsmouth 133, 149, 155, 157, 160,
    163
dates 123, 181
Death Duty registers 12, 84–7, 169,
    181, 182
deaths 137; abroad 60–3, 66, 96;
    Ireland 22; Royal Marines 157;
    Royal Navy 160, 163, 164–5;
    Scotland 22; at sea 55–9, 66, 93; war
    deaths *see* war deaths
Debt of Honour Register of the
    Commonwealth War Graves
    Commission 46, 47, 50, 63, 66, 152,
    156, 158, 165
deciphering documents 20–1
declarations of alienage 103, 105
decree nisi 87
deeds of enfeoffment 128
deeds poll 69–70
denizations 101, 102–4, 104–5
denizens, tax of 170, 174
deportees 110
depositions 113, 115, 184
description books: dockyard
    employees 90, 91; Royal Marines
    154, 155
Dictaphones 19
Dictionary of National Biography 29

digital images, indexed 9, 12, 13, 23,
    66, 67, 186
Directorate of Personnel Support
    (Navy), Swadlincote 91
directories of names 27–9
disablement pensions 40, 51, 134, 153,
    164
discharged merchant seamen 130–1
disputed wills 114
dissenters' chapels 24, 138–43
distraint 174
district probate registries (DPRs) 26,
    176
district registries 87–8, 89
Division of the Royal Marine Artillery
    (Blue Marines) 154
divorce *a mensa et thoro* 88
divorce petitions 87–90
dockyard employees 90–2
Document Reading Room 19, 20
Dominions Office 98
double taxation 110, 142–3, 170, 174
Dr Williams's Registry 24, 62–3, 142
Dublin Gazette 69, 70
Duchy of Lancaster 111, 112
Durham, Palatinate of 77, 79, 111
Dutch Walloons 108

Earl of Hardwicke's Act 1753 121
East India Company 100
East India Register 100
Edinburgh Gazette 29, 70
1837 Commission 139
electoral registers 27, 119, 120
emigrant labourers' applications 98
emigrants 92–101
Emigration Commission 98
Emigration Entry Books 98
employment voucher 102
enclosures 119
engineers 132
entry books (Chancery decrees and
    orders) 115–16
enumeration books 66–7
Equity Pleadings database 15, 114
equity suits 111–17
Estate Duty 84
Exact Searches 67

Exchequer, Court of 115, 124, 125
Excise Entry Papers 83
Excise Life Assurance and Benevolent Fund Society 84
excise officers 83–4
exemption certificates 172

family historians' societies 107–8
Family Records Centre 9, 10, 23, 27, 60–1, 63, 66, 67–8, 121, 136–7
Federation of Family History Societies 25, 108
feet of fines 128
Fencible Infantry and Cavalry 52–5
feudal aids 126, 170, 173
Feudal Aids 1284–1431 127, 173
final decrees 116
Finance Act 1909/10 118
Fine Rolls 126, 127
First World War 12, 29, 39, 56, 109, 152, 153; army records 43–51
fishing vessels 132
Fleet Air Arm (FAA) 149
'Fleet' marriages 120–2
foam wedges 20
food and drink 18
Foot Guards 44, 45, 49
Foreign Office (FO) 60–1; General Correspondence 109
foreign Protestant congregations 108, 140
forfeited estates 143
four-year search 26
Freedom of Information Act 2000 11, 17
freehold land 177
French refugees 108

gallantry awards 41, 50, 51–2, 153, 158
gaol calendars 78–9
Genealogical Research Directory, National and International 96, 107
General Railway Workers' Union (GRWU) 148
General Register Office for England and Wales 9, 10, 157; army records 40, 43, 48, 52; Consular Returns 60, 61; Marine Returns 55, 165; war deaths 48, 50–1, 52, 152, 157
General Register Office of Ireland 22
General Register Office (Northern Ireland) (GRONI) 22
General Register Office for Scotland 10
General Service Medal 47
German Lutherans 108
Gibson guides 13
good conduct medals 41, 52
Grants of Life Annuities Act 1776 168
gravestone inscriptions 65
Greenwich Royal Hospital 65, 75, 164, 165
Griffith's Primary Valuation of Ireland 23
Guards Regimental Headquarters 45, 49
Guildhall Library 28, 29, 59, 62, 138, 182

habitual criminals register 82
half-pay 43
Ham's Customs Year Book 83
Ham's Inland Revenue Year Book 83
Harleian Society 122
hearing problems 18
Hearth Tax 170, 171–3, 173
heir-at-law 176
hereditament numbers 118
hidage and carucage 170
High Court of Admiralty 112
High Court of Delegates 89, 112, 184–5
High Court of Justice 111, 115
Historial Manuscripts Commission 9
Holborn Lying-In Hospital 140
holographic wills 178
Holy Trinity Minories 121
Home Children database 100
Home Guard 52–5
Home Office 102, 103–4, 105, 106, 109
hospital records 31
House of Commons Journal 102
House of Lords Journal 102
House of Lords Record Office 87, 102

Household Battalion 38
Household Cavalry 45
'How to ...' leaflets 18, 21, 186
Huguenot refugees 108
Huguenot Society of London 108, 140

images, indexed digital 9, 12, 13, 23,
    47, 50, 66, 67, 75, 156, 186
immigrant arrival lists 93, 95, 107
immigrants 23, 101–11
*Immigrants to the New World
    1600s–1800s* 96
Immigration and Nationality
    Directorate 102, 105
Imperial Certificates of Naturalization
    103
Imperial War Museum 46, 48
impressment 159
income/wealth tax 170
Increment Value Duty 118
indentures *see* apprenticeship
    records
Independents 138
indexed digital images 9, 12, 13, 23,
    66, 67, 186
India 100
India General Service Medal 47
India Office 100
Indian Army 39, 42, 44
Indian Army Lists 100
indictments 78
Information Points 19
inheritance disputes 114
Inheritance Tax 84
Inquisitions post mortem (IPMs) 123,
    125–6, 127
interlocutory orders 115–16
International Council of the Red
    Cross 110
International Genealogical Index 24,
    25, 59, 62, 96, 108, 122, 140
'International memoranda' 59, 62
International Vital Records Handbook
    62
internees 97–8, 109–10
Interregnum 70–3
inventories, probate 182–3, 184
Irish ancestors 22–3

Irish Constabulary 144
*Irish Immigrants to North America
    1803–71* 96
Irish state tontines 166, 168
Irish Wills Index 23

Jacobite rebellion 143
Jews 121, 139
joiners, registers of (police) 144
Judicial Committee of the Privy
    Council 89–90, 112, 184–5

King's Bench Prison 120–2
King's German Legion 106

Lambeth Palace Library 112, 184
Lancaster, Palatinate of 77, 79, 111
land taxes 170, 174–5
landowners 124–6, 127, 170
laptop computers 19
Latin documents 123
Law Lists 28
lawsuits *see* legal proceedings
lawyers 34
lay subsidies 126, 170, 171
leather and beaded weights 20
leavers, registers of (police) 144
Leeson, F. 168
Legacy Duty 84, 85, 87, 178
legal proceedings: causes 183–5; civil
    actions 111–17, 122; criminal courts
    77–82
letters of administration *see*
    administration grants
Library and Resource Centre 18
lieutenants' passing certificates 161,
    163
life annuities 166–9
Life Guards 38
Life-Saving Apparatus Companies 75
limited administration grants 180
Limited Probate Act Books 178
list books 160
List and Index Society 184
Liverpool 93
livery company records 33
Lloyd's Captains' Registers 138
Lloyd's Register of Shipping 135

Local Defence Volunteers (LDV) 53
local newspapers 75–6, 78, 89
local reference libraries 13
locker 20
log books 59, 134–6, 163
London directories of names 27–8
London Gazette 29, 47, 50, 69, 70, 106, 153
London Metropolitan Archives 87
London Metropolitan Police 143–6
long service medals 41, 52
lord lieutenant of the county 53
Lord Lyon King of Arms 69
Lutherans 108

magistrates' courts 77
magnification of documents 18
male servants, number of 175
manorial courts 30, 77, 112, 124
Manorial Documents Register 9, 30–1, 126–7
manorial index 30
manorial records 30–1, 72–3, 122–3, 124–6
Map and Large Document Room 19, 20
maps 117–20
Marine List 156, 157
Marine Returns 55–9, 93, 137
Maritime History Archive 136
marriage settlements 176–7
marriages 139, 157, 164; abroad 60–3, 96; clandestine 120–2; Ireland 22; Nonconformists 138–42; parish registers 23–5; Scotland 22; at sea 55–9, 93
masters, index of 33
masters, register of 132
MayFair Chapel 121
medals 12, 75; army 40–1, 46, 47, 50; Merchant Navy 137; RAF 153; Royal Marines 156, 158; Royal Navy 163–4
Medical Directories 28
medieval ancestors 122–9
memorials 103–4
Mentions in Dispatches 50
Mercantile Marine Medal 137
Mercantile Marine Reserve 129

Mercantile Navy List 132, 135
Merchant Navy 12, 22, 35, 55–9, 129–38, 160; apprentices 35; masters and mates 1845 onwards 132–8
Merchant Navy Reserve Pool 131, 133
meritorious service awards 51–2, 153
Methodist Movement 139
Metropolitan Police Force 109
Metropolitan Police Museum 145
microform records 9, 13, 21
Middle East Centre, St Antony's College, Oxford 144
Middlesex 127
Middlesex Sessions 77, 79
Military General Service Medal 40–1
militia 35, 52–5, 72, 128
militia muster rolls 53, 54, 128
Million Bank 169
Minories 120–2
Mint 120–2
minute books 148
Mobile Naval Base Defence Organization 154
Modern Records Centre, University of Warwick 148
Mormon Immigration Index 96
Morton Allan Directory of European Passenger Steamship Arrivals 95
muster books/rolls: army 39; militia 53, 54, 128; ships 91, 134–6, 156, 160

names, directories of 27–9
National Advisory Service 9
National Archives 8–9, 10–21, 119, 186–7; arrangement of records 13; catalogues 8, 13, 21, 186; closure dates 18; details of opening 11; enquiries by post/phone/fax/email 16–17; facilities for people with special needs 17–18; home page 14; monthly magazine 186; online newsletter 186; ordering documents in advance 8, 16, 21; ordering documents on site 11, 19, 20; practical advice on research 21; preparing for a visit to 8, 12; public access computer terminals 19;

reader's ticket 8, 11; searching the catalogue 14–16; step-by-step guide to visiting 19–21; using public search areas 11; what to take on a visit to 17

National Archives of Ireland 22

National Archives of Scotland 10

National Burial Index 25, 63, 141

National Council of Voluntary Child Care Organisations 100

National Debt Office 166

National Index of Parish Registers 24, 63, 141

National Library of Wales 10, 77, 111

National Maritime Museum 136

National Register of Archives 9, 31, 127, 142, 147

National Union of Railwaymen (NUR) 148

Naturalization Act 1870 97, 103

naturalization certificates 95, 97, 102, 103

naturalizations 101, 102–4, 104–5

Naval Dockyards Society 91

Naval General Service Medal 164

Naval Pay and Pensions (Accounts) 131

Naval Signalling Force 74

Navy Board 158

Navy Lists 90, 133, 149, 151, 156, 157, 159, 160–1

Navy Pay Office 182

New Navy Lists 156, 161

New South Wales 80–2

New Zealand Company 98

Newspaper Library 30, 60, 76, 89, 99

newspapers 29–30, 69, 75–6, 99; local 75–6, 78, 89; overseas 60, 99

next of kin 176, 178

1914 Star 47

1914–15 Star 47

Nonconformist Registers of Wales 141

Nonconformists 24, 64, 65, 138–43

notes, taking 20

nuncupative wills 178

NUR Orphan Fund 148

Office for National Statistics 65

officers: army 41–3, 48–51, 51–2; Merchant Navy 133; Royal Air Force 151–4; Royal Marines 154, 156–8

officers' service returns 161–3

Old Bailey 77, 79, 121

Old Dissenters 138

online application forms 17

online catalogues 8, 13, 21, 186

online documents 9, 12

online newsletter 186

online Research Guides 8, 14, 21

Operations Record Books 152–3

ordering documents 19, 20

Ordnance Survey maps 117–20

palaeography 123

Palestine, British Police in 144

Pallot's Marriage Index 25, 122

pardons 82

parish constables 53, 143

parish copies of indentures 33

parish index 30

parish registers 23–5, 65, 70, 122, 141

parishes: and Valuation Office district offices 119

Parliamentary county committees 71–2, 170

parochial overseers of the poor accounts 33

Passenger and Immigration Lists Index 96

passenger lists, ships' 92–3, 95, 104, 105, 107, 110

passing certificates *see* certificates of competency

Patent Rolls 102, 126, 127

pedigree chart 10

pedigrees 122, 124

pension records: army 36–7, 39, 40, 43, 46, 47, 51; Coastguard 75; customs officers 83; dockyard employees 91; excise officers 83–4; militia 53; police 145–6; RAF 153

personal effects and wages of dead seamen 55, 56, 57

personal-names 16

personal taxes 170
personalty 176
personalty valuation 178
Phillimore Atlas and Index of Parish Registers 25, 63, 86, 121, 122, 127, 141, 176
police 143–6
poll books 119
poll taxes 110, 170–1, 173
Poor Law Union papers 99, 99–100
postal enquiries 16–17
pouches, seamen's 131
Prerogative Court of Canterbury (PCC) 26, 59, 71, 84, 112, 124, 176, 178; 183; administration grants 178–81
Prerogative Court of York (PCY) 176
Presbyterians 138
Preventive Water Guard 74
Principal Probate Registry (PPR) 26, 176, 181
Principal Registry of the Family Division 88, 89
prison hulks 80
prison registers 80
prisoners of war 110
private Acts of Parliament 69, 87; naturalization 101, 102
private annuities 168–9
Privy Council, Judicial Committee of the 89–90, 112, 184–5
Privy Council registers 73
Privy Council Unbound Papers 73
probate accounts 183
Probate Act Books 178, 180
probate courts 12, 176
probate grant 177
probate inventories 182–3, 184
Probate Jurisdictions: Where to Look for Wills 26, 59, 86, 96, 127, 176
probate records 22, 175–85; *see also* wills
Probate Searchroom 26
Probate Sub-Registry four-year search 26
professional researchers 17, 21, 31, 123
professionals, directories of names of 28

provincial directories of names 27–8
public access computer terminals 19
Public Record Office of Northern Ireland (PRONI) 10, 22–3

Quakers 65, 121, 139, 140, 141
Quarter Sessions 33, 77, 79
RAF Innsworth 149, 150, 152
RAF Museum 152
Railway Benevolent Institution 148
railway company records 147, 148
railway workers before nationalization 146–8
Ranked Searches 67
rate books 120
ratings 158, 159–60
reader's ticket 8, 11
realty 176
reference libraries, local 13
references, noting 21
refugees 108
Regimental List, The 47
regimental museums 48
regimental registers 40, 52, 54
regiments 35, 38–9
register tickets (Coastguard) 76
Registrar General's Miscellaneous Non-Statutory Foreign Returns 55, 56, 60, 61, 66, 96
registration district maps 120
Registry of Shipping and Seamen 129, 131, 133, 136, 137
relief of the king's distressed subjects in Ireland 71, 72, 174
religious census of churchgoers 138
Religious Society of Friends (Quakers) 65, 121, 139, 140, 141
Religious Society of Friends Library 141
rent books and rolls 30
Requests, Court of 114–15, 124
Research Enquiries Room 20
Research Guides 8, 14, 15, 18, 21, 186
residence, certificates of 173
residuary accounts 86–7
residuary legatee 178
return of officers' services 42

Revenue Cruisers 74, 75
Riding Officers 74
Rifle Volunteers 52–5
Rocket Life Saving Apparatus Long
    Service Medal 75
Rolls of Honour 137
Roman Catholics 138–9, 140, 141,
    142, 142–3; taxation 142–3, 170,
    174, 175
Royal Air Force (RAF) 22, 56, 148–54;
    airmen and airwomen 149–50;
    officers 151–4
Royal Army Medical Corps 50
Royal Artillery 37
Royal Bounty 165
Royal Corps of Sappers and Miners
    35
Royal Courts of Justice 70
Royal Dockyards 90–2
Royal Engineers 35, 37–8
Royal Fleet Auxiliaries 129, 133
Royal Fleet Reserve 159
Royal Flying Corps (RFC) 12, 148,
    149, 150, 151, 153
Royal Horse Artillery 37
Royal Horse Guards 38
Royal Irish Constabulary 23, 143–6
Royal Licences 69
Royal Marine Artillery 156–7
Royal Marine Light Infantry (Red
    Marines) 154
Royal Marines 22, 56, 154–8, 182;
    officers 154, 156–8
Royal Naval Air Service (RNAS) 56,
    148, 150, 151, 153, 153–4
Royal Naval Reserve (RNR) 129, 130,
    131, 133, 137, 159
Royal Naval School 35
Royal Naval Volunteer Reserve
    (RNVR) 159
Royal Navy 12, 22, 35, 56, 59, 91, 129,
    130, 158–65; commissioned officers
    and warrant officers 160–5;
    immigrants 106; wills 182
Royalist Composition Papers 71

Scots ancestors 22–3
scutage 170

sea: births, marriages and deaths at
    55–9, 66, 93
seamen's services registers 129–30,
    131, 133, 159–60
searching the catalogue 14–16, 20;
    problems in 16
Second World War 12, 29, 56, 57,
    109–10, 152
Sequestration of Delinquents' Estates
    committees 71–2, 73
Sheerness dockyard church 92
sheriffs 125
ships' arrivals lists 95
ships' crew agreements 59, 134–6
ships' crew lists 59, 134–6
ships' logs 59, 134–6, 163
ships' musters 91, 134–6, 156, 160
ships' pay books 91
ships' passenger lists 92–3, 95, 104,
    105, 107, 110
Sick and Hurt Board 158
Signet Bills 104
silver plate 175
Silver War Badge 47, 153
Society of Friends 65, 121, 139, 140,
    141
Society of Genealogists 66, 121, 141,
    168
Soldiers Died in the Great War 46, 153
solicitors 34
South African Aviation Corps 150
South African Constabulary 144
South London Burial Ground 64
Southwark New Burial Ground 65
Spa Fields cemetery 65
special administration grants 180
special needs, facilities for people with
    17–18
Special Reserve 53
Special Reservists 150
Squadron Operations Record Books
    152–3
St James's Duke's Place 121
Stamp Duty 34, 35, 84
Star Chamber, Court of 115
State Papers 73
State Papers Colonial: America and
    West Indies 73, 97

State Papers Foreign 97
state tontines 166–9
statutory declarations 69
submariners 56
succession books 74, 75
Succession Duty 84, 85, 87
superannuation allowances 83
Supplementary Reserve 53
Supreme Court of Judicature 111
surnames 123
Surrey 127

tallage 170
Tasmania 80–2
tax assessments 1642–1660 71, 170
tax lists 15, 71–2, 110, 126, 142–3,
    170–5
temporary commissions 49
tenants-in-chief 123, 125
Territorial Army 49, 53
Territorial Force War Medal 47
Texts and Calendars: An Analytical
    Guide to Serial Publications 128, 173
tickets, merchant seamen's 129,
    129–30
tickets of leave 82
Times, The 29, 48, 51, 52, 60, 69, 114,
    152, 156
Tithe Applotment Books 23
Tithe apportionments 118
Tithe maps 117–20
TNT Archive Service (Navy),
    Swadlincote 54, 91, 131, 133, 149,
    157, 160, 163
tontines, state 166–9
trade unions 147–8
Transport Board 158
transportation 80–2, 95
'Travel to the UK' project 105
Trinity House Petitions 134

Ulster King of Arms 69
ultra-violet lamp 20
Underwood, J. 83
United Pointsmen's and Signalmen's
    Society (UPSS) 147
UPS Mutual Aid and Sick Society
    147

Valuation Books 118–19
Valuation Office Records 117–20
Victoria Cross 41
Victoria Park Cemetery, Hackney 65
Victory Medal 47, 50
Victualling Board 158
victualling yard records 91
visitation pedigrees of heralds 122
Vital Records Indexes 62; Australia 62,
    81, 96; British Isles 24–5, 96, 122,
    142
voluntary enlistment 44
Volunteers 52–5
voters, registers of 27, 119, 120

wages and effects of dead seamen 55,
    56, 57
war deaths 56; army 47–8, 50–1, 54;
    Merchant Navy 137; RAF 152,
    153–4; Royal Marines 156, 157–8;
    Royal Navy 164–5
war diaries 12, 47, 50, 51
War Graves Roll 137, 153, 158,
    164
Wards and Liveries, Court of 126
warrant officers: Royal Marines
    156–8; Royal Navy 158, 160–5
Watchers and Intelligence Section
    75
Waterloo Medal 40
wealth/income tax 170
weights 20
Welsh Assize courts 77
Wesleyan Methodist Metropolitan
    Registry 24, 62–3, 142
Westminster Great Hall 111
wheelchairs 17–18
wheeled vehicles 175
Who Was Who 29
Who's Who 29
widow's pensions 43, 146, 165
Willing's Press Guide 29, 76
wills 12, 34, 114, 174, 175–85; Civil
    War and Interregnum 70–1, 73;
    Death Duty registers 84–7; deaths at
    sea 59; emigrants 95, 96; medieval
    ancestors 123–4, 127; proved locally
    in England and Wales before 1858

26; proved locally in England and Wales from 1858 onwards 26; Scotland 22

witness depositions 113, 115, 184

wives: naturalization 101; petitions to accompany husbands in transportation 81; settlements on 176–7

women 27, 68; and wills 176–7, 181; *see also* wives

Women's Army Auxiliary Corps (WAAC) 49; Forms of Enrolment 46

Women's Auxiliary Air Force (WAAF) 149, 150

Women's Royal Air Force (WRAF) 149

yard pay books 90

Year Books 84

Yeomanry 52–5